Marxis... ...d Medieval History

≈

Essays on the crusades and medieval society

Conor Kostick

First published 2021 by Curses & Magic, Dublin, Ireland.

© Conor Kostick

Dewey: 321.3
ISBN 978-1-7399385-0-5

AA	Albert of Aachen, *Historia Ierosolimitana – History of the Journey to Jerusalem*, Susan B. Edgington (ed. and tr.), Oxford: Clarendon Press, 2007
AC	Anna Comnena, *The Alexiad*, E.R.A. Sewter (tr.), Middlesex: Penguin, 2003 [1979]
BD	*Baldrici episcopi Dolensis Historia Jerosolimitana, RHC Occ.* IV.1–111
BEO	*Bulletin d'Etudes Orientales de l'Institut Français de Damas*
BnF	Bibliothèque nationale de France
BSOAS	*Bulletin of the School of Oriental and African Studies CCCM Corpus Christianorum, Continuatio Mediaevalis*
EA	Ekkehard of Aura, 'Chronica', *Frutolfs und Ekkehards Chroniken und die Anonyme Kaiserchronik*, Franz-Josef Schmale and Irene Schmale-Ott (eds), Darmstadt: Wissenschaftliche Buchgesellschaft, 1972
EHR	*English Historical Review*
Fath	Imad al-Din al-Isfahāni, *Kit āb al-Fath al-Qussi fi' l-Fath al-Qudsi*, H. Massé (tr.), as *Conquête de la Syrie et de la Palestine par Saladin*, Paris: Paul Geuthner, 1972
FC	Fulcher of Chartres, *Historia Hierosolymitana (1095–1127)*, H. Hagenmeyer (ed.), Heidelberg: Winter, 1913
GF	*Gesta Francorum et aliorum Hierosolimitanorum*, R. Hill (ed.), Oxford: Clarendon Press, 1962
GN	Guibert of Nogent, *Dei Gesta per Francos*, R.B.C. Huygens (ed.), *Corpus Christianorum Continuatio Medievalis* 77a, Turnhout: Brepols, 1996
JK	John Kinnamos, *Epitome rerum ab Ioanne et Alexio Comnenis gestarum*, Augustus Meineke (ed.), *Corpus Scriptorum Historiae Byzantinae* 28, Bonn, 1836 *JSAI Jerusalem Studies in Arabic and Islam*
JSAI	*Jerusalem Studies in Arabic and Islam*
ME	Matthew of Edessa, 'Chronicle', in *Armenia and the Crusades: Tenth to Twelfth Centuries*, A.E. Dostourian (ed. and tr.), Lanham, MD: University Press of America, 1993 *Monumenta Germaniae Historica Scriptores, Scriptores* in *Folio*, 32, Berlin: Weidmann, 1826–1934
NC	Niketas Choniates, *Nicetae Choniatae Historia*, Jan Louis van Dieten (ed.), *Corpus Fontium Historiae Byzantinae*, 11, Berlin: Walter de Gruyter, 1975

OD   Odo of Deuil, *The Journey of Louis VII to the East*, V.G. Berry (ed.), New York: W.W. Norton, 1948

OV   Orderic Vitalis, *The Ecclesiastical History of Orderic Vitalis*, Marjorie Chibnall (ed.), 6, Oxford: Oxford University Press, 1968–80
J.P. Migne (ed.), *Patrologiae cursus completus: Series Latina*, Paris: Migne, 1844–66

RA   Raymond of Aguilers, *Historia Francorum qui ceperunt Iherusalem*, *RHC Oc.*, III.235–309

RC   Ralph of Caen, *Gesta Tancredi in expeditione Hierosolymitana auctore Radulfo Cadomensi*, *RHC Oc.*, IV.587–716 *Repertoire Chronologique d'Epigraphie Arabe*

RH   Roger of Howden, *Chronica magistri Rogeri de Houedene*, William Stubbs (ed.), Rolls Series 51, 4, London: Longman, 1868–71

RHC Arm.   *Recueil des historiens des croisades: documents armeniens*, 2, Paris: Académie des inscriptions et belles-lettres, 1869–1906

RHC Lois   *Recueil des historiens des croisades: les Assises de Jérusalem*, 2, Paris: Académie des inscriptions et belles-lettres, 1841–3

RHC Oc.   *Recueil des historiens des croisades*, *Historiens occidentaux*, 5, Paris: Académie des inscriptions et belles-lettres, 1841–95

RHC Or.   *Recueil des historiens des croisades*, *Historiens orientuax*, 5, Paris: Académie des inscriptions et belles-lettres, 1872–1906

RM   Robert the Monk, *Historia Iherosolimitana*, *RHC Oc.*, III.717–882

WT   William of Tyre, *Chronique*, R.B.C. Huygens (ed.), *CCCM*, 63, Turnhout: Brepols, 1986

Marxism and Medieval History

Conor Kostick

Table of Contents

I grew up in Chester, England. Once *Deva*, an important Roman town, Chester preserved its medieval character by an accident of geography. The River Dee on which the town is located silted up in the Early Modern period and thus the Industrial Revolution, which should have made it a Liverpool or Manchester – a great entrepot focused on sea-lanes running through the Irish Sea – passed the city by. It became, instead, a marketplace, a garrison town and a tourist attraction. With the UK's only complete circuit of medieval walls, shops stacked on top of each other in two rows, a race-course, and mock-Tudor housing the city has learned that it has an international appeal.

My dad was a tour guide, giving walking tours of the city and coach tours of the environs, sometimes all the way to his home country of Ireland via the Holyhead ferry. And while he preferred a good fiction to a dull fact (and I suspect the tourists appreciated the same), our house was stocked with history books. I too had my own little collection: the Ladybird book of *The Crusades* was one of them. In it were such classic apocryphal stories as the time Richard the Lionheart met Saladin. The king of England demonstrated how powerful was his two-handed sword, so Saladin issued a challenge, throwing up a piece of silk. No matter how hard Richard tried, he couldn't cut the silk. Then Saladin drew his razor-sharp scimitar and effortlessly cut the silk in two.

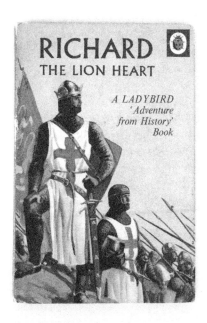

I loved stories like these. And every day I was walking to school past Roman columns; medieval town walls; and a medieval cathedral. My route took me close to a Roman amphitheatre (in which I could imagine gladiators fighting one another while the crowd cheered). After walking past the rows of mock-Tudor shops I came to the river Dee and the spot at which in 973 King Edgar the Peaceful was supposed to have taken the helm of a skiff rowed by rulers from Wales and Scotland, in a symbolic demonstration of their pledge to be his allies.

I always had an interest in ancient and medieval history as a result. But apart from a memorable visit to my school by a Roman soldier in authentic armour, this was not the history I learned about. History, it is often said, is taught by the winners. And while the actual mechanism by which bias emerges in the teaching of history is obviously more subtle than direct appointments of 'winners', in spirit, this statement is true. I deeply disliked history in school, because all I got to learn about was how great Britain was. I learned about the development of the canal system; the railroads; the application of steam power; the banking system; three-course crop rotation and a long list of inventors and industrialists whose years of birth and death I memorised for exams. Even now, nearly fifty years since I learned it, I can remember a few lines that were written in code to the English ambassador in Holland, which I used to 'explain' the rivalry between those countries:

> *In matters of commerce the fault of the Dutch,*
> *Is offering too little and asking too much.*
> *The French are with equal advantage content.*
> *So we clap on Dutch bottoms just twenty per cent.*

I'd been brought up to be aware that my dad was Irish and although I don't remember making an issue of this, my nickname on the school football team was 'Iro'. Not one mention of Ireland arose in a history class in my entire time at school. This is the sense in which the winners teach history. Throughout the world, teachers follow curricula that have evolved with enormous cultural biases in favour of their local ruling elites. Of course, there is room for alternative views in the more liberal and democratic countries (less so under dictatorships) but typically these are marginal and sanitised. All my generation were brought up to consider ourselves lucky to be living in the greatest country in the world. And it was quite a shock when we went abroad and found out that it wasn't.

I moved to Ireland in 1990 and there in 1997 I went to university thanks to an usually enlightened social welfare scheme. 'The Back to Education' allowance was aimed at the long-term unemployed and it allowed you to retain your benefit while at university. Suddenly, it became viable for me to get a degree. The only difficulty was to gain a place somewhere as a mature student. I applied to Trinity College and was allowed to try for a place on two courses: Philosophy and History. The first hurdle for entrance was that mature students had to take an aptitude test. It was the kind of test that used to be called an IQ test and consisted of verbal, visual and mathematical questions of the kind: complete the series: 2, 5, 7, 12 ... I was not daunted by these tests, being quite practiced at them.

There was a boy in my school who in the mornings used to be taken out of the assembly, conspicuously, and given IQ tests. He was scoring genius level results and the headmaster was very pleased with him. My school, Queens Park High, had no great academic reputation. At that time only three per cent of the students would go on to get a university degree. One time, I took him aside and said, 'Carl, you're no genius, what's going on?' His answer was that his mum was training him intensively in these tests. Contrary to the idea that they were measuring an innate intelligence, they were mostly measuring how much practice you'd put in at doing such tests. I'd done a fair few of these over the years and was able to surmount the first hurdle.

Hurdle two was a fair one in Philosophy: write an essay on the ethics of cloning someone from Hitler's DNA (assuming that to be possible). Dolly the sheep was in the news and the angle I took on the question was to say that your politics had nothing to do with your DNA, so the resulting human would not share Hitler's fascism. It would pose ethical questions, however, to have an apparent reincarnation of Hitler, around whom modern-day Nazis would rally. I couldn't imagine, either, the poor person involved being able to have a happy life. I put some serious work into the essay and was accepted. In History, however, the second step was an interview.

My interview panel consisted of Professor Aidan Clarke, as chair, Associate Professor David Fitzpatrick and Senior Lecturer Katharine Simms. It began badly. I was nervous and they were bored by a long day of interviews. We ran through some basic questions without me offering anything worthwhile and then Aiden Clarke gently asked what topics in history interested me.

'I'm interested in medieval society and especially in the struggle of the peasantry against their masters.'

Immediately David Fitzpatrick bristled and poured scorn on this subject. 'There are hardly any sources for that; you won't be able to study that in much depth.'

I was floundering a bit but referred to Rodney Hilton. My difficulty was not only was I relatively poorly informed – it was a topic I wanted to learn about, not one I'd already mastered – but there was very little archaeology taught at TCD and yet investigations of peasant life, especially in the early medieval period, leaned more on archaeology than historical sources.

Katharine Simms tried to help and interjected that, in fact, there were such sources. She was an expert in old Irish and well aware of the highly detailed legal tracts from which one could certainly explore the theoretical legal position of the lower social orders. But Fitzpatrick, enjoying himself now, talked right over his more expert colleague (his era was the early twentieth century) and rounded off his mini-polemic by decrying my interests as hopeless, to his own great delight and satisfaction.

It felt to me like that Fitzpatrick would put a red cross on my application and I doubted that anyone would make it through the interview stage with even one of the panel making an objection. I might have been wrong about David Fitzpatrick as later, when I wrote an essay that disagreed with his lecture on the Easter Rising, he gave me a first class mark. But at the time I thought I was sunk.

There was one more question, however: 'why have you chosen Trinity College?'

'My father came here and studied history under F.S.L. Lyons.'

Well, it was as though the sun had come out. Suddenly, everyone, Fitzpatrick included, were beaming at the mention of their former Provost. Having earlier not had a grasp on who I was, they now thought they understood: I was one of them. For some unfathomable reason, I had not, at the age of 32, yet obtained a degree. But now I was making good and of course I would want to follow a family tradition of coming to Trinity.

The next week I got the letter in the post, announcing that I had been accepted to study History at TCD. In fact, I got two letters, the other accepting me on the Philosophy course. I chose History.

The fact about my dad having gone to Trinity was true although I think making it up would have worked just as well, nobody would have checked. Being Jewish and growing up in a corporation house in Cabra, getting into Trinity in 1940s was a challenge. My dad was smart and determined and interested in literature and history, so the academic side of the challenge wasn't the issue. Rather it was a question of money. The Kostick family solved the issue with an agreement that Evan, my uncle, and Gerry, my dad, would support each other through college.

Evan, the older brother, got in to do Medicine and my dad worked to pay his way. Much to my dad's fury, as it consigned him to another year in purgatory when the heaven of sports in college beckoned, Evan failed a year. At last, six years on, it was dad's turn to study Humanities. Only, Evan reneged on the deal and after a stint in Dr Steevens' Hospital left Ireland for America, to seek his fortune. Dad never forgave his brother for this, reasonably enough I think.

Left with a small amount of savings, my dad reckoned he had one twelfth of the money necessary to complete his degree. He took it all to a bookies and having found a horse offering 12/1 odds, bet the lot. He won.

I once asked my dad about F.S.L. Lyons and what he was like as a teacher. Dad replied that he didn't really know, as the one encounter between them ended with Lyons throwing a book at dad's head and saying not to come back until he had read it.

I had gone to TCD anticipating I would be making good on all the Irish history I had missed out on by getting my education in England. And I took all the Irish courses I could. While I found David Dickson on the Famine and the nineteenth century more generally to be thoroughly engaging, moving even, I struggled with topics around the revolutionary history of Ireland. The problem being that those teaching the subject despised the revolutionaries and it showed. The year above mine walked out on David Fitzpatrick as he gave a lecture on the 1916 Rising, so disagreeable did they find his portrayal of the leaders.

The topic that really caught my interest was one that I thought would be utterly tedious: the medieval papacy. I went to my first lecture on the subject and an elderly professor in very proper dress, inclusive of waistcoat, was writing the names and dates of popes on the blackboard.

The lecture was fascinating. Rome in 1046 had three popes, arising from a factional struggle of the Roman aristocracy: Benedict IX of the Tusculani; Sylvester III of the Crescentii; and Gregory VI, also aligned to the Tusculani. This was a particular headache for the German King Henry III, who had undertaken the risky journey out of his core lands to claim the Italian crown and the title of emperor. He needed a pope who could legitimise his claim and so backed a German bishop who was acceptable to the senior clergy. Clement II lasted long enough to crown Henry as emperor, but not much longer, as he died of lead sugar poisoning.

The lecturer was Professor I.S. Robinson (subsequently, Lecky Chair of History) and in hindsight, I was very fortunate to have met him. He was very tolerant, encouraging even, of my enthusiasm for Marxist-influenced writers like Marc Bloch and Georges Duby and of my own desire to get below the surface of the sources to discover the impact of the lower social orders on events and to include the role of women in my accounts. So even though Professor Terry Barry's lectures on medieval archaeology would have brought me into a direct line of thought that ran from his supervisor Rodney Hilton and the Deserted

Medieval Village Research Group (which was very influenced by Marxism), I ended up doing my undergraduate final year thesis and then my PhD under the supervision of Ian Robinson.

Ian Robinson had a very gentle way of correcting my mistakes. I had to learn Latin, for example (it's surprising how many medieval Latin sources are still not translated), and we would meet every week and consider my understanding of the Latin I'd read. Invariably, in the early weeks he would find himself having to steer me in the right direction as a result of my having made a howler and would say something like, 'that's a fascinating way of putting things, but I think you'll find it more customary to translate *capellanus* as chaplain, rather than goat.'

Intellectually, Ian Robinson's influence on me was to cause me to devote much more time than I previously would have to appreciating the belief systems held by the writers of medieval texts and how they evolved with surprising rapidity in an era considered on the whole to be fairly static. I was coming to the subject steeped in the writings of Marx and Engels (in 1989, with the collapse of Communism, the Birmingham Communist Party bookshop put the Marx and Engels collected works up for sale at the bargain price of £5 each. I still couldn't afford them all at once, but bought about twenty and had them keep the rest out back for me to buy at that £5 when I had the money. I got the full set and over the subsequent years read them). To look at the material interests of people and their place in a social structure, with its tensions and rivalries, is a very useful way of understanding the past. I consider myself a Marxist in the sense of having enormous respect for Marx and in appreciating the value of this approach. But I'm not convinced by the periodisation of history in the *Communist Manifesto*, taken to deterministic extremes in the hands of theorists like David Liabman (see chapter 2). And I'm certainly much more appreciative of the importance of the intellectual formation of those writing medieval sources as a result of my weekly meetings with Ian Robinson throughout four years of PhD and two years of Post-Doctoral study.

I've called this book *Marxism and Medieval History*, because these are essays in medieval history, and the crusades especially, written from what can broadly be considered a Marxist approach. But by this, I do not mean that these are the sorts of essays that begin by discussing the medieval plough and end by declaring the need for a modern revolutionary socialist party. I wrote an essay like that in my first year at TCD, much to the amusement of Professor Christine Meek, another medievalist whom I learned to admire greatly. Mostly, these essays concern very specific subjects, the events of a few years, rather than some sweeping system of history. I do begin, however, with two chapters that might interest you if you are looking for a more general discussion about the patterns in history and the Marxist conceptual tools for understanding them.

Chapter 1 Marxism, Idealism and the Crusades

My PhD was an examination of the social ideas of the authors of the early accounts of the First Crusade. Having done my best to understand what these authors meant by *pauperes, mediocres, milites, iuvenes, principes*, etc. I then applied this understanding to the narrative of the events of that crusade. This research was written up as *The Social Structure of the First Crusade* (2008) and if you are interested to read more from it, it is available online or as a PDF under an open access, Creative Commons licence at https://library.oapen.org/handle/20.500.12657/31507.

The following discussion comes from the conclusion of that book, in which I attempted to defend the idea that a Marxist approach to the study of the crusades was possible.

In popular culture, certainly in the Muslim world, but even in the West, the crusades are largely viewed as disreputable adventures in which, under the guise of piety, Christian knights slaughtered and plundered their way through the lands of non-Christians and heretics. This was essentially the view of the crusades created by enlightenment historians, especially Voltaire, Gibbon and Hume. For these authors the crusades were useless expeditions, organised by popes and the Catholic Church to satisfy an instinct for domination. They were cruel displays of fanaticism whose achievements were performed by strength, described by ignorance. Gibbon considered it absurd that 'six succeeding generations should have rushed headlong down the precipice that was open before them; and that men of every condition should have staked their public and private fortunes on the desperate adventure of possessing or recovering a tombstone two thousand miles from their country.'[1]

A consensus that the crusades were a negative phenomenon lasted until the 1960s, with Steven Runciman concluding his famous work on the subject with the summation that 'in the long sequence of interaction and fusion between Orient and Occident, out of which our civilization has grown, the crusades were a tragic and destructive episode. High ideals were besmirched by cruelty and greed, enterprise and endurance by a blind and narrow self-righteousness, and the Holy

---

[1] E. Gibbon, *The Decline and Fall of the Roman Empire*, 6 (Everyman's Library reprint: London, 1994), p. 116.

War itself was nothing more than a long act of intolerance in the name of God.'[2]

This consensus has broken down. Many of the dominant writers in the field and the most prominent members of the Society for the Study of the Crusades and the Latin East now hold to what is, essentially, a positive view of the crusades. Famously, it has been argued that crusading should be seen as 'an act of love.'[3] Jonathan Riley-Smith, the author of this formulation and Dixie Professor of Ecclesiastical History at Cambridge University is quite open about the fact he is writing from a Christian, indeed Catholic, perspective. He is a member of two religious orders that have their roots in the crusading era, being a Knight of the Sovereign Military Order of Malta and of the Most Venerable Order of St John. He is the standard bearer for a certain group of Western historians, for whom the crusades are to be seen in a favourable light.

What Jonathan Riley-Smith and his students have brought to the motivation debate is new source material and in historical debate such material is decisive. Upon leaving for the crusade, very many property owners made substantial donations to the church, in return for ready coin with which to finance their involvement on the expedition. These transactions were recorded and churches and monasteries preserved the charters throughout the centuries, being ever diligent on such matters.

Methodologically, the inclusion of such charters in a discussion of the First Crusade is unfaultable; the database created as a result of research into donation charters is extremely valuable. By the mid 1990s, for the period 1095–1131, it comprised 549 men and women who definitely took the cross, 110 who probably did so, and 132 who might have become crusaders.[4] Insofar as such a database helps reveal the geographical and familial networks of the nobles who participated in the First Crusade, charter evidence is a welcome addition to the crusading sources. But their use as the key evidence in refuting the popular notion that crusaders were greedy knights, who cloaked their desire for booty in a pretended piety, is problematic.

Essentially, the argument in favour of seeing the motivation of the crusaders as primarily spiritual consists of three observations based on the charter evidence. Firstly, the cost of going on the crusade was shown to be extremely high; four times a knight's annual income.[5] The enterprise was not 'cost effective'. Secondly, the proportion of second sons going on the crusade was demonstrably low. Therefore the theory that those who had no other prospects were the main driving force behind the crusade was rejected. Thirdly, the charters are

---

[2] S. Runciman, *A History of the Crusades*, 3 (fifth edition: London, 1991), III, 480.

[3] J. Riley-Smith, 'Crusading as an Act of Love' in T. F. Madden ed., *The Crusades*, (Oxford, 2002), p. 38.

[4] M. Bull and N. Housley ed., *The Experience of Crusading 1: Western Approaches* (Cambridge, 2003), p. 7.

[5] J. Riley-Smith, *The First Crusade and the Idea of Crusading* (London, 1986), p. 43.

consistent in expressing a deep concern for the salvation of their soul and a love of Christ. The core of the 'act of love' position rests on the point that, in the absence of material motivations, the professed piety of the first crusaders must be considered to be the best guide to their outlook. Those who set forth on the First Crusade did so out of love of Christ and their neighbour.

So powerful was this argument, presented above all in Jonathan Riley-Smith's *The First Crusaders, 1095–1131* (1997), that it gathered a seemingly irresistible momentum, to the point where alternative perspectives have been swept aside. Not only have the notions of 'profit' and 'second sons' been considered to have been refuted, but so too the sophisticated and strongly sourced arguments of Carl Erdmann and George Duby. Carl Erdmann saw the First Crusade as an evolving from new notions of knightly vocation developed by the papal reformers of the eleventh century, in particular by Pope Gregory VII.[6] George Duby's contention, not necessarily in contradiction to Erdmann, was that the great popular peace movements of the eleventh century formed the most important context for the launching of the First Crusade. Both these theories have important implications for the motivations of the First Crusader and, to a certain degree, both are uncomfortable for the school of thought that emphasises piety. The first, because it places an emphasis on the political, rather than spiritual, goals of the papacy and its followers; the second because of its portrayal of the knightly class of France as coming into conflict with the Church for their turbulent, exploitative and unruly behaviour.

The divergence between Erdmann, Duby and the Riley-Smith school is a relatively subtle one that will not be developed further here. Rather, it is necessary to address the core argument: is the 'act of love' contention with regard to the motivation of the First Crusaders as strong as its popularity at the time of writing would suggest?

One obvious point that seems to have been lost in the debate, is that any discussion based upon the charters of departing crusaders can only concern a small minority of those who participated. Whilst the knights formed the key fighting forces of the expedition and their military role was out of all proportion to their numbers, it is important to remember that they formed a relatively small part of the whole expedition. The others on the First Crusade—the footsoldiers, artisans, former peasants and townspeople, women and clergy—made up the overwhelming majority of the army. To discuss the motives of those knights who made donations to the church before departing, therefore, is not the same thing as discussing the motives of the majority of crusaders. What was the outcast woman thinking, who having been renounced by her husband in the name of clerical reform, attached herself to the crusade through the following of Peter the Hermit? What

---

[6] C. Erdmann, *The Origin of the Idea of Crusade*, trans. M. W. Baldwin and W. Goffart (Princeton, 1977), *passim*.

interpretation was put on the crusading message by the farmer who despaired of managing his land following a year of famine and the death of his relatives by plague? Or the serf, against the will of her owner, who ran away to join the expedition? Can the donation charters of departing nobles speak for them?

Moreover, even for those who did append their names to donation charters, it cannot be assumed that the spiritual outlook documented was theirs. Jean Flori has drawn attention that these charters invariably contain statements that are legal formula belonging to a tradition that predates the crusades by several centuries. The emphasis of the charter documents is generally on the act of donation being meritorious, not the fact that the knight was departing on crusade. Furthermore, as Flori puts it, 'the need for money and support of all kinds would have led some crusaders to allow themselves to be depicted as repenting and penitent.'[7]

There is a methodological weakness in the first strand of the argument, that based on cost-effectiveness. Suppose future historians were to debate the US and UK-led invasion of Iraq in 2003 and ask whether the motives of those involved were self-interested or not. A short-term cost-benefit analysis would clearly point away from avariciousness as the motive. The enormous outlay of expenditure on the invasion will not be regained by those states in the foreseeable future, if at all. Should the future historians therefore conclude that the ostensible, documented, reasons for the invasion therefore be taken at face value? That those who initiated the invasion sincerely believed that it was a matter of urgency to deprive Saddam Hussein of weapons of mass destruction? Or would these future historians be better advised to look at a variety of pressures on those who launched the war, to try to build up a more complex picture that included the state of domestic political affairs and the strategic importance of oil resources.

The point of this analogy is not in any way to cast the nobles of the First Crusade as some kind of imperialist force. It is a methodological one. To rule out immediate financial gain as a motive for war, does not rule out other material and strategic considerations. In the case of the First Crusade, to add up the costs incurred by those knights who went on the expedition and compare it to the booty they returned with does not tell us a great deal about their motives on setting out. It does not even rule out the possibility that knights did anticipate considerable material reward, but that most of them were disappointed. Nor can the cost-benefit approach take into account the unquantifiable value to a knight's reputation of having been a crusader. What historians can see, however, is the reverse: opprobrium heaped on those who abandoned the crusade. A

---

[7] J. Flori, 'Ideology and Motivations in the First Crusade' in H. Nicholson ed., *The Crusades* (Basingstoke, 2005), pp. 15–36, here p. 21.

generation after the event those writing about the First Crusade were well aware of the 'rope-dancers', the scathing nickname for those knights who let themselves down from the walls of Antioch at a time when it looked like the expedition was doomed.[8] In an era where a reputation played an important political role in the manoeuvres of the nobility, self-interest may have played a part in the thinking of the first crusaders, not necessarily in the form of their anticipating a return laden with booty, so much as the prospect of glory and the approval of the church.

In any case, not all modern historians have given up the thought that considerations of plunder might well have made up part of the attraction of the crusade for the nobility. So, for example, John France has seen the First Crusade as offering 'something for everyone— salvation, cash, land, status.'[9] After pointing out that one of the leading crusader princes, Tancred, treated the Church of the Nativity at Bethlehem as a mere prize of war, France concluded 'the lure of booty, the hope perhaps of land or position in the exotic east, personal or institutional advantage, a whole spectrum of motives drove men to the east.'[10]

He pointed out that piety and material aspirations are not mutually exclusive with a very convincing example. Famously, the author of the *Gesta Francorum* reported the rallying cry of Bohemond at the battle of Dorylaeum, 1 July 1097: 'stand fast all together, trusting in Christ and in the victory of the Holy Cross. Today, please God, you will all gain much booty.'[11]

The cost-effectiveness argument also ignores evidence that not all departing crusaders financed themselves in a suitably pious manner: that of making a donation to the church. Some used the opportunity provided by the expedition to raise funds by increasing local levels of exploitation. At the peak of the social structure there is the example of Duke Robert II of Normandy who mortgaged his duchy to his brother, King William II of England. The ten thousand silver marks were raised from the English population by a harsh and much resented tax.[12] Guibert of Nogent, an eyewitness, provided evidence that at a more lowly level the departure of knights on crusade could be paid for by fierce extractions from the poor. William Carpenter, one of the knights active in the People's Crusade who eventually abandoned the expedition at Antioch, plundered from the *pauperes* of his region to obtain his provisions for departure.[13] Guibert also wrote about other unnamed knights from France, who before setting out on the

---

[8] AC xi.6 (348); OV 6, 18.

[9] J. France and W. G. Zajac ed., *The Crusades and their sources: Essays Presented to Bernard Hamilton* (Aldershot, 1998), p. 19.

[10] J. France, *Victory in the East. A military history of the First Crusade* (Cambridge, 1994). p. 16.

[11] GF 19–20.

[12] *The Anglo-Saxon Chronicles*, ed. and trans. Michael Swanton (London, 2000), p. 233.

[13] GN 178–9.

expedition had been fighting unjustly and were creating poverty by their criminal plundering.[14]

The cost-benefit argument does not apply to such figures. Their departure for Jerusalem cost them nothing of their own resources. By going on crusade these knights were simply transferring their depredations from the local peasantry to those they encountered en route.

There were another body of crusaders, outside the knightly class, to whom it is worth turning in any discussion of the economic gains and losses of the First Crusade. By the end of the eleventh century a growing social milieu was beginning to assert itself in parts of Europe: the urban manufacturer and merchant. In France, Germany and Italy, a number of major towns had formed communes and in some instances fought for control of the town against the previous, often clerical, authorities. Notable examples were the effort of the citizens of Worms to throw off the rule of their bishop in 1073, and the less successful attempt the following year in Cologne.[15] In Italy, a number of cities were beginning to emerge as independent powers; importantly for the history of the First Crusade, Genoa was already organising itself into a commune in 1052 and by 1095 was governed by elected consuls. Sources nearly contemporary with the First Crusade noticed the *consules* of Genoa as the leading figures of city.[16] The significance of this development for the motivation of the first crusaders has not yet been explored in depth, but Abram Leon, who during the course of his classic work The Jewish Question observed that the crusades were the expression of the will of city merchants to carve a road to the Orient, has pointed to a potentially very fertile line of investigation.[17]

Working very firmly within the 'act of love' framework, a former pupil of Jonathan Riley-Smith, Christopher Marshall, has examined the question of the motivation of the Italian city republics with regard to crusading. Marshall drew the conclusion that since the speech of the bishops of Grenoble and Orange to the citizens of Genoa (1097) to encourage them to participate in the First Crusade made no mention of material gain 'it is therefore safe to assume that the recorded Genoese response reflected their religious fervour.'[18] Marshall examined the sources for the First Crusade to show that many contemporary authors treated the Genoese fleet as fellow crusaders. But no one, even the crudest advocate of the 'booty' position, would expect eleventh century sources to do otherwise. The point here, as with the argument about

---

[14] GN 179.

[15] For the context of these revolts see Robinson 1999, pp. 93–4.

[16] CA I, 5; FC II.viii.2 (396–7).

[17] A. Leon, *The Jewish Question* (New York, 1970), p. 138.

[18] C. Marshall, 'The crusading motivation of the Italian city republics in the Latin East, 1096–1104, in M. Bull and N. Housley eds., *The Experience of Crusading 1: Western Approaches* (Cambridge, 2003), pp. 60–79, here p. 67.

motivation in general, is to ask whether there were contemporary social and economic trends which would contribute to an enthusiasm, sincere or otherwise, for the First Crusade among the *consules* of Genoa? In other words, whatever the formulations of the preaching by the bishops, was the city predisposed to support the crusade? If the sailors of the commune were acting out of a love of Christ that was detached from the strategic benefits that accrued to their city through controlling a greater share of trade to and from the east, then why, with the pilgrimage complete, did they insist upon trading privileges in return for their assistance for the newly founded Principality of Antioch and Kingdom of Jerusalem?[19]

When, in 1101, a fleet from Genoa made a convention with King Baldwin I of Jerusalem, the agreement is another good illustration of how contemporaries had no difficulty combining their religious beliefs with their own material interests. The treaty was made, reported Fulcher, with the consuls of the fleet. If, out of the love of God and with His assistance, they and the king could take any of the cities of the Saracens, a third of the wealth of the inhabitants would go to the Genoese, the other two thirds to the king. Additionally, a section in each captured city would be given to the Genoese in perpetuity.[20]

This agreement became a standard one for relations between Italian cities and the Kingdom of Jerusalem, leading to considerable long-term benefit for the cities. Is it plausible to deny that the prospect of such arrangements formed part of the considerations of the Italian republics when they heard and accepted the crusading message?

The second strand of the idealist argument, the refutation of the 'second son' contention, is much stronger, as the evidence of the charters does not provide evidence for it being the younger sons of noble families who departed on the First Crusade. Not all modern historians, however, have dismissed the contention as being a consideration for some crusaders. H. E. Mayer, for example, has cited the case of the Mâconnais family of La Hongre, which successfully avoided the fragmentation of their allodial wealth through the participation of two males in the First Crusade and one in the Second Crusade.[21]

Nevertheless, it is generally accepted that the numbers of noble crusaders who had nothing to lose and everything to gain from the expedition was nothing like the size portrayed in the nineteenth century sources. The 'act of love' school of thought therefore concludes that the crusading image of the spirited young warrior, more interested in fame and glory than the salvation of their soul, is a fictional one. They have consistently overlooked, however, the significant presence of those knights who were described as *iuvenes*

---

[19] H. Hagenmeyer, *Epistulae et Chartae* pp. 155–6; FC II.viii.2 (396–7).
[20] FC II.viii.2 (396–7).
[21] H. E. Mayer, *The Crusades* (seventh edition: Oxford, 1993), p. 24.

and the pattern of behaviour they displayed which earned them such an epithet.

Chapter Six of this book draws attention to a number of these magnates, not always young in age, who were described by the early crusading sources as *iuvenes*.[22] These warriors were brave, but extremely violent. They sought glory in battle, slaughtered both combatants and civilians and revelled in displays of their riding ability. Their motivation for joining the crusade was not strictly material, in the sense of a search for land and booty. But there was nevertheless a structural consideration at work in their behaviour. Georges Duby explored the position of the unmarried sons of the magnates of a slightly later era and he drew attention to the way that bands of 'youths' would draw together to fight in tournaments and in the wars of their elders, in order to win fame, followers and if possible, the biggest prize of all, an heiress whose lands would allow them to become magnates in their own right.[23]

The violence of these bands of knights in search of the opportunity to prove their military prowess was destabilising and more than one clerical author breathed a sigh of relief that the destructive energy of the knightly order had been deflected by the idea of crusading onto an external non-Christian enemy.[24] For the *iuvenes* who took the cross, they not only had the opportunity to earn salvation without having to give up their customary military lifestyle: but they could advance their fame while simultaneously winning the approval of the church. One of the results of the investigation in *The Social Structure of the First Crusade*, was to put back into an understanding of the mentality of those participating in the First Crusade the presence of the worldly and ambitious knight, having reinterpreted their behaviour as arising out of their particular social situation rather than it being a simple reflection of a desire for booty or the 'second son' syndrome.

Overall, the motivation of those on the First Crusade was as heterogeneous as the various social classes who took part. Not only did the balance between spiritual and material considerations vary considerably from social group to social group, within each stratum could be found figures displaying considerable devotion to the spiritual goals of the expedition and those of a more cynical disposition. And no doubt there were those whose outlook changed during the course of the expedition.

Methodologically, the school of crusading historiography that is currently dominant in the Western world can appropriately be termed

---

[22] AA ii.23 (100).

[23] 'Les "jeunes" dans la société aristocratique dans la France du Nord-Ouest au XIIe siècle,' *Annales: Economies, Sociétés, Civilisations* 19 (5), 1964, pp. 835–846. Reprinted in Georges Duby, *The Chivalrous Society*, trans. C. Postan, University of California Press (Berkely, 1977). Also G. Duby, *William Marshal—The Flower of Chivalry*, trans. R. Howard (London, 1986), passim.

[24] GN 87; RM 748.

'idealist' as a result of its philosophical approach, its attribution of pious ideals to early crusaders and a quite conscious rejection of materialism. Marcus Bull has written the following explanation of why historians with a Marxist background have been incapable of analysing the crusades: 'there is no serious Marxist interpretation of the crusade and its motivations—perhaps because problems of human agency obtrude a little too disconcertingly when large numbers of people consciously engage in something that on the surface appears so eccentric in relation to the broad trends of social change. Perhaps, too, because the "poor" are seldom more than a shadowy presence in the dynamics of a crusade, cultural Marxist analysis is a lost cause.'[25]

Bull's portrayal of the methodology of Marxist historical writings here seems rather narrow. If everybody's behaviour always conformed to the broad trends of social change, there would be no political conflict. Human history would be very simple, smooth and mechanical. There certainly are historical works in the Marxist tradition that reduce the complexities of a historical phenomenon to overly crude economic generalisations. But equally, it is often the subtle dynamics and peculiarities of certain periods of history that has stimulated the more important investigations in the Marxist tradition, not least those of Marx himself. For example, Marx's study of Louis Bonaparte is an appraisal of the colourful events of 1848–52 in France, many of which seemed extremely eccentric in relationship to the broad trends of social change, but which still leant themselves to an analysis rooted in an assessment of the material position of the various classes of the era.[26]

Moreover, Bull's assertion about the 'poor' is exaggerated. It has been shown in *The Social Structure of the First Crusade* that for the First Crusade at least, *pauperes* played a significant and notable role in the dynamics of the movement. The statement about the 'poor' also indicates that for Bull, a Marxist approach is one that focuses narrowly on the lower social orders. In most Marxist historical works, however, while the writers are indeed often interested in the classes at the bottom of society, their studies are typically attempts to understand the totality of a particular historical phenomenon.

For Norman Housely, the absence of a materialist tradition of analysis with regard to the crusades is something to be regretted, but even if it did exist, it would probably not lead to a challenge to the current consensus. 'It is unlikely that the emphasis placed by recent research on devotional motivations will be overturned and that a materialist interpretation will be put forward with authority. This is not because it is inherently misguided to explain crusading in materialist

[25] M. Bull, 'Muslims and Jerusalem in miracle stories,' in Marcus Bull and Norman Housley eds., *The Experience of Crusading 1: Western Approaches* (Cambridge, 2003), pp. 13–38, here p. 18.

[26] K. Marx, 'The Eighteenth Brumaire of Louis Bonaparte' in K. Marx and F. Engels, *Collected Works* (London, 1979) XI, 99–197.

terms . . . rather, it is because the devotional motivations that have been put forward are both appropriately nuanced and firmly embedded in broader contexts, cultural as well as economic and social.'[27]

It is regrettable that the great medievalists best equipped to put forward a materialist interpretation of the crusades, figures such as Georges Duby or Rodney Hilton, never did so. Regrettable, because approaching the subject with an interest in social dynamics unlocks a great deal of unappreciated content in the source material. There is a rich, stimulating, wealth of information to be studied from such a perspective. Looking at the sources with an eye for what they reveal about social structure can bring a fresh approach to old debates, even ones that seemed to have been resolved, and stimulate new ones, to the benefit of all those interested in the crusades and in approaches to history that take social conflicts as integral to a persuasive account of events.

---

[27] N. Housely, *Contesting the Crusades* (Oxford, 2006), p. 79.

Chapter 2 Deep History

David Laibman is a Marxist economist based in New York. Editor of the journal for Marxist scholarship, *Science & Society*. He was also associate editor of *New World Review*, a journal associated with the Communist Party of the USA. And I think it would be fair to say that Laibman was a supporter of the former Soviet Union. For some reason, I was on his radar, I forget how we were introduced, perhaps because of an article I'd written on Irish Marxism for *Rethinking Marxism*. We met in 2007, when I was in New York for a history conference and I had a pleasant evening, chatting and being introduced to other Marxist colleagues of his.

That year too, Laibman wrote a book, *Deep History: A Study in Social Evolution and Human Potential* and asked would I review it. I did and the review was published in the *Review of Radical Political Economics*. I very much doubt that it was the review that Laibman anticipated. As you'll see, it is critical of the entire project of his system for the motion of history. Yet I'm grateful for the engagement. Before grappling with *Deep History*, if you'd have asked me to explain Marxism and history in just a few bullet points I'd have said that history was a history of class struggle. And that epochs of history are defined by the relationship between the owners of the means of production and those who do the work. And that at a certain stage an historical epoch passes from a period of advancement into a period of decay, which is resolved by revolution and a move to the next stage, or a catastrophe.

Each of these statements is interesting and can be a valuable concept through which to approach an actual historical moment. Taken together, however, they often become formula that are imposed on the source material, with distorting effects. In reading *Deep History* I encountered the most extreme 'stages' of history formulations that I'd ever come across. And in thinking about why my intuition told me they were wrong, I realised that Laibman was wearing the garb of Marxism inside out. Marx himself loved the detail, the incident, the moment – especially quirky ones or where some leading political figure makes an idiotic mistake - and was very reluctant to derive 'laws' of history. The famous summary that Marx gave in 1859 in his Preface of *A Contribution to the Critique of Political Economy* was a rare example of such laws in Marx's overall body of work. For Laibman, as for many other Marxist theorists, (rather than Marxist historians), this summary marks the point of departure for a grand scheme by which history unfolds.

'My project is to reach behind the rich veins of human experience, in all its forms, through the entire time of our existence on Earth, and seek out explanatory principles that might help organise our understanding of that record—our basic sense of ourselves, where we have been and where we are going.'

Except for those still enjoying the wordplay of postmodernism, political theorists will appreciate opening a book with such a stated goal. And the main strength of the book is that it lives up to its promise, offering nothing less than a total conception of the pattern of history.

David Laibman is a Marxist and the explanatory principles that he offers are derived from Marx's writings. But this book is not an exegesis of Marx's model of history; it is an adoption of these conceptual tools to entirely new formulations and ways of looking at the evolution of human societies. Direct quotes from Marx are few because the author does not want to reheat past debates about orthodoxy, but rather knuckle down to the substantive issue: what concepts explain the deep structural evolution of human history?

Laibman's answer is that there is a high level construct, the 'abstract social totality' (AST), that explains the logic of historical development. To be clear, for Laibman the AST is not a metaphor or helpful illustration; it is an explanatory, scientific, testable theory.

Philosophically, the AST model is based on a particular notion of dialectics. The author believes in 'transcending' contradictions. Most importantly for his project, Laibman believes he has found a way to transcend the apparent dichotomy between theories about history and the 'tangle of formless empirical material'[1] that arises from the study of specific historical moments.

The notion of transcendence of contradiction is, of course, perfectly orthodox in Marxism's Hegelian inheritance. But an insightful transcendence of the Hegelian kind is, in fact, relatively rare in human thought. We are talking of radical shifts of perspective that allow us to see that what had formerly appeared to be irreconcilable concepts are in fact one-sided features of a more dynamic, dialectical, totality. By contrast, for example, to say that the difference between apples and pears can be resolved by understanding them both as fruit is not very profound or dialectical in the above sense. Several times while reading this book I felt that the author was offering us apparently transcendent solutions to problems, but that his actual formula lacked the penetration necessary to really convince the reader that they were fundamental resolutions of contradictions rather than metaphysical constructions.

With regard to the critical question of whether the dynamics of history can be explained at an abstract high level, without their having to

---

[1] David Laibman, *Deep History* (New York: State of New York Press, 2007), p. 4.

be adapted to specific historical detail in such a way as they lose their explanatory power, Laibman writes as follows:

> My suggestion is to overcome this dichotomy, by developing a theory that is simultaneously 'hard' and 'soft'. I posit level of abstraction, and arrange these into a hierarchy, so that at the 'highest' level we find the abstract social totality (AST) and at a 'lower' level the (more) concrete social formation reflecting geo-climatic and developmental variation. At still 'lower' levels numerous contingent and accidental factors, including the personalities and capacities of individuals, come into play and infuse variety into the picture, which thus approaches the concreteness of the actual historical record.[2]

The idea then is that the two opposites (crudely: theory and data) affect each other, but not equally. The AST encompasses both the next level down, social formations, and below that, very particular events. This schema is consistent with Laibman's notion of dialectics. 'Dialectics refers not simply to mutual interaction, but to interaction between unequal poles. In a dialectical interaction, dominant determination runs from one pole to the other; without this, the dialectic characterizes the mutual conditioning of the poles, their relational consistency, but does not reveal a dynamic movement in the system that they constitute.'[3] This formulation is different to the Hegelian–Marxist tradition and the worry here is that we are being offered a metaphysical construction that asserts the primacy of the AST rather than demonstrating how it arises from the concrete historical record.

The most important theoretical assertion by Laibman is that the abstract social totality (AST) explains the pattern of history. Given 'perfect' conditions, human society would necessarily go through certain historical periods: primitive communism, slavery, feudalism, and capitalism. This periodization is derived not from historical observation, but from the logic of the structures of the AST.

What are those structures? They are the 'productive forces' (PF) and the 'production relations' (PR) that are derived from the works of Marx and Engels and the huge subsequent literature about them. The PFs and PRs form a consistent whole, the 'mode of production' (MP). Laibman, probably wisely given that it would lead away from his main purpose, does not spend a great deal of time on the debates about these concepts. Rather he formulates two propositions that are important for developing his logical stages view of history: first, that PRs are progressively

---

[2] *Ibid.*
[3] *Ibid*, 51.

replaced over time with ever more sophisticated PRs, and second, there is a tendency to development in the PFs. Because any particular set of PRs tend to stasis, a tension develops within a mode of production, resolved if a revolution takes place leading to a new mode of production.

The first transition Laibman believes arises from AST considerations is that from primitive communism to the slave mode of production. Laibman asserts that slavery is logically and necessarily the first form of systematic surplus extraction. But no argument is provided to explain why the first form of class society has to be slavery rather than, say, one based on the extraction of tributes from peasants. Suppose agriculture to have reached the point that it is possible to generate significant surpluses and suppose coercion necessary to gather this surplus to a ruling elite, why would the person being exploited be, in the first instance, a slave, the chattel of another person? Is it not as likely, in fact, that initially the first elites would not be able to leap from primitive communism straight to owning other human beings, but rather, and perhaps over many centuries, their privileged position would have arisen through the gradual tightening of their control over the limited surplus available to society?

If we leave the terrain of logic and structure to follow E. Gordon Childe's account of the actual origins of class society on this planet, then as well as the appearance of slavery we find examples, such as that of ancient Egypt, where tomb paintings show 'peasants coming in to pay their rent or dues, always in kind, while a scribe notes down on papyrus what each man brings and an overseer with a whip keeps the tributaries up to the mark.'[4] This latter source of wealth was almost certainly far more important initially than that created by slaves.

It is possible for Laibman's schema to be adjusted to take into account the above point, but this shaky start undermines confidence in the whole model. Nevertheless, accepting then that a slave mode of production has come into being, is there a dynamic, at the AST level, that explains what will happen to it? Laibman follows earlier Marxist historians in saying that there is a fundamental problem for the stability of a slave mode of production in that it is continually obliged to seek outside its own territory for new sources of slaves and to devote an increasing share of the surplus to supporting this activity. The slave MP also, because of the lack of incentive for the slave to develop the productive forces intensively, has a tendency to expand them extensively: larger agricultural holdings, construction projects, etc. The PF–PR model therefore points towards a crisis of the mode of production, as more and more of the share of the surplus is devoted to the means of coercion and control in this expanding system. For Laibman, the explanation for the overrunning of Rome by Germanic and other peoples ultimately lies at the level of the AST.[5]

There are many accounts of the fall of Roman civilization as well as an increasing number of both Marxist and non-Marxist studies that argue

---

[4] E. Gordon Childe, *Man Makes Himself* (London: Fontana, 1966), p. 166.

[5] Laibman, *Deep History*, p. 30.

the fall has been exaggerated.[6] My own preference is for that of G. E. M. de Ste Croix. This differs from Laibman's AST explanation in one very important aspect. The author of *Deep History* believes that the backdrop of small-scale peasant production against which the gangs of slaves are working is an 'inert medium within which the slave dynamic occurs.' For Ste Croix, on the other hand, the decline of the importance of slave-generated surpluses (for, approximately, the reasons given above) caused a massive tightening of the screw by the Roman elite on the non-slave lower social classes. The ruination and demoralisation of the once-free Roman peasantry is what contributed, above all, to the inability of the empire to save itself from invasion.[7] The difference is important for the question of methodology. Laibman's book is an attempt to distil a few high level explanations for the pattern of history; it does not suit this project to have to constantly adjust 'hard' theory with 'soft' lower-level historical data. But without amendment, the explanation offered for the conquest of the Western Roman Empire in *Deep History* seems inadequate.

According to the AST model, the crisis of the slave mode of production gives way to the feudal mode. Laibman argues that this change is a necessary one because it is not possible for a slave mode of production to move directly to a capitalist mode. Now again, adhering strictly to the logic of the model and setting aside actual historical events for the moment, why must the end of slavery mean specifically feudalism? There are several theoretical ways in which surpluses could be extracted from a labouring class. Excluding the possibility of a capitalist form does not necessitate a feudal form; that needs to be demonstrated.

In Laibman's discussion of the economic dynamics of feudalism, he convincingly demonstrates that their most important feature is that, by contrast with slavery, there is an incentive for the producers to improve the techniques of production. As a consequence, the PFs advance to what Laibman terms 'the second-most-difficult of the revolutionary transitions: to capitalism.'[8]

Capitalism is the next mode of production for the AST treatment. The model suddenly becomes less compelling, however, when Laibman wants to distinguish the capitalist mode of production from the other modes of production on the grounds that it has within it a nest of evolutionary stages. The justification for this layering is that of complexity: there are long cycles at the level of AST, within which are shorter cycles of structures that still remain above the level of full historical contingency. But Laibman does not address why, intrinsically, capitalism deserves this treatment and not the other modes of production.

According to the author's system, we are in Stage III of capitalism, one where there is a troubled and protracted move from the Cold War

---

[6] Bryan Ward-Perkins, *The Fall of Rome and the End of Civilization* (Oxford: Oxford University Press, 2007).
[7] G. E. M. de Ste Croix, *The Class Struggle in the Ancient Greek World* (London: Duckworth, 1980), pp. 453–503.
[8] Laibman, *Deep History*, p. 36.

towards a totalized global capitalist world, Stage IV. 'Stage IV would involve a global, passive, state, an end to diffusion.' It 'requires the global state that transnational capitalist class theorists observe as immanent in the emerging world institutions (World Bank, IMF, etc.).'[9]

It is strange, having discussed history at a very philosophical level up until now, to suddenly find the book invoking specific historical institutions. Once again the reader is told that this model is genuinely theoretical in the sense that the move from one stage to another is chain linked. But then very distinct political beliefs are given to the reader as being derived from the model, such as the author's belief that Islam is fundamentally more reactionary than Judaism and Christianity;[10] that a very long time period must elapse before an end to the capitalist mode of production is possible;[11] that the Gorbachev era represented a mature version of socialism in Soviet Russia;[12] and that even now the post-Soviet Russian social formation is not capitalist.[13]

Surely these relatively 'low level' statements (compared to the book's entire theme of deep history) have to be analysed at a much more historically concrete level, or we end up having an AST theory that threatens to become crudely determinist. A theory intended to operate over ten thousand years is suddenly applicable to decades.

All in all, there is a fundamental difference in approach to making generalizations about history between that of Marx and that evident in *Deep History*. Marx's generalizations about history were derived by examining particular historical moments, their contradictions, and thus arriving at powerful insights that were sometimes at a very high level, such as his famous *Preface to A Contribution to the Critique of Political Economy*. By contrast *Deep History* takes the methodologically opposite approach of starting with an abstract schema and attempting to fit historical evidence into it.

To finish, however, on a positive note: *Deep History* is a very refreshing book. It is rare these days to encounter historiographical works of any sort that deal with an entire, totalising, conception of history.

---

[9] *Ibid.*, p. 136.
[10] *Ibid.*, p. 139.
[11] *Ibid.*, p. 137.
[12] *Ibid.*, p. 181 – 2.
[13] *Ibid.*, p. 183.

Chapter 3 Women and the First Crusade

You would think that by now it was would be obvious that there is a need to make a particular effort to redress the gender discrimination that was a feature of history writing for centuries. Surely, it does not need pointing out that most modern academic historians are males, reading sources mainly written by males and that therefore a considerable bias exists? Yet, those writing 'women's history' are struggling in the face of continued resistance to recognising the value of their work.

True, in the West there has been an increase in the number of centres for women's and gender studies. But this is not the same as developing women's history: often gender studies means social science research or literary criticism, with historians interested in restoring the gender balance of their discipline relatively marginalised. At the time I wrote this article on women and the First Crusade (2003) a UK national committee report noted that women's history was typically part of a women's studies programme, rather than a history programme. In 2004, the Association of German Historians rejected every paper with a gender theme.

Thanks especially to the efforts of Professor Christine Meek, gender history was largely integrated into the courses and research conducted at TCD while I was there, without any particular battles that I was aware of. It was an interest of mine because the oppression of any group, let alone half of humanity, is anathema to socialists.

In reading the crusade sources while asking what are they saying about women, I was able to unlock a relative wealth of relevant material: material which I gathered for a presentation at a PhD seminar on the topic of this chapter.

The room was packed that night, with many attendees having to stand at the back. This was largely because most of those doing medieval research at post-graduate level were women and many of them, if not all, were encountering exactly the same issues as me: a relative neglect of the role of women both in the original sources and by very many male historians of an earlier generation. The talk went well and several of those in attendance expressed interest in my argument that we should recognise the presence of large numbers of women as crusaders on the First Crusade. A less enthusiastic question, however, came my way from senior lecturer (now professor) Seán Duffy: 'so what?'

Despite his negative tone, that was an important question. Academia discourages history with purpose and it has evolved into a kind of game where ever narrower topics are chosen for PhD topics and expertise is acquired in a topic for no other sake than playing the game of getting sufficient papers published and conference talks delivered to have a chance of a permanent post. In this case, however, there is a definite answer to 'so what?' The First Crusade provides yet another case study of how for decades expert historians can read source material with a blind spot for what the sources are saying about the presence and activity of women. Not only should we see those women when we imaginatively reconstruct the past (with implications for what women's role was then and can be in the future), but it's a reminder that historians must consciously strive to address gender in their research or risk perpetuating a male-centred narrative in their own fields.

The general view of the First Crusade is that it was an entirely male affair, and this is not surprising given that even eminent experts in the history of the crusade can begin articles by saying that 'the history of the First Crusade is, in large part, the history of mass movements of men'.[1] Yet the sources for the crusade give ample and overwhelming evidence that 'innumerable'[2] numbers of women joined the movement. A typical, if rather salacious, comment for example occurs in the history of Albert of Aachen as he talks about the setting forth of the crusade:

> Crowds from different kingdoms and cities gathered together, but in no sense turning away from illicit and sexual intercourse. There was unbridled contact with women and young girls, who with utter rashness had departed with the intention of frivolity; there was constant pleasure and rejoicing under the pretext of this journey.[3]

Albert of Aachen's description of the immorality and licentiousness of the crusade is coloured by the morality of a celibate male infused with the characteristic misogyny of monasticism. But it is nevertheless a striking passage by an eyewitness to the departure of the First Crusade that raises interesting questions. What motivated women to join the First Crusade? Was the undertaking an opportunity for them to escape a sexually restrictive society? Did they see themselves as participants or were they camp followers?

Firstly, to establish that there were indeed thousands of women involved in the crusade, and that their presence is well attested, the sources can quickly be surveyed. Orderic Vitalis, who wrote his

---

[1] J. A. Brundage, *The Crusades, Holy War and Canon Law*, (Aldershot, 1991), II p. 380. An unfortunate beginning to his 1960 article, which is more than redressed in the pathbreaking 'Prostitution, Miscegenation and Sexual Purity in the First Crusade' *Ibid*. XIX, pp. 57-65.

[2] Bernold of St Blaisen (Constance), *Chronicon*, 1096, *Die Chroniken Bertholds von Richenau und Bernolds von Konstanz 1054-1100*, ed. I. S. Robinson, *MGH Scriptores Rerum Germanicorum nova series* 14 (Hanover, 2003), p. 529: *innumerabiles*.

[3] AA 125.

Ecclesiastical History between 1125 and 1141, noted that the determination to either go to Jerusalem or to help others who were going there affected 'rich and poor, men and women, monks and clerks, townspeople and peasants alike. Husbands arranged to leave beloved wives at home, the wives, indeed, sighing, greatly desired to journey with the men, leaving children and all their wealth.'[4] That many women acted on this inclination is clear. Guibert, abbot of Nogent's history, written to provide the monastic reader with a set of moral standards[5] is full of (usually derogatory) references to women and is an important source more generally for the theological and moral view of women in the early twelfth century. Guibert was another eyewitness to the departure of those participating in the expedition and described how 'the meanest most common men and even unworthy women were appropriating to themselves this miracle [the mark of the cross].'[6] Ekkehard, abbot of Aura and crusader on the 1101 expedition alongside many of those who had participated in 1096, wrote that of the common people, 'a great part of them were setting out with wives and offspring and laden with the whole household.'[7] In a manner very similar to that of Albert of Aachen, Ekkehard condemned the 'degraded women' (*inhonestas feminei*) who had joined the Lord's host under the guise of religion.[8] The Anglo-Saxon chronicler, writing in Peterborough, had very little to say about the Crusade, but he did think it noteworthy that countless people set out, with women and children (*wifan and cildan*).[9] The near contemporary Annals of Augsburg say that along with warriors, bishops, abbots, monks, clerics and men of diverse professions, 'serfs and women' (*coloni et mulieres*) joined the movement.[10]

The epic poem, the *Chanson d'Antioche*, which, it is generally accepted, contains eyewitness material, has the lines: 'There were many ladies who carried crosses, and the (freeborn) French maidens whom God loved greatly went with the father who begat them.'[11] Anna Comnena, the daughter of the Byzantine Emperor, Alexius I, writing in the 1140s gave a brief description of the People's Crusade whose unusual make-up must have been a striking feature. She remembered seeing 'a host of civilians,

---

[4] OV 5, 17: *Diuitibus itaque et pauperibus, uiris et mulieribus. monachis et clericis, urbanis et rusticis, in Ierusalem eundi aut euntes adiuuandi inerat voluntas mirabilis. Mariti dilectas coniuges domi relinquere disponebant, illae uero gementes relicta prole cum omnibus diuitiis suis in peregrinatione uiros suos sequi ualde cupiebant.*

[5] J. G. Schenk, *The Use of Rhetoric, Biblical Exegesis and Polemic in Guibert of Nogent's 'Gesta Dei per Francos'* (unpublished M. Phil thesis: TCD, 2001).

[6] GN 330: *... quilibet extremae vulgaritatis homines et etiam muliebris indignitas hoc sibi tot modis, tot partibus usurpavere miraculum.*

[7] EA 140.

[8] EA 144.

[9] *The Anglo-Saxon Chronicles*, ed. Michael Swanton (London, 2000), p. 323.

[10] *Annales Augustani, MGH SS* 3, 134.

[11] *Chanson d'Antioche*, II.2, 9-12: *Des dames i ot maintes qui ont les crois portées; Et les frances pucieles que Diex a moult amées O lor pères s'en vont quit les ont engenrées.* See also Susan B. Edgington, '*Sont çou ore les fems que jo voi la venir?* Women in the *Chanson d'Antioche*', in *Gendering the Crusades*, ed. S. B. Edginton and S. Lambert (Cardiff, 2001), pp. 154-62, here p. 155.

outnumbering the sand of the sea shore or the stars of heaven, carrying palms and bearing crosses on their shoulders. There were women and children too, who had left their countries.'[12] In his description of the disastrous aftermath of the battle of Civetote, 21 October 1096, Albert of Aachen wrote of the Turks who came to the camp of the crusaders: 'Entering those tents they found them containing the faint and the frail, clerks, monks, aged women, young boys, all indeed they killed with the sword. Only delicate young girls and nuns whose faces and beauty seemed to please the eye and beardless young men with charming expressions they took away.'[13] This description by Albert is particularly important in that it draws attention to the previously barely noticed fact that nuns (*moniales*) came on the crusade.

Even after the slaughter at Civetote, many women were assimilated into the Princes' Crusade. It is clear, indeed, that large numbers of women were travelling with the Princes' contingents. In Brindisi the first ship of those sailing with Robert of Normandy capsized (5 April 1097). Fulcher of Chartres wrote of the incident that four hundred 'of both sexes' perished by drowning.[14] Fulcher described the united army at Nicea as containing women and children.[15] The *Chanson d'Antioche* indicated that the camp of the crusaders had a particular women's section, which was raided by the Turks shortly after the siege of Nicea:

> 'Firstly, turning their violence on the ladies,
> Those who attracted them they took on
> horseback,
> And tearing the breasts of the old women,
> When the mothers were killed their children
> cried out,
> The dead mothers suckled them, it was a very
> great grief,
> They climbed up on them seeking their breasts,
> They must be reigning [in heaven] with the
> Innocents.'[16]

The anonymous author of *Gesta Francorum* reported that at the battle of Dorylaeum (1 July 1097), the women in the camp were a great help, for they brought up water for the fighting men to drink and bravely always

---

[12] Anna Comnena, *The Alexiad*, X.5, trans. E. R. A. Sewter (Middlesex, 1979) p. 309.

[13] AA 119: *tentoria vero illorum intrantes quosquos repererunt laguidos ac debiles, clericos, monachos, mulieres gradeuas, pueros, sugentes, omnen vero etatem gladio extinxerunt. Solummodo puellas teneras et moniales quarum facies et forma oculis eorum placere videbatur, iuvenesque inberbes et vultu venustos adbuxerunt.*

[14] FC I,VIII,2 (169).

[15] FC I, X, 4 (183).

[16] *Chanson d'Antioche*, III.4, 15-21: *Premièrment aus Dames vont leur regne tournant, Celes qui lor contequent es sieles vont montant, Et aus vieilletes vont les mamelles torgant. Quant les mères sont moretes, si crient li enfant, Sor les pis lor montoient, les mameles querant, La mère morte alaitent; ce fu dolor moult grant, El regne aus innocents doivent estre manans.* See also Susan B. Edginton, 'Women in the *Chanson d'Antioche*', p. 155.

encouraged them, fighters and defenders.[17] The *Chanson d'Antioche* has a description of the same scene:

> 'The baronage was thirsty, it was greatly
> oppressed;
> The knights of Tancred strongly desired water.
> They were greatly served by them who were
> with them.
> The ladies and maidens of whom there were
> numerous in the army; Because they readied
> themselves, they threw off their cloaks,
> And carried water to the exhausted knights,
> In pots, bowls and in golden chalices.
> When the barons had drunk they were
> reinvigorated.'[18]

During the battle, Turkish horsemen were sent to cover a possible line of retreat, and the near contemporary *Historia Vie Hierosolimitane* recorded that they 'cruelly put to the sword almost a thousand men, women, and unarmed, common folk.'[19] Further along the march in the arid stretches of Asia Minor, in July 1097 William of Tyre noted the presence of women on the crusade, and their suffering: 'Pregnant women, because of the rigours of both thirst and of the intolerable heat were forced to expel the foetus before the time decreed by nature. Through sheer mental distress they cast them out in coverlets, some of them alive, some half dead. Others with more humane feelings embraced their offspring. They fell down along the route and forgetful of their feminine sex exposed their secret parts. To a great extent they were more apprehensive about the immediate risk of death than that about the preservation of the reverence that was due to their sex.'[20] Albert of Aachen referred to there being thousands of women and children at the siege of Antioch that began 21 October 1097.[21] The *Gesta Francorum* had a description of a woman in the camp of Bohemond being killed by an arrow during that siege.[22] In the plague that followed the capture of the

---

[17] GF 19.

[18]*Chanson d'Antioche*, III.11, 3-10: *Li barnages ot soif, si fu moult oppressés; Forment desirent l'aigue li chevalier Tangrés. Mestier lor ont éu celes de leur regné, Les dames et pucieles dont il i ot assés; Quar eles se rebracent, les dras ont jus jetés, Et portèrent de l'aigue aus chevaliers lassés, As pos et as escueles et as henas dorés: Quant ont bu li baron tout sont resvigorés.* See also Susan B. Edginton, 'Women in the *Chanson d'Antioche*', p. 155.

[19] GP 86-7: *crudeliter ense necauit, Mille viros ferme, mulieres, vulgus inerme.*

[20] WT 217-18: *pregnantes pre sitis angustia et caloris intemperie ante tempus a natura decretum fetus edere compellerentur, quos pre anxietate spiritus quosdam vivos, extinctos quosdam, alios etiam semineces in strate proiciebant; alie, ampliore habundantes humanitate proles suas circumplexe, per vias volutabantur et sexus oblite feminei archana denudabant, magis pro instante mortis periculo sollicite quam ut sexui debitam conservarent reverentiam.*

[21] AA 252.

[22] GF 29.

city women were notably more likely to be victims.[23] At the climactic denouement of the First Crusade, the capture of Jerusalem (13-15 July 1099), women were still present in considerable numbers, sharing the work and bringing water and words of encouragement to the men. Indeed, according to William of Tyre, who although writing some three generations after the events had access to local traditions in Jerusalem, the women even presumed to take up arms.[24]

This by no means exhaustive selection of references to women on the Crusade, from a range of sources, establishes without a doubt that women were present in large numbers. But is it possible to focus more closely on the women present in the First Crusade and indicate something of their motivation?

One group of women whose presence and role is most easily understood are those who were members of the aristocracy.[25] Because the sources were largely written for the benefit of the aristocracy and because historians such as William of Tyre were interested in the genealogy of the leading noble families in Outremer, we are in a position to name some of the aristocratic women involved in the Crusade. Raymond of Toulouse brought with him on the Crusade his third wife, Elvira, daughter of Alfonso VI of Castile by his mistress, Ximene.[26] Baldwin of Boulogne, later Count of Eddessa, also brought his wife, Godehilde of Tosny, 'an illustrious lady of high rank from England' wrote William of Tyre.[27] Godehilde's first cousin, Emma of Hereford came on the crusade with her husband Ralph I of Gael.[28] Bohemond brought his sister with him on Crusade and once he and his nephew[29] Tancred had obtained their impressive landholdings in Outremer, he sought and received suitably prestigious marriage partners. Bohemund married Constance and Tancred her half-sister Cecilia, both daughters of Philip I of France. It is likely that Count Baldwin of Bourcq brought at least one of his sisters with him as she later (12 September 1115) married Roger, Prince of Antioch.[30] Walo II, lord of Chaumont-en-Vexin brought his wife, Humberge, daughter of Hugh Le Puiset and sister of the crusader Everard.[31] On the deatho of Walo, Humberge was described as being supported by a band

---

[23] WT 344.

[24] WT 403.

[25] For a full discussion of their presence on the crusade see S. Geldsetzer, *Frauen Auf Kreuzzügen 1096-1291* (Darmstadt, 2003) esp. Appendix 2, pp. 184-7.

[26] FC I, XXXII, 1 (320); GN 134.

[27] AA 139; WT 453. See also S. Geldsetzer, *Frauen Auf Kreuzzügen*, p. 186.

[28] OV 2, IV, 318. See also S. Geldsetzer, *Frauen Auf Kreuzzügen*, p. 185.

[29] The relationship that historians have generally reached consensus upon, see R. L. Nicholson. *Tancred: A study of his career and work in their relation to the First Crusade and the Establishment of the Latin States in Syria and Palestine* (Chicago, 1940) p. 3-15, who opts, based on a discussion of the contemporary evidence, for Tancred being the son of Bohemund's half sister Emma, whereas she is shown as a full sister to Bohemund but without supporting evidence in the Hauteville family tree in E. van Houts, *The Normans in Europe* (Manchester, 2000) p. 298.

[30] WT 498.

[31] RM 794 – 6; GP 127. See also S. Geldsetzer, *Frauen Auf Kreuzzügen*, p. 186.

of mature ladies (*matres*).[32] In all likelihood the wives and sisters of many other lesser nobles intending to stay in the newly won crusader states were present, but by and large they did not come to the attention of the chroniclers of the Crusade. We know that Hadvide of Chiny, for example, journeyed with her husband Dodo of Cons-la-Grandville only due to charter evidence.[33] Emeline, wife of Fulcher a knight of Bullion only appears in the historical record as a crusader, due to Albert of Aachen taking an interest in the story that although she was captured, because of her beauty an illustrious Turkish knight, a general of Omar, lord of Azaz fell in love with her. At the suggestion of Emeline, this Turkish general contacted Duke Godfrey of Lotharingia with a view to leading a revolt against Ridwan of Aleppo.[34] Other than this example, aristocratic women seem to have played no independent role in the Crusade. Their actions or words are not mentioned. This is hardly surprising given that for an aristocratic woman to have a measure of authority c.1100 she would have had to be a widow with a sizeable patrimony or a mother with significant influence over powerful sons. It was the next generation of aristocratic women who controlled property in the Kingdom of Jerusalem who were able to wield some political power, or indeed those women left behind by their noble husbands. The women of the nobility present on the initial expedition were brought to generate families should the conquest be successful and were not in a position to play an independent political role during the campaign. Indeed if their male guardian died on the crusade such aristocratic women could be placed in a difficult position, Humberge was given a speech on the death of Walo that includes the question: 'other than with a man, can a woman live following the camp?'[35] Although dependent on Ovid for the phrase, Gilo posed the question in the contemporary setting of the Crusade, using the classical reference to indicate the dependency of the position of aristocratic women on their guardians.

Beyond the aristocratic women there were far greater numbers of women of the other social orders. There is no possibility of finding out their names or much detail concerning their backgrounds. Eyewitness descriptions of the gathering of forces for the First Crusade, however, have important information to offer. It is clear, first of all, that women from the social order of *pauperes*, both urban and rural poor, came with their husbands and children on the crusade. Guibert of Nogent, for example, was amused at the setting forth of entire families of the poor from southern France: 'you were seeing extraordinarily and plainly the best of jokes; the poor, for example, tied their cattle to two-wheeled carts, as though they were armoured horses, carrying their few possessions, together with their small children, in the wagon. And these

[32] GP 126.

[33] *Chartres de l'abbaye de St-Hubert-en-Ardenne*, ed. G. Kurth, I (Brussels, 1903), p. 81. For Dodo of Cons-la-Grandville see J. Riley-Smith, *The First Crusaders,* p. 203.

[34] AA 380. See also S. Geldsetzer, *Frauen Auf Kreuzzügen*, p. 185.

[35] GP 128 – 9.

infants, when coming to a castle or a city, enquired eagerly if this were the Jerusalem to which they strained.'[36]

From Pope Urban II's letter to the clergy and people of Bologna of September 1096, it is clear that the unexpected departure of large numbers of non-combatant forces was a concern and a development to be restrained.[37] But it is hardly surprising that peasants undertaking the crusade with the expectation of finding a better life moved in entire families. As Ekkehard disapprovingly observed, 'the farmers, the women and children, roving with unheard of folly, abandoned the land of their birth, gave up their own property and yearned for that of foreigners and go to an uncertain promised land.'[38] There can be no question of describing such women as prostitutes or camp followers. These married women were non-combatant participants like the elderly, the clergy and the children on the crusade.

In addition to married women of urban and rural poor families, there is also evidence that unattached women participated in the Crusade. For this there are five important and interesting sources. The first has already been presented: Albert of Aachen's anger that what should be been a chaste undertaking in the manner of all pilgrimages was contaminated by licentiousness.[39]

The second was a description of the recruiting activities of Peter the Hermit by Guibert of Nogent. Peter was an enormously influential figure in generating support for the crusade and led the People's Crusade: '[Peter the Hermit] was liberal towards the poor showing great generosity from the goods that were given to him, making wives of prostitutes [*prostitutae mulieres*] through his gifts to their husbands.'[40]

Guibert's use of the term *prostitutae* needs to be put in context. In contemporary ideology, particularly that of a monk, for a woman to fail to give an appearance of modesty, let alone for her to engage in sexual activity outside the bonds of marriage, meant she was considered a prostitute.[41] In fact canonists found it very difficult to define prostitution. A letter by Jerome's (ca.342-420) contained the definition that 'a whore is one who lies open to the lust of many men'. In the same letter Jerome clarifies this by saying that 'a woman who has been abandoned by many lovers is not a prostitute.'[42] It was the first formulation that was to be

---

[36] GN 120: *Videres mirum quiddam et plane ioco aptissimum, pauperes videlicet quosdam, bobus biroto applicitis eisdemque in modum equorum ferratis, substantiolas cum parvulis in carruca convehere et ipsos infantulos, dum obviam habent quaelibet castella vel urbes, si haec esset Jherusalem, ad quam tenderent rogitare.*

[37] Urban II, letter to the clergy and people of Bologna, H. Hagenmeyer ed. *Die Kreuzzugsbriefe aus den Jahren 1088 – 1100* (Innsbruck, 1901), p. 137-8.

[38] EA 140.

[39] See above, note 3.

[40] GN 121: ... *dilargitione erga pauperes liberalis, prostitutas mulieres non sine suo munere maritis honestans.* For Peter the Hermit see above p. xxx.

[41] As summarised in J. A. Brundage, *Sex, Law and Marriage in the Middle Ages* (Aldershot, 1993) I, p. 378.

[42] Jerome, *Epistula*, 64.7, *PL* 22, col. 611: *Meretrix, quae multorum libidini patet*; col. 612: *Non meretricem, quae multis exposita est amatoribus.*

used by Gratian for his widely distributed *Decretum* (ca.1140).[43] In other words, the early twelfth century concept *prostitutae* was far broader and much more detached from financial exchange than the modern term prostitute. The term was used by church reformers to refer to priests' wives, women who would have considered themselves entirely respectable. Given this context, it seems reasonable to understand Guibert's *prostitutae mulieres* as wandering women – his sense of proper place being offended in a manner similar to his attitude towards runaway monks – rather than their literally being 'prostitutes'.

In an article unrelated to the crusade, Georges Duby made a comment that is extremely helpful in analysing the description given by Guibert of the activities of Peter the Hermit. In discussing the consequences of the drive to reform the church from 1075-1125, Duby wrote: 'Prostitution flourished in the rapidly expanding towns, thronging with uprooted immigrants. Above all, there were those women without men that the reform movement had itself thrown out onto the street, the wives abandoned by husbands because they were priests, or if laymen, because they were bigamists or had contracted an incestuous union. These women were to be pitied, but they were also dangerous, threatening to corrupt men and lead them astray...'[44]

The fact that Peter the Hermit was providing dowries to 'prostitutes' has been noted by E. O. Blake and C. Morris as showing that his was an urban audience.[45] But it seems possible to draw a further conclusion, that Peter the Hermit was using his gifts to gather a following amongst marginalised women. Those who accompanied him on crusade should therefore, once more, not be considered camp followers in the conventional sense. In the period of the First Crusade these women were *prostitutae* only in the sense that they were unmarried and as such a cause for concern, particularly to the clergy who were anxious at the potential social disorder they might cause and the contamination of the purity of the pilgrimage. The reforming concept of pilgrimage was closely related to that of the Truce of God, a clerically led peace movement that emphasised chastity and abstinence during the period of peace.

The third source, Raymond of Aguilers, gave very detailed accounts of the speeches of peasant visionaries, from which it is possible to detect elements of the political programme of the poor crusader. In one vision of St Andrew to Peter Bartholomew (30 November 1098), we have evidence that the body of unmarried women was still a cause for concern, as the saint says 'amongst your ranks is a great deal of adultery, though it would please God if you all take wives.'[46] This idea seems remarkably similar to the aims of Peter the Hermit who was closely linked to the

[43]Gratian, *Decretum*, C.XVI. See J. A. Brundage, *Sex, Law and Marriage in the Middle Ages*, p. 827.

[44] G. Duby, *Women of the twelfth century, I: Eleanor of Aquitaine and six others*, trans. J. Birrell (Cambridge, 1997), p. 36.

[45] E. O. Blake and C. Morris, 'A hermit goes to war: Peter and the origins of the First Crusade', *Studies in Church History* 22, 1984, 79-107.

[46] RA 171: *Inter vos caedes et... plurima adulteria: quum Deo placitum sit, si uxores vos omnes ducatis.*

pauperes, for whom, in part, Peter Bartholomew was speaking. Guibert of Nogent, writing for the edification of his congregation of monks, says that the measures taken on the crusade against unmarried women were far more severe than desiring they be married off. Having made the point that those requiring the protection of God should not be subject to lustful thoughts, he wrote that 'it happened there that neither a mention of harlot or the name of a prostitute was tolerated... because if it was found that any of those woman was found have become pregnant, who was proven to be without husbands, she and her procurer were surrendered to atrocious punishments.... Meanwhile it came to pass that a certain monk of the most famous monastery, had the cloister of his monastery and undertaken the expedition to Jerusalem, being inspired not by piety but by shallowness, was caught with some woman or other. If I am not mistaken he was found to be guilty by the judgement of red-hot iron, and finally the Bishop of Le Puy and the others ordered that the miserable woman with her lover be led naked through all the corners of the camps and be most fearfully lashed by whips, to the terror of the onlookers.'[47] That Guibert is particularly vehement on this point is unsurprising given his purpose. As Brundage has noted, the incident is likely to have some basis in fact given that Albert of Aachen tells a similar story.[48]

Fourthly, a more precisely observed episode of relevance occurred at a moment of great strain for the crusade, January 1098, during the siege of Antioch, when famine was causing the movement to disintegrate. During this crisis the higher clergy managed to gain an influence over the movement, which they were not subsequently able to maintain. Their argument that to weather the crisis particularly devout behaviour was required carried the day and therefore their hostility to the presence of unmarried women on the crusade surfaced in the form of a decision that women should be driven from the camp. Fulcher – at the time in Edessa – wrote that 'the Franks, having again consulted together, expelled the women from the army, the married as well as the unmarried, lest perhaps defiled by the sordidness of riotous living they should displease the Lord. These women then sought shelter for themselves in neighbouring towns.'[49] William of Tyre describes the same incident as being a more limited purge of solely 'light foolish women' (*leves mulierculae*).[50] This incident reveals the presence of significant numbers of unmarried women

---

[47] GN 196: *Unde fiebat ut ibi nec mentio scorti nec nomen prostibuli toleraretur haberi...quod si gravidam inveniri constitisset aliquam earum mulierum, quae probantur carere maritis, atrocibus tradebatur cum suo lenone suppliciis. Contigit interea quemdam predicatissimi omnium coenobii monachum, qui monasterii sui claustra fugaciter excessarat et Iherosolimitanam expeditionem non pietate sed levitate provocatus inierat, cum aliqua femina ibi deprehendi, igniti, nisi fallor, ferri iudicio convinci ac demum Podiensis episcopi ceterorumque precepto per omnes castrorum vicos miseram illam cum suo amasio circumduci et flagris nudos ad terrorem intuentium dirissme verberari.*

[48] AA 261-2.

[49] FC I, XV, 14 (223): *tunc facto deinde consilio, eiecerunt feminas de exercitu, tam maritatas quam immaritatas, ne forte luxuriae sordibus inquinati Domino displicerent. Illae vero in castris adfinibus tunc hospitia sibi adsumpserunt.*

[50] WT 264.

on the Crusade and that given the opportunity the senior clergy moved to drive them away and give the movement a character more in keeping with the reforming military pilgrimage that Pope Urban II had envisaged.

Finally, the fifth piece of direct evidence for the presence of large numbers of unmarried women on the crusade, an excerpt from the chronicle of Bernold of St Blaisen (Constance): 'At this time a very great multitude from Italy and from all France and Germany began to go to Jerusalem against the pagans in order that they might liberate the Christians. The Lord Pope was the principal founder of this expedition ...an innumerable multitude of poor people leapt at that journey too simple-mindedly and they neither knew nor were able in any way to prepare themselves for such danger... It was not surprising that they could not complete the proposed journey to Jerusalem because they did not begin that journey with such humility and piety as they ought. For they had very many apostates in their company who had cast off their monastic habits and intended to fight. But they were not afraid to have with them innumerable women who had criminally changed their natural clothing to masculine clothing with whom they committed fornication, by doing which they offended God remarkably just as also of the people of Israel in former times and therefore at length, after many labours, dangers and death, since they were not permitted to enter Hungary they began to return home with great sadness having achieved nothing.'[51]

The importance of Bernold's work is that it is the most contemporary eyewitness account of the setting forth of the Crusade. He did not wait for the end of the year to write up his chronicle and therefore it is particularly valuable in recording the immediate response to events. It is notable that he shared with Guibert of Nogent and Albert of Aachen a sense that women leaving their allocated social position are similar to monks casting off their habits. Bernold's description of women dressing as men in order to go on crusade is supported by an entry in the Annals of Disibodenberg which states that news of the expedition depopulated 'cities of bishops [and] villages of dwellers. And not only men and youths but even the greatest number of women undertook the journey. Wonderful indeed was the spirit of that time in order that people should be urged on to this journey. For women in this expedition were going forth in manly dress and they marched armed.'[52]

---

[51] Bernold of St Blaisen (Constance), *Chronicon*, 1096, pp. 527-9: *His temporibus maxima multitudo de Italia et omni Gallia et Germania Ierosolimam contra paganos, ut liberarent christianos, ire cepit. Cuius expeditionis domnus papa maximus auctor fuit... Nimium tamen simpliciter innumerabilis multitudo popularium illud iter arripuerunt, qui nullomodo se ad tale periculum praeparare noverunt vel potuerunt...Non erat autem mirum, quod propositum iter ad Ierosolimam explere non potuerent, quia non tali humilitate et devotione, ut deberent, illud iter adorsi sunt. Nam et plures apostatas in comitatu suo habuerunt, qui abiecto religionis habitu cum illis militare proposuerunt. Sed et innumerabiles feminas secum habere non timuerunt, quae naturalem habitum in virilem nefarie mutaverunt, cum quibus fornicati sunt; in quo Deum mirabiliter, sicut et Israheliticus populus quondam offenderunt. Unde post multos labores, pericula et mortes, tandem, cum Ungariam non permitterentur intrare, domum inacte cum magna tristicia ceperunt repedare.*

[52] *Annales s. Disibodi*, MGH SS 17, 16: *regna rectoribus, urbes pastoribus, vici vastantur habitatoribus; et non tantum viri et pueri, sed etiam mulieres quam plurimae hoc iter sunt aggressae. Mirabilis enim*

It is possible to see women taking men's clothing as a form of protection for their journey. Their action could also be a form a social statement, indicating a desire to be considered pilgrims. Both ideas are present in a twelfth century saint's life, that of St Hildegund, who is disguised by her father, a knight, during their travels on crusade to Jerusalem and who retains her garb to become a famous monk whose secret is only revealed upon her death.[53]

The prescriptions against women wearing men's clothes would have been well known at the time of the First Crusade, for example that in Burchard of Worms' widely disseminated *Decretum*: 'if a woman changes her clothes and puts on manly garb for the customary female clothes, for the sake, as it is thought, of chastity, let her be anathema.'[54] Guibert of Nogent also told an interesting story in his autobiography in which men and women overcome their fear and distaste of cross-dressing in order to disguise themselves for an escape.[55] Nevertheless by this time there was an almost respectable tradition of pious women disguising themselves as men to escape persecution or to live like monks, for example, Pelagia, Thecla, Anastasia, Dorothea, Eugenia, Euphrosyne, Marina and Theodora.[56] Whether these tales had any influence over the cross-dressing crusaders is entirely speculative, but it is possible to draw at least one unambiguous conclusion from the description in Bernold and the Annals of Disibodenberg, which is that these women did not attach themselves to the movement as prostitutes – male attire and the bearing of arms being completely inappropriate for such a role.

Insofar as historians have considered the role of women on the First Crusade they have tended to make the assumption that the majority of women were associated with the movement as camp followers, prostitutes. A closer examination of the evidence suggests that this is an error and that the thousands of women who went on the Crusade – to find a promised land, or to get away from the towns in which many of them had been abandoned – did so as participants, as pilgrims.

---

spiritus illius temporis homines impulit ad hoc iter aggrediendum. Nam feminae in hanc expeditionem exeuntes virili utebantur habitu et armatae incedebant.

[53] A. Butler, *Butler's lives of the Saints, April* (London, 1999), p. 141-2. See also V. L Bullough and B. Bullough, *Cross Dressing, Sex and Gender* (Philadelphia, 1993) p. 54.

[54] Buchard of Worms, *Decretum*, VIII.60, *PL* 140, col. 805A: *Si qua mulier propter continentiam quae putatur, habitum mutat, et pro solito muliebri amictu virilem sumit, anathema sit.*

[55] Guibert of Nogent, *Monodiae*, III.9.

[56] D. Farmer, *Oxford Dictionary of Saints* (Oxford, 1997), p. 396 (Pelagia), p. 462 (Thecla). J. Coulson ed., *The Saints – a concise biographical dictionary* (London, 1958), p. 28 (Anastasia), p. 160 (Eugenia), p. 177 (Euphrosyne), p. 300 (Marina), p. 428 (Theodora). See also V. L Bullough and B. Bullough, *Cross Dressing, Sex and Gender*, p. 51.

Chapter 4   Eleanor of Aquitaine and the women of the Second Crusade

In a search for powerful medieval women, whose lives demonstrated agency and the possibilities open to women, many historians and readers have gravitated towards Eleanor of Aquitaine. It is certainly true that her long political career demonstrates a great deal about the role of aristocratic women in the twelfth century. On the whole though, Eleanor's autonomy has been exaggerated and the history around her often mythologised to present her as a Amazon for feudal times. I follow George Duby, however, in seeing her as very much constrained by the men around her and only rarely able to escape their control.

One such moment in which the circumstances allowed her to steer her own course was during the Second Crusade, where for a brief moment she was leading a faction of the French army against the wishes of her husband, the French king, Louis VII. Understanding those circumstances and how quickly the conditions that allowed Eleanor to steer her own course is useful for shedding light on the situation of elite medieval women more generally and how unusual it was for them to grasp the reins of power.

Moreover, a study of Eleanor and the question of women on the Second Crusade allowed me to compare their participation with the women of the First Crusade. It is sometimes thought that there has been incremental progress in the rights of women from severe oppression in the distant past to a much less onerous inequality today. The comparison between the two crusades suggests that in the period c.1100 – 1150 in Europe, there might in fact have been a development of more restrictive rules around women at the time of the Second Crusade.

There is a very striking contrast between the sources of the First Crusade (1096–9) and those for the Second (1147–8). It is hard, although some narrative historians of an earlier era did so, to miss the references to women in all the sources for the First Crusade. In even the tersest accounts of the Crusade there can be found mention of women participants. So, for example, The Anglo-Saxon chronicler, writing in Peterborough, had only a few lines of comment about the Crusade, but he did think it noteworthy that countless people set out, with 'women and children'.[1] The near contemporary *Annals of Augsburg* stated that along with warriors, bishops, abbots, monks, clerics and men of diverse

---

[1] Michael Swanton (ed.), *The Anglo-Saxon chronicles* (London, 2000), p. 323: *wifan and cildan*.

professions, 'serfs and women' joined the movement.[2] When the longer accounts of the expedition are examined it becomes clear that women participated in the First Crusade in their thousands and they even led popular contingents of departing crusaders.[3]

The sources for the events of 1147–8, however, very rarely mention women. The presence of women on the Second Crusade is only evident from a small number of references and even then in more fragmentary fashion than is the case with regard to the material concerning the First Crusade. This contrast provokes the question that is investigated here.

Does the absence of women in the sources for the Second Crusade genuinely reflect the fact that fewer women participated in it? Or is it that those contemporaries who wrote about the Second Crusade paid less attention to the presence of women and therefore created a false impression that there were fewer women crusaders than in the expedition of 1096-9?

For the First Crusade historians have a relative abundance of source material. Fulcher of Chartres, Raymond of Aguilers and the anonymous author of the *Gesta Francorum* were all crusaders who wrote substantial accounts of the expedition.[4] Soon after its completion, a well-informed Lotharingian monk, Albert of Aachen, also wrote a very rich and valuable history.[5] But for an account of what happened to the major armies of the Second Crusade there is only one history of comparable length written by a participant: Odo of Deuil's *De profectione Ludovici VII in Orientem*.[6] The other participant historian, Otto of Freising, was so disheartened by the experience that when he came to the year 1147 in his history of Frederick I, king of Germany, he stated that he would leave the subject to others, as he had not set out to write a tragedy.[7] So for eyewitnesses we are left with Odo, a monk from the monastery of St Denis, who accompanied King Louis VII on the Second Crusade as his chaplain. In 1152, Odo replaced the very important figure of Suger, regent of France and confidant of the king, as abbot of St Denis, a position he retained until his death in 1162.

The structure of Odo's work is that of an extended letter, as if he were explaining events for the benefit of Suger back in France. It covers the events from the large assembly on Easter Sunday in 1146 at Vézalay,

---

[2] *Annales Augustani, MGH SS* 3, 134: *coloni et mulieres*.

[3] Baldric of Dol, *Historia Hierosolymitana, RHC Oc*. ▨, ▨–▨▨▨, hereafter BD, here 17. For women and the First Crusade see C. Kostick, *The social structure of the First Crusade* (Leiden, 2008), pp. 217–86. See also S.B. Edgington, '*Sont çou ore les fems que jo voi la venir?* Women in the *Chanson d'Antioche*', in S.B. Edgington and S. Lambert (eds), *Gendering the Crusades* (Cardiff, 2001), pp. 154-62.

[4] Fulcher of Chartres, *Historia Hierosolymitana (1095-1127)*, ed. H. Hagenmeyer (Heidelberg, 1913); Raymond of Aguilers, *Historia Francorum qui ceperunt Iherusalem*, ed. John France (Ph.D. thesis, University of Nottingham, 1967); R. Hill (ed. & trans.), *Gesta Francorum et aliorum Hierosolimitanorum* (London, 1962). For the complex relationship between the *Gesta Francorum* and a very similar account by the eye-witness Peter Tudebode, see J. Rubenstein, 'What is the *Gesta Francorum*, and who was Peter Tudebode?' *Revue Mabillon* 16 (2005), 179–204.

[5] Albert of Aachen, *Historia Ierosolimitana*, ed. S.B. Edgington (Oxford, 2007), hereafter AA.

[6] Odo of Deuil's *De profectione Ludovici VII in Orientem*, ed. V.G. Berry (New York, 1968), hereafter OD.

[7] *Ottonis et Rahewini Gesta Frederici I. Imperatoris*, G. Waitz and B. Simson (eds), *MGH Scriptores rerum Germanicarum in usum scholarum*, vol. 46, 3rd ed. (Hanover, 1912), hereafter OF, p. 65.

where Louis launched the French contingent by distributing crosses, to the king's arrival at Antioch in March 1148, at which point Odo probably wrote his history. Frustratingly, it therefore says nothing of the subsequent political crisis at Antioch in which Louis' wife, Eleanor of Aquitaine, played an important part, nor the siege of Damascus in 1148.

There is only one clear reference to the presence of women on the Second Crusade in the *De profectione Ludovici VII in Orientem*. In writing of the negotiations between Louis and Manuel I Comnenus, the Byzantine Emperor, Odo reported that the emperor demanded two things: a kinswoman of the king's, who accompanied the queen, as wife for one of his nephews and the homage of the French barons. While the French crusading nobility were considering these demands, Robert, count of Perche, Louis' younger brother, took matters into his own hands. He 'secretly abducted his kinswoman from the queen's retinue, thereby releasing himself and certain barons from paying homage to the emperor and his relative from marrying the emperor's nephew.'[8]

It is not possible to identify the Capetian noblewoman at the centre of this dispute. But the example is crucial nonetheless as it shows the participation of the French queen, Eleanor of Aquitaine, was not an isolated example of a noblewoman being present on the crusade: she had a female retinue with her. This information derived from the key source, although only momentarily drawing attention to the presence of women on the crusade, is sufficient to substantiate the later and more distant reports that have to be examined to flesh out the issue.

Henry of Huntington, the influential English historian, wrote, c.1154, a very brief summary of the events of the Second Crusade in his *Historia Anglorum*. He contrasted the success of the humble naval expedition that captured Lisbon in 1147 with the failure of the great armies led by kings and explained this by the fact the humility of the former earned God's favour, while the pride of the latter caused God to despise them. Moreover, their incontinence, open practice of fornication and adulteries rose up in the sight of God.[9] That this sinful activity involved women who had departed with the crusading armies was a major theme of another English historian, William of Newburgh.

William wrote a history of England at his priory in the final years of his life, around 1196–8, in other words, some 50 years after the events, although with an interest in Eastern affairs. In his youth, William had met a monk who had lived at Antioch for many years.[10] When William described the departure of the Second Crusade he wrote that following the example of Louis and Eleanor, 'many other nobles followed this example and brought their wives with them.'[11] Since the wives of princes

---

[8] OD 57: *cognatam suam reginae clam subripit se cum quibusdam baronibus illius subducens hominio et cognatam suam nepotis eius matrimonio.*

[9] Henry of Huntingdon, *Historia Anglorum* ed. D. Greenway (Oxford, 1996), p. 752.

[10] William of Newburgh, *Historia Rerum Anglicarum*, ed. R.G. Walsh and M.J. Kennedy (Warminster, 1988), hereafter WN, p. 96.

[11] WN 92: ... *multi alii nobiles uxores suas secum duxerunt.*

could not be without ladies-in-waiting, he explained, the resulting multitude of women (*feminarum multitudo*) brought about licentiousness in the Christian camp: a lack of chastity that polluted the army and resulted in the withdrawal of God's favour.[12] William then continued with a more convincing historical and political explanation of the failure of the expedition, but his attempt to offer a reason for why the Christians lacked God's favour draws attention to a wider body of women participants in the crusade than is visible from the work of Odo of Deuil alone.

Rather closer to the events of 1147–8 was William of Tyre. William was Chancellor of the Kingdom of Jerusalem from 1174 and Archbishop of Tyre from 1175 to his death *c.*1185. Thus he was familiar with the traditions of the region and explicitly stated that he had heard accounts from those who had participated in the events of the Second Crusade.[13] William of Tyre's *Chronicon* was commissioned by King Amalric of Jerusalem in 1167 and took its final form after redrafting by William in 1184. The presence of women among the crusading army is quite explicit in the *Chronicon*. In describing the enormous numbers who came with Conrad III alone, William of Tyre wrote that there were 'up to 70,000 with breastplates, not including the footsoldiers, infants and women and riders with light armour'.[14]

On 7 January 1148, the French contingent split. The vanguard, having ascended Mount Cadmus (about 25 miles south east of Laodicea in Phrygia), pushed on in search of a better camping place, leaving a considerable gap to the baggage train and the rearguard. A Turkish force that had been monitoring the Christian army seized the opportunity and attacked from the heights of the mountain, inflicting great losses on the French. That night, wrote William of Tyre, those in the camp waiting for news of the battle were oppressed by grief. 'This man sought his father, that his lord; that woman sought her husband, this her son and when they did not find what they sought, they spent the night kept awake by the burden of their cares.'[15] William therefore believed that considerable numbers of women, of unspecified social rank, were accompanying the French army.

In these sources then, the evidence for women on the Second Crusade indicates that noblewomen were present, along with their ladies-in-waiting, but – apart from the deduction that female servants of these noble ladies were likely to have been present – there is no indication of the presence on the crusade of a large body of women of the lower social orders, such as was the case on the First Crusade. Since we have only a limited number of near contemporary sources it cannot necessarily be

---

[12] WN 92-4, 128.

[13] William of Tyre, *Chronicon*, ed. R.B.C. Huygens, CC Vols LXIII and LXIII A (Turnholt, 1986), hereafter WT, pp 742, 747.

[14] WT 742: ... *exceptis peditibus, parvulis et mulieribus et equitibus levis armature.*

[15] WT 752-3: *Hic patrem, ille dominum; illa filium, hec maritum cuncta lustrando perquirit; dumque non inveniunt quod querunt, noctem percurrunt pondere curarum pervigilem.*

concluded that such women were not present: it might be that the lack of information concerning lower class women reflects more on the interests and outlook of these particular medieval historians than the actual role of women on the crusade.

A survey of the annalistic sources offers some insight into this question. As noted above, two chroniclers specifically noted the presence of large numbers of women among the popular contingents of the First Crusade setting out in 1096, and their testimony is supported by the chronicle of Bernold of St Blaisen (Constance), as well as eyewitnesses to the departure of the crusade who subsequently wrote histories of the expedition.[16] Do we have similar information in the annals of 1147? Certainly we get a picture of a huge popular response to the appeal for a new crusade: German and Lotharingian annals in particular emphasized the great numbers of people of all social backgrounds who participated in the Second Crusade. The *Annals of Aachen*, the *Annals of St Peter of Erfut*, and those of the Premontre Continuator of Sigebert of Gembloux all refer to an 'innumerable multitude' taking part in the journey.[17] The later works of Lambert of Ardres and the *Historia Welforum Weingartensis* state that those setting out included 'uncountable thousands of people'[18] and 'men of every condition'.[19] The near contemporary *Annals of Klosterrad* (just north of Aachen) talk of a tenth of the entire land participating.[20] This corresponds with an 1147 letter from Bernard of Clairvaux, the main preacher of the crusade, who rather proudly wrote to his fellow Cistercian, Pope Eugenius III that as a result of his agitation for the expedition 'towns and castles are emptied, one may scarcely find one man amongst seven women, so many women are widowed while their husbands are still alive.'[21] It is notable that Bernard reported men leaving women to participate and not entire families joining the movement.

More precise detail about the departing crusaders is available in the description provided by the eyewitness Gerhoch, provost of Reichersberg (in 1162) of the gathering of the crusading forces:

> There was not a city that did not send forth multitudes or a village or town that did not at least send a few. Bishops together with magnates were each setting out with his own squadrons, carrying shields, swords, armour and other instruments of war with abundant

[16] Bernold of St Blaisen (Constance), *Chronicon*, 1096, pp. 527-9; *Historia peregrinorum euntium*, *RHC Oc.* 3, 167–229, here 174; AA i.25 (48); Ekkehard of Aura, 'Chronica', in F-J Schmale and I. Schmale-Ott (eds), *Frutolfs und Ekkehards Chroniken und die Anonyme Kaiserchronik* (Darmstadt, 1972), pp. 140, 144; Guibert of Nogent, *Gesta Dei per Francos*, ed. R.B.C. Huygens, *CC* LXXVIIa (Turnhout, 1996), hereafter GN, p. 331; BD 17.
[17] *MGH SS* 16, 686; *MGH SS* 16, 20; *MGH SS* 6, 453: ... *multitudine innumerabili*.
[18] *MGH SS* 24, 633: ... *innumeris populorum milibus*.
[19] *MGH SS* 21, 468: ... *cuiuscumque conditionis hominibus*.
[20] *MGH SS*, 16, 718.
[21] Bernard of Clairvaux, *Epistola* 247.2 in J. Leclercq, H.M. Rochais & C.H. Talbot (eds), *Sancti Bernardi opera*, 9 (Rome: Cistercienses, 1957-77), pp 8, 141.

preparation of finances and of tents, which they convoyed with carts and innumerable horses. The highway and that of the neighbouring plains could scarcely contain the innumerable carts and horses; the breadth of the Danube could hardly hold the multitude of boats. For so infinite was the army that from the times when nations began to exist I should have thought that never had so great a multitude of knights and footsoldiers been concentrated together. No markets of goods were lacking for the sale of the necessities, nor were there any fields that lacked carts or horses for conveying food. No lack either of peasants and serfs, the ploughs and services due to their lords having been abandoned without the knowledge or against the will of their lords.[22]

It is clear from these sources, particularly Gerhoch, that in a similar manner to the First Crusade, the preaching of the Second inspired great crowds of all social condition to take up the cross. This seems especially true of the Rhineland, where a Cistercian monk Radulf, responded to the idea of the crusade by preaching his own agitational message against the local Jewish population with considerable destructive effect until checked by Bernard of Clairvaux. But it is less obviously the case that women of the lower social orders participated in the same proportions as they did in 1096. In fact the impression, especially from Bernard's letter, is that the crowds who set out in 1147 were overwhelmingly male. In contrast to the First Crusade, where it was a much-commented on phenomenon, only a handful of annalists explicitly mentioned the presence of women among the departing crowds of the Second Crusade. The *Annals of St Giles of Brunswick*, although heavily dependent of the *Annals of Pöhlde* for its account of the Second Crusade, deviated from the latter in making the point that in 1147 'an infinite number of people of both sexes were inspired' to take the cross.[23] The *Annals of Würzburg* stated that 'both sexes of mankind therefore hurried unwisely [to join the crusade], men with women, poor with rich, princes and great magnates of the realm with

---

[22] Gerhoch of Reisenberg, *De Investigatione Antichristi Liber I, MGH Historica Libelli de Lite Imperatorum et pontificum, Saeculis XI et XII conscripti* 3 (Hannoverae, 1897), p. 374: *Non fuit civitas, que multitudines, non villa seu vicus, que non saltim paucos emitteret, episcopi cum magnates singuli cum suis turmis incedebant, scuta, gladios et loricas aliaque belli vasa secum perferentes cum capiosa preperatione sumptuum ac tabernaculorum, que plaustris et equis innumeris subvehebant. Vix terrestris via simul et campi contigui per terram gradientes, vix Danubii decursus navium multitudines capiebat. Tam enim erat infinitus exercitus, quod, ex quo gentes esse ceperunt, numquam tantam hominum, equitum simul et peditum, multitudinem in unum congregatam estimarverim. Nulla earum necessitatibus venalium rerum fora, vix ulli campi cui plaustra et equi victualibus perferendis deerant, non rusticanorum ac servorum, dominorum suorum relictis aratris ac servitiis, ignorantibus quoque nonnulli vel invitis dominis.*
[23] *MGH SS* 30.1, 14: ... *populus infinitus sexus promiscui animatur.*

the king himself, clergy, monks with abbots and bishops.'[24] The *Chronicle of Hainaut* by Giselbert of Mons is less valuable, being written more than a generation later, *c.*1193. Giselbert echoed the theme of Henry of Huntingdon in saying that 'but because very many had their wives and their company marched women of every condition, marching in rows neither sensible nor lawful, they accomplished nothing.'[25] Writing with a similar theme, but significantly closer to events was Vincent of Prague, chaplain to Bishop Daniel I (1148–67), whose annals noted that 'in as much as the aforementioned kings together with their wives and other barons did not reject the company of foolish women when they took hold of so great a journey, they generated much filthiness which was detestable to God. It is well known that nothing good comes of having military equipment and foolish women in the same tent.'[26]

This survey of the chronicle evidence then suggests that there were women among the popular crowds that took up the crusading message in 1146 and 1147, but they represented – probably – a smaller proportion of the crusade than in 1096.

Why was this? In part the explanation might lie in the message of the crusading preachers. Although the official papal message with regard to the First Crusade, as evidenced from Pope Urban II's letter to the clergy and people of Bologna,[27] was to dampen down the unexpected enthusiasm of non-combatants, the itinerant popular preacher, Peter the Hermit, consciously sought a following among women.[28] Bernard of Clairvaux, however, checked the activities of Radulf, the most notable popular preacher of 1146, and so the main recruiting message for the Second Crusade was more definitely the official voice of the papacy. Ideologically, therefore, it might have been more difficult for women in 11146 to claim that they too were to be included than those women who in 1096 claimed to found a cross fallen from heaven as a signal they should set off for Jerusalem.[29]

Bernard's boast that he had left towns abandoned by their men indicates he was not attempting to give the mobilization the emigratory character it had for thousands of peasants in 1096. The Second Crusade was a more strictly military undertaking and one from which on the whole the Christian forces seem to have intended to return. In 1096 there were many who brought their plough teams and sold their land before departing, providing evidence that they intended to settle in the Near

---

[24] *MGH SS* 16.3: *Currit ergo indiscrete uterque hominum sexus, viri cum mulieribus, pauperes cum divitibus, principes et optimates regnorum cum suis regibus, clerici, monchi cum episcopis et abbatibus.*

[25] *MGH SS* 21.516: *... sed quia uxores suas quamplures secum habebant et in eorum comitatu cuiusque conditionis mulieres incedebant, ipse non sano vel iusto ordine incedentes, nihil profecerunt.*

[26] *MGH SS* 17.633: *... predicti namque reges cum uxoribus suis aliique barones consortia muliercularum non repudiantes, talem viam arripuerunt, ubi plurime Deo abhominabiles oriebantur spurcicie; non autem bene conveniunt nec in unu sede morantur arma bellica et muliercularum contubernia* [Ov. Met. II.846].

[27] Urban II, letter to the clergy and people of Bologna: Hagenmeyer, *Epistulae et Chartae*, pp. 137-8.

[28] GN 121.

[29] BD 17.

East.[30] A far larger proportion of such crusaders would be accompanied by women than those who planned to return once the military pilgrimage was concluded.

Does the difference in the numbers of women noted among the popular crowds also reflect a tightening of social roles in the 50 years since 1096? Had the lives of women become more regulated in the first half of the twelfth century? Was there less opportunity for women to act in the independent manner, such as was reflected in reports of women dressing in manly attire in order to participate in the First Crusade? There is a considerable literature on the evolution of marriage in the twelfth century.[31] The wider issues cannot be entered into here, but insofar as an comparison of the role of women on the First Crusade and the Second offers any material for the discussion, it suggests that there was less freedom for independent action by women of the lower social orders in 1147 than in 1096.

In regard to one particular woman, however, the Second Crusade shows a marked contrast with the First. From 1096 – 9 no Christian woman played a significant role in directing the course of events of the expedition. Only one incident – and that suspiciously like an episode from a *chanson* – showed a woman crusader affecting the strategic considerations of the expedition. Albert of Aachen reported that a certain Emeline, wife of Fulcher a knight of Bouillon, was captured by the illustrious Turkish knight, a general of Omar, lord of Azaz. At the suggestion of Emeline, this Turkish general contacted Duke Godfrey of Lotharingia with a view to leading a revolt against Ridwan of Aleppo.[32] For the Second Crusade, however, there is the very interesting issue of the role played by Eleanor of Aquitaine, the queen of France. Eleanor's long and colourful career has attracted a great deal of attention both from scholars interested in the role of noble women in the medieval period and from a wider public interest.[33]

One problem with establishing Eleanor's role on crusade with any clarity is that our main source, Odo of Deuil did not care to comment on the queen's activities and he never named her. This may well reflect the fact that Odo had a rather idiosyncratic notion of the *libra vita*, the 'book of life' mentioned in a letter of Paul to the Phillipians and in Apocalypse.[34] Odo seems to have treated his history as a part of the *libra vita* and was very anxious that only worthy persons be named in it. Several pious individuals were described as being 'worthy of mention', while other, less

[30] GN 120.

[31] See especially Georges Duby, *Medieval marriage: two models from twelfth-century France* (Baltimore, 1978); Georges Duby, *The knight, the lady and the priest: the making of marriage in medieval France* (New York, 193); James A. Brundage, *Law, sex and Christian society in medieval Europe* (Chicago, 1987); J. Goody, *The development of the family and marriage in Europe* (Cambridge, 1983); D. Herlihy, *Medieval Households* (Cambridge, MA, 1985); C.N.L. Brooke, *The medieval idea of marriage* (Oxford, 1989); R.F. Berkhofer III, 'Marriage, lordship and the "greater unfree" in twelfth-century France', *Past and Present* 173 (2001), 3-27.

[32] AA v.7 (346). See also S. Geldsetzer, *Frauen Auf Kreuzzügen* (Darmstadt, 2003), p. 185.

[33] For Eleanor of Aquitaine see Jean Flori, *Aliénor d'Aquitaine: La Reine insoumise* (Paris, 2004).

[34] Paul to Phillipians, 4:3, Apocalypse 13:8.

reputable figures were not named since they 'did not deserve to be in the book of life'.[35] Eleanor of Aquitaine seems to have belonged in the latter category and if this was conscious censorship by Odo, it was almost certainly because he was writing in the aftermath of the events in Antioch described below: events that were very damaging to Louis, the subject of Odo's devotion.

On 31 March 1146 at Vézelay in the presence of Bernard of Clairvaux, King Louis VII took the cross and when he departed on the expedition he took his wife Eleanor with him, because, wrote William of Newburgh much later, he could not bear to leave her at home. There is a version of this event which has been repeated for some 70 years now and remains the dominant one in the public domain, which is that Queen Eleanor, along with many companions among the women of the French aristocracy formed a distinct female company, compared to the classical Amazons, with Eleanor their Penthesilia, riding around handing out spindles and distaffs to those reluctant to commit themselves.[36] Even academic writing that avoids such fanciful speculations has nevertheless repeated that several noblewomen came on the expedition with Eleanor, those most frequently named being Sybilla, countess of Flanders; Mamille, or Maybel of Roucy; Faydide of Uzés, countess of Toulouse; Florina of Bourgogne; the countess Torqueri of Bouillon; and the countess of Blois.

The problem here is that there is no evidence for any of these individuals having been present on the crusade and quite strong evidence that the whole idea of a contingent of noblewomen has arisen through a mistaken assembly of certain associations between some of these women and crusading. Mamille was a crusader, but she came to the Kingdom of Jerusalem in 1107, not 1146.[37] A Florina of Burgundy appears in Albert of Aachen's history, dying in Anatolia in the winter of 1907, ambushed while travelling with a company of Danes who were attempting to catch up with the main army of the First Crusade.[38] Sybilla did travel with her husband, Thierry I of Flanders to the Kingdom of Jerusalem, but not until 1157. In 1147 she was acting as regent of Flanders and Lambert of Waterlos describes her as defending the territory from incursions by rivals.[39] Faydide was married to Alphonse-Jordan of Toulouse, who was a participant in the Second Crusade and might have travelled with him but there is no record of this, such as might be expected to appear in William of Tyre's history. Nor is there any contemporary record of the presence of Torqueri, but Sabine Geldsetzer notes that she might be connected to Emeline of Bouillon, the participant in the First Crusade mentioned above.[40]

---

[35] OD 10, 12, 20.
[36] For example, A. Weir, *Eleanor of Aquitaine* (London, 2000), p. 51.
[37] WT 14.15.
[38] AA 224.
[39] *MGH SS* 16, 516 – 7.
[40] S. Geldsetzer, *Frauen Auf Kreuzzügen*, p. 185.

Curiously, while admirers of Eleanor of Aquitaine have tended to exaggerate her enthusiasm for the crusade and attribute to her much more initiative than the sources allow for they have tended to slide over the one clear period in which she appears on the crusade as a political leader in her own right, that of the sojourn of the French forces in Antioch, in the spring of 1148. On Louis' arrival at the port of Saint Symeon on 19 March 1148, Raymond, the prince of Antioch rode to meet the French army with his household to give them an enthusiastic welcome. Hopes were high in the Latin principality that the united French – Antiochene army could reverse the gains of Nur ad-Din, the emir of Aleppo, who had been successfully capturing Christian towns and castles on the Christian frontier east of the Orontes. As the uncle of Eleanor of Aquitaine, Raymond had every reason to anticipate close collaboration with the newly arrived knights. But Raymond's fellow Christian magnates based around Jerusalem also desired the assistance of the French army for their own goals. They considered it would be a waste if Louis campaigned in the region of Antioch and sent envoys to him urging that he come to the Holy City. The greatest concern of the Jerusalem magnates was that Louis would be detained in Antioch especially because of the 'intervention of the queen.'[41]

As it became clear that Louis favoured taking his forces to Jerusalem and did not intend to fight in the region of Antioch, Raymond made plans to salvage something from the situation. According to William of Tyre:

> Frustrated in his hope, [Raymond], changing his efforts, began to hate the ways of the king and to openly construct ambushes and to arm himself to harm the king. For he planned, either violently or with secret machinations, to seize from the king his wife [Eleanor] who consented in this same plan as she was a foolish woman. For as we deduce, she was an imprudent woman, as she demonstrated both before and afterwards with clear evidence: contrary to the dignity of royalty, the law of marriage was neglected and the fidelity of the con- jugal bed forgotten. After the king learned of this, forestalling the efforts of the prince, taking measures for his life and safety, on the advice of his magnates, hastening his journey he secretly left the town of Antioch with his followers.[42]

---

[41] WT 16.29, p. 757: ... *interventu regine.*

[42] WT 16.27, p. 755: *Spe frustratus mutato studio regis vias abhominari et ei prestruere paten- ter insidias et in eius lesionem armari cepit: uxorem enim eius in idipsum consentientem, que una erat de fatuis mulieribus, aut violenter aut occultis machinationibus ab eo rapere proposuit. Erat, ut premisimus, sicut et prius et postmodum manifestis edocuit indiciis, mulier imprudens, et contra regiam dignitatem legem negligens maritalem, thori*

John of Salisbury, the celebrated English philosopher, spent the years 1149–53 at the papal court in Rome, and wrote an account of his experience there, the *Historia Pontificalis*, c.1163–7. From the perspective of a papal insider, John gave some attention to the Second Crusade and provided a version of the events at Antioch that matches that of William of Tyre. According to the *Historia Pontificalis* the constant conversations between Raymond and Eleanor made the king of France suspicious. When Raymond asked Louis for consent to keep the queen at Antioch, Louis prepared to bring her away, only to be confronted by Eleanor raising the question of consanguinity. At this the king, though he loved the queen, was shaken and would have been willing to consent to divorce if his advisors hand not pointed out that if, in addition to the military disasters, it was reported that Louis had also been deserted by his wife, it would bring everlasting shame to France. Moreover, argued one particular hostile knight, the queen might be party to incest, for, 'guilt under kinship's guise could lie concealed' (as Ovid put it in the *Heroides*, IV. 138). As a result of the policy of the king's French counsellors, Eleanor was forced to leave Antioch when the king departed.[43]

Georges Duby, in an important essay on Eleanor of Aquitaine, held to a theme that historians have tended to exaggerate her independence of action in a search for an example of a strong twelfth-century woman. In the main his argument is convincing, but for this particular incident Duby probably went too far in describing the conflict as entirely between Raymond and Louis.[44] William of Tyre explicitly stated that Eleanor colluded with Raymond and that it was her intervention with the French army that the nobles of Jerusalem feared, while John of Salisbury attributed the raising of the issue of divorce to Eleanor herself.

It probably is the case here that, for the first time, a woman of the nobility was an important figure in the strategic direction of a crusade. Eleanor found herself in a situation where she could threaten to break away from Louis and take her vassals into alliance with her uncle, Raymond of Antioch, and, indeed, she came close to implementing this threat. But it has to be recognised that a very particular set of circumstances gave rise to the opportunity for Eleanor to raise her own political and military agenda: the hegemony of the king over the French army had been undermined by the great losses it had experienced and the shameful abandonment of many of the foot soldiers; Eleanor as an heiress had the vassalage of many crusading knights in her own right, a minority faction of the army but an important one; and two powerful male figures, the king of France and prince of Antioch, were in conflict, creating space into which she could assert her own goals. The moment was short-lived. With what was effectively a kidnapping – the forcible removal of

coniugalis fide oblita. Quod postquam regi compertum est, principis preveniens molimina, vite quoque et saluti consulens, de consilio mag- natum suorum iter accelerans urbe Antiochena cum suis clam egressus est.
[43] John of Salisbury, *Historia Pontificalis* ed. M. Chibnall (London, 1956), pp. 51–3.
[44] Georges Duby, *Women of the twelfth century* (Cambridge, 1997), pp. 9–11, 16.

Eleanor from Antioch by Louis' advisors – this combination of circumstances collapsed and she once more became an invisible appendage of the king's. There are no other references to the queen on the crusade.

One final piece of evidence worth noting with regard to women on the Second Crusade comes from the naval expedition that in 1147 captured Lisbon for an alliance of Christian forces. An Anglo–Flemish fleet had sailed to the city from Dartmouth, arriving on 28 June and, with the assistance of the Christian king of Portugal, had captured the city on 24 October. To ensure discipline across the disparate force the various regional factions agreed to a common set of laws by which to regulate their conduct. Among these statutes was a decree that women should not go out in public.[45] This decree provides a useful summary of the contrast between the First Crusade and the Second. Without doubt women were present on the Second Crusade, but in much fewer numbers and – but for a moment of political crisis in which Eleanor of Aquitaine briefly strove to implement her own goals – very much more under the direction of men than had been the experience of women on the First Crusade.

---

[45] Raol, *De Expugnatione Lyxbonensi*, ed. C.W. David (New York, 2001 [1936]), p. 56.

Monty Python had a strong engagement with medieval history and this has coloured popular perceptions of the era. Not necessarily for the worse either. Terry Jones in particular devoted a lot of time to understanding medieval life from a viewpoint that was sympathetic to the peasant and hostile to the knight, whom he essentially saw as a thug. Jones also described the fall of Rome 24 August 410 to Alaric the Visigoth as an invention of propaganda. He was trying to shock those for whom the idea of the barbarian at the gate was as horrifying as a punk band playing at the local venue. And he had a valid point. So onerous was the burden of Roman aristocratic rule on their population that not only did tens of thousands of slaves escape to join invading barbarian armies, but even Roman citizens crossed sides, 'preferring poverty and freedom among the barbarians to putting up with the duty of paying taxes among the Romans', as Orosius of Spain wrote in 417.

One memorable moment in *Monty Python and the Holy Grail* comes when the peasants, guided by a knight, put a woman on trial for being a witch. The absurdity of the trial is the source of the humour of the scene, with the 'proof' that the woman is a witch being utterly illogical. The idea of undergoing an ordeal to prove you are speaking the truth, however, is not nonsense. It can have an emotional honesty, especially in circumstances where the formal legal procedures are hopelessly against you. And when I came across a vivid account of a trial by fire that occurred during First Crusade, I saw another side to the farce, a tragic one. The test of Peter Bartholomew revealed to me that in the late eleventh century at least (long before witch trials became a means of social control and to expropriate women of their property) these trials were as much a test of the mood of a community as of the individual. The setup of the ordeal and the extent to which it could be surmounted without harm had a social context. There were social conflicts at play in this event and undoubtedly many similar ordeals.

> If Omnipotent God talked to this man face to
> face, and Saint Andrew revealed the Holy Lance
> to him when he was keeping vigil, let him walk
> through the fire unhurt; but if this is a lie let him
> and the Lance he will carry in his hand be
> consumed by fire.[1]

---

[1] J. France, *A Critical Edition of the* Historia Francorum *of Raymond of Aguilers.* Unpublished PhD. Thesis, University of Nottingham (1967) [hereafter RA]. I am grateful to John France for permission to quote from his thesis. References to the more easily accessible RHC edition, Raimundi de Aguilers, *Historia Francorum qui ceperunt Iherusalem*, Recueil des historiens des croisades: Historiens occidentaux III (1841-1895) [hereafter

The ordeal by fire of Peter Bartholomew during the course of the First Crusade (1096-1099) is one of the more dramatic examples of a medieval trial by ordeal. Much discussed by historians of the crusades, it deserves wider attention as a case study of a particular type of legal case: one where contending political and social factions agree to put their dispute to a test, a test whose outcome they then attempt to influence.

Despite the canonical hesitancy over the legitimacy of the practice of the ordeal,[2] at the time of the First Crusade the trial by ordeal was a powerful tradition, invoked especially in circumstances where other evidence was lacking.[3] In his *An Introduction to English Legal History*, however, J.H. Baker notes that in the last days of the ordeal the acquittal rates were surprisingly high and concludes that this suggests that those who administered the ordeal began to feel a responsibility to facilitate the result they felt right.[4] A well-documented ordeal that gives a useful case study for examining this suggestion is the trial by fire of Peter Bartholomew on 8 April 1099, Good Friday, during the course of the First Crusade.

Our main source for the ordeal of Peter Bartholomew was a Provençal cleric, Raymond of Aguilers. Raymond was a canon of the cathedral church of St Mary of Le Puy, in the Auvergne region of France, who was ordained a priest during the course of the First Crusade and became chaplain to one of the main princes of the crusade: Count Raymond IV of Toulouse.[5] The *Historia Francorum* was Raymond of Aguilers's account of the First Crusade, written soon after the completion of the expedition. The finished history, as John France has noted, seems to be based on notes that Raymond wrote during the course of the expedition.[6] The main theme expressed by Raymond in writing his account was a sincere belief that the First Crusade was an *iter Dei* and that God was working miracles through the participants of the journey.[7]

Raymond's belief that divine interventions were taking place to assist the Crusade are no more evident than in the priest's attitude towards one of the most interesting characters to emerge as a leading figure during the course of the three-year expedition: the lowly visionary Peter Bartholomew. Thanks to Raymond's adoration of Peter, with whom he shared a tent for some nine months, we are given a great deal of information about the visionary that would have been lost, had we to depend on other sources for the First Crusade.

RHC Oc.], are in brackets. 283 (289): '*Si Deus omnipotens huic homini locutus est facie ad faciem, et beatus Andreas lanceam dominicam ostendit ei, quum iste vigilaret, transeat iste illaesus per ignem. Sin autem est mendacium, comburatur iste cum lancea quam portabit in manu sua.*'

[2] J.W. Baldwin, 'Preparation for the Canon of 1215 against Ordeal', *Speculum* 36.4 (1961), 613-636: 627-628.

[3] R. Bartlett, *Trial by Fire and Water: the Medieval Judicial Ordeal* (Oxford 1986), 26.

[4] J.H. Baker, *An Introduction to English Legal History* (Oxford 2000), 5.

[5] RA 5 (235), RA 11-12, 17 (237-238), RA 100 (255).

[6] RA cxxxix-cxliii.

[7] *Itinere Dei* see RA 202 (276); 'miracles' see RA 59 (247).

Peter Bartholomew was a servant of William Peyre of Cunhlat, from Provençe.[8] Peter's humble social status made him an unlikely candidate for a leader of the Crusade, but in the eyes of Raymond of Aguilers it was entirely appropriate someone so modest should be favoured by God. For the Crusade was echoing the journey of the Children of Israel, and far from poverty being a barrier to divine approval, it was the fact that the Christian army as a whole was suffering and in poverty that brought it close to God.[9]

Although a servant, Peter Bartholomew entered the battlefield alongside the professional combatants. He was among those who went out of the recently captured city of Antioch on 10 June 1098 to skirmish with the vanguard of a newly arriving army command by the atabeg of Mosul, Kerbogha. When the Christian forces beat a hasty retreat to the protection of the city, Peter Bartholomew became trapped between two knights and was nearly crushed to death in the confusion.[10] After this harrowing experience, Peter, in keeping with the rest of the Christian army, suffered from famine conditions that developed as the crusaders found themselves trapped by the Muslim army outside Antioch. Their enemies were also inside the city walls, as the remnants of the former garrison retained control of the mountainside citadel.

The three weeks before the crusaders finally reached a decision to confront Kerbogha were the low point of the crusade. From the perspective of many, the situation was hopeless and those with the means to escape began to do so. Several Christian knights lowered themselves by rope from the walls of the city and escaped during darkness. According to Albert of Aachen – not an eyewitness, but someone writing a history based on his interviews with crusaders – when it was discovered that even illustrious lords had fled the city, many people considered making a similar escape.[11] Worse, there were princes so terrified of the plight of the crusade that, unknown to the commoners, they had formed a conspiracy to leave the city together.[12]

In these desperate circumstances, Peter Bartholomew gathered his nerve and came forward with a set of policies at whose core was the idea that the army should march out against Kerbogha before it disintegrated. At first, Peter's approach to the senior princes was hesitant. After all, a servant who dared advise his masters on their conduct was liable for a

---

[8] For Peter Bartholomew see J. Riley-Smith, *The First Crusaders 1095-1131* (Cambridge 1997), 216; C. Morris, 'Policy and Visions – The case of the Holy Lance at Antioch' in: J. Gillingham and J.C. Holt ed., *War and Government in the Middle Ages: essays in honour of J.O. Prestwich* (Woodbridge 1984), 33-45; J. France, 'Two Types of Vision on the First Crusade: Stephen of Valence and Peter Bartholomew', *Crusades* 5 (2006), 1-20; R. Rogers, 'Peter Bartholomew and the Role of "The Poor" in the First Crusade' in: T. Reuter ed., *Warriors and Churchmen in the High Middle Ages* (London 1992), 109-122; C. Kostick, *The Social Structure of the First Crusade* (Leiden 2008) 134-149; J. Rubenstein, *Armies of Heaven: the First Crusade and the Quest for Apocalypse* (New York 2011), 157-262.

[9] Kostick, *The Social Structure of the First Crusade*, 31-36.

[10] RA 89 (253).

[11] Albert of Aachen, *Historia Iherosolimitana*, S.B. Edgington ed. (Oxford 2007) [hereafter AA], 307.

[12] AA 309.

beating, if not worse. At a meeting with those senior leaders who shared his own Provençal language – namely, the papal legate, Bishop Adhémar of Le Puy, Count Raymond of Toulouse and Peter Raymond of Hautpoul (one of the Count's leading vassals) – the servant claimed that he had seen Saint Andrew in five separate visions.[13] As proof of the visions, Peter Bartholomew said that St Andrew had revealed to him the hiding place of a valuable relic that would save the crusaders: the Lord's Lance.[14]

There was a problem with this announcement, as Steven Runciman first noted, which is that Constantinople already housed a relic that was supposedly part of the Lance that had pierced Christ's side.[15] And, indeed, at first Adhémar and his clerical entourage expressed his mistrust of the servant and his visions. This hesitancy, Peter later claimed, was to cost the papal legate three days in Hell's fires.[16] But as Peter's revelations became public and were met with popular enthusiasm, it suited Adhémar and all those leaders of the crusade wanting to rally the army to fight Kerbogha to allow the story to go unchallenged in the hope of reviving the flagging morale of the knights. Moreover, Raymond of Toulouse was willing to back the servant with enthusiasm, since one of the major themes of the visions described by Peter Bartholomew was that God had allocated a special role in the expedition to the count.[17] This bid for the patronage of a prince who already saw his role on the expedition as being that of another Moses was entirely successful and Peter Bartholomew was taken into the care of Count Raymond's chaplaincy and thus into the companionship of the person who would document his rise and fall: Raymond of Aguilers.[18]

On 14 June 1098, digging began in the Church of St Peter in order to unearth the Holy Lance. Having locked out all other persons, Count Raymond himself undertook the work, along with his most important lay and clerical followers. But by evening these men were overcome with tiredness. And here we have the first sign that despite an utter conviction in the belief that God was actively assisting the crusade, Raymond of Aguilers had not lost his critical faculties. Raymond, although desperate to believe in Peter Bartholomew, nevertheless noted a contradiction in Peter's story. According to Peter's account of the vision in which St Andrew showed the servant where the Lance was buried, the saint placed the Lance in the ground while the visionary was watching, implying that it was close to the surface; but the initial twelve men had dug a considerable hole and found nothing. Indeed 'by evening some had given up hope of unearthing the Lance.'[19] A new set of men were asked to take over the digging, until they too became tired. Finally, Peter Bartholomew

---

[13] RA 254 (284). For Peter Raymond of Hautpoul see: Riley-Smith, *First Crusaders*, 217.

[14] RA 94 (295).

[15] S. Runciman. 'The Holy Lance Found at Antioch', *Analecta Bollandiana* 68 (1950), 197-205.

[16] RA 138–140 (263).

[17] RA 93 (254).

[18] RA 100 (255).

[19] RA 257 (285): *In vespere desperare quidam de inventione lanceae coeperunt.*

dropped into the deep hole and urged everyone to pray at length, which conveniently meant that no one was standing and looking down at him. A moment later the visionary hailed the discovery of the Lance, whose point was protruding from the earth. The dubious circumstances of the find were not lost on Raymond of Aguilers, who is all the more convincing for having to acknowledge a fact that went against his religious beliefs: namely that while everyone else present was above the pit, praying on their knees, Peter alone discovered the Lance.[20]

Despite the unconvincing manner in which the Lance was found, as several modern historians have noted, all the crusading army at the time united in acclaiming the discovery of the Lance.[21] So, for example, the view expressed in the *Gesta Francorum*, the work of an Italian-Norman eyewitness, was that – as foretold by Peter Bartholomew – the relic had been found with subsequent boundless rejoicing.[22] A letter to Pope Urban II of the united princes, headed by Bohemond, leader of the Normans, the faction that was later the most hostile towards Peter Bartholomew, also referred favourably to the Lance, reporting that through its discovery and many other divine revelations the Christians were much strengthened and more willing to do battle.[23]

The enthusiasm for the relic and its discoverer was to soar stratospherically as a result of the relief felt by all factions after their successful confrontation of Kerbogha's huge army in the battle of 28 June 1098. The great Muslim army, however, was less of a fighting force than it appeared, for there were deep divisions between the Muslim lords present outside Antioch. In particular, Duqāq of Damascus was more concerned about the consequences of Kerbogha being victorious and thus uniting Mosul with Antioch than with the victory of the Christians. Other Muslim rulers, such as Janāh ad-Daulah of Homs, also had fears for their future in the event of Kerbogha being victorious.[24]

As soon as he could decently do so, Duqāq took his troops from the field and the rest of the Muslim cavalry soon followed, leaving their infantry to be destroyed and their camp to be overrun, with Kerbogha's own tent a prize of battle. From the Christian perspective it was an astonishing victory with very few casualties. More than astonishing, it was a miracle. The Holy Lance had been carried into the battle by our historian, Raymond of Aguilers, who felt that it had protected him.[25] Above all, it was the Christian poor who rejoiced in the victory and celebrated the fact that they had not been stranded in Antioch by the

---

[20] RA 203 (276).

[21] For example, C. Morris, 'Policy and Visions', 36; J. France, *Victory in the East. A Military History of the First Crusade* (Cambridge 1994) 278-279.

[22] *Gesta Francorum et aliorum Hierosolimitanorum*, R. Hill ed. (London 1962) [hereafter GF] 65.

[23] Letter of Bohemond and the other princes to Pope Urban II, H. Hagenmeyer ed., *Epistulae et Chartae ad Historiam Primi Belli Sacri Spectantes Quae Supersunt Aevo Aequales ac Genuinae: Die Kreuzzugsbriefe aus den Jahren 1088-1100* (Innsbruck 1901), 163.

[24] Ibn al-Athīr, *al-Kamil fi'l-ta'rikh* I, D.S. Richards tr., (Aldershot 2006), 16-17; K. al- Din, *Extraits de la Chronique d'Alep*, RHC Oc. 1-5: 3 (Paris 1841-1895), 577-690: 582- 583.

[25] RA 263 (286).

knights. As a result of his association with the miracle, Peter Bartholomew found himself in a position of great authority. He could now speak to the other princes as an equal, knowing that a large part of the poor and the clergy were devout enthusiasts of his visions.

After the death of Adhémar on 1 August 1098 during the outbreak of plague in Antioch, Peter Bartholomew made a bid to fill the leadership role formerly given by the legate. The night that Adhémar's body was buried, 3 August 1098, Peter Bartholomew claimed that both St Andrew and Adhémar came to talk with him in the chapel of Count Raymond of Toulouse. Speaking to Peter from beyond the grave, Adhémar explained that he had been in Hell for the period between his death and his burial due his lack of belief in the Holy Lance. As a result, he appeared before Peter Bartholomew, showing horrific burns on his head and face, which would have been even worse but for the intervention of the Lord Himself, who presented Adhémar with a robe that protected him from the fire. The robe was that which the legate had given away to a poor person on the occasion of his ordination as bishop of Le Puy. Moreover, a candle, offered in prayer by the bishop's friends, and three *denari* that the legate himself had offered to the Holy Lance, were the most effective items in restoring him as he departed Hell.[26]

These aspects to the vision served – somewhat crudely – to reinforce the importance of the Holy Lance as a relic, as well as to point out the spiritual value of supporting the poor. The message was directed in particular to the relatively large body of Provençal clergy who had come with Adhémar on the crusade and were now leaderless. Adhémar had a message for them and the knights of his household (*familia*), which was that they should follow Count Raymond of Toulouse. In return for his services to them the Count would be rewarded by God. This was in fact the arrangement that was adopted up until the death of Peter Bartholomew and it seems natural enough that crusaders of the same language group, travelling from the same region of France, should amalgamate together. But there was at least one major fault line between these two Provençal contingents: Count Raymond and his vassals intended to settle in the region while Adhémar's followers, on the whole, wanted to complete their vows and return to France. This difference would become a significant factor in the political struggle surrounding the trial of Peter Bartholomew. For now, though, Peter had successfully offered a way forward for the crusade, one that appealed to Count Raymond's desire to be the leading figure of the whole expedition.

That the visionary felt secure in his political position within the crusade is evident from the surprisingly confident tone in which one of the poorest of the crusaders felt he could address the mighty Count Raymond, who although singled out for a leading role on the crusade by the vision was also publicly reminded of his faults and given instructions by Peter. The reception of this vision, with its demand for the public accounting of the wealth of the princes and bishops, among the main

[26] RA 138–140 (263).

body of the crusading army was initially enthusiastic. But the faction of Provençal clergy and poor crusaders that was most dedicated to the cause of the visionary were unable to impose the practical elements of policy contained in the message from Heaven upon the princes. Instead, the whole expedition stalled while the princes wrangled over the ownership of Antioch and over the question of whether to acknowledge the Byzantine emperor as overlord.[27]

As time passed, with no sign of the crusade uniting in order to continue on to Jerusalem, the poor quickly used up the few resources they had and famine conditions developed in Antioch, leading to an outbreak of plague that killed an uncountable multitude.[28] Throughout this period, August to October 1098, Peter Bartholomew consolidated his position within the Provençal contingent with further visions. One, in mid September, had a very strong message for Count Raymond coming directly from the Lord Himself, speaking in the company of St Andrew. Peter Bartholomew announced to the crusading army that although Count Raymond had received the gift of the Holy Lance he had nonetheless sinned badly. The crusade should be marching towards Jerusalem. Christ and St Peter declared it was now necessary that the count perform a penance: a penance that effectively would set by Peter Bartholomew.[29] The political content of the vision consisted of a demand for an immediate resumption of the crusade and an attack on the advisers of the count for their evil counsel.

On 5 November 1098 the senior princes, their immediate followers, and the clergy met in the cathedral of St Peter. The people (not merely the *pauperes* but the broader *populus*) gathered outside and threatened to choose one of their own as leader to take them forward and even to tear down the walls of the city if the princes could not agree to resume the march.[30] As we shall see below for Ma'arra, this was no idle threat and this incident helps illustrate that some six months before his ordeal, Peter Bartholomew was far from isolated: there were a considerable body of crusaders expressing even greater determination to press on to Jerusalem than that articulated by Peter. Under such popular pressure, the princes announced that the expedition be resumed and that their first goal would be the reduction of the town of Ma'arra. On 23 November 1098, the crusade resumed and a week later Peter Bartholomew had a new vision to report to a mass assembly outside the walls of Ma'arra. The visionary had been met by Saints Peter and Andrew, with the saints initially clad in the ugly and filthy clothing of *pauperes*. The saints made an important point about God's favour being with the poor, when they explained that this dress was the garb in which they came to God.[31] Their initial appearance also gave an answer to the critics of Peter Bartholomew

[27] RA 264 (286).
[28] AA 341.
[29] RA 265 (286).
[30] RA 163–4 (264–7).
[31] RA 269 (287)

who could not believe that God would reveal himself to one so lowly.[32] The saints then outlined their criticisms of the crusade and demanded that the poor be protected from the violence of the rich crusader. The saints also called upon the army to tithe all wealth to provide sustenance for the poor.

Between Raymond of Aguilers' report of this vision and a corroborative one from the eyewitness Peter Tudebode,[33] we can detect four policy ideas that give us absolute clarity that at this point Peter Bartholomew was articulating the views of the poor crusader, his main political base. Firstly, justice was required on behalf of the poor, to defend them from violence from their fellow Christian oppressors. Secondly, that the solution to the presence of large numbers of unmarried women on crusade was that they be married, a response that contrasts with the policy of the senior clergy who were more inclined to drive unattached women from the crusade altogether.[34] Thirdly, again Peter Bartholomew raised the idea of a public accounting of the resources available to the crusaders, this time of those suspected of taking goods from the poor. Lastly, the vision raised the idea of taking a tithe for the church and the poor. These ideas addressed the harsh poverty that existed among the Christian forces at the siege: conditions were so desperate that some of the poorest crusaders were shortly to be driven to acts of cannibalism.[35]

At a council of the united Provençal faction the following day, which was attended by the common people as well as the nobles, a partial concession was made to Peter Bartholomew's demands. A collection was taken to which the faithful offered generous alms.[36] Having been inspired by this vision of Peter Bartholomew, the army was now aroused and willing to attempt to seize the city.[37] The subsequent attack, 11 December 1098, convinced the population of Ma'arra that they could not hold out any further and although the city survived until nightfall, the Christian poor broke in that night, for once obtaining the best of the booty.[38] In the aftermath of the crusader victory at Ma'arra a major political crisis emerged. Count Raymond had hoped to use the town as a base for a principality that he could hold as a vassal of the Byzantine emperor. But in the harsh circumstances of December 1098 this was an ambition that neither the poor nor the majority of the knightly class could

---

[32] RA 229–30 (280–1).

[33] Peter Tudebode, *Historia de Hierosolymitano Itinere*, J.H. Hill and L.L. Hill ed. (Paris 1977) [hereafter PT], 122.

[34] Guibert of Nogent, *Gesta Dei per Francos*, R.B.C. Huygens ed., CC LXXVIIa, (Turnhout 1996) 196. For women and the First Crusade see also: J.A. Brundage, *The Crusades, Holy War and Canon Law* II (Aldershot 1991) 380 and XIX, 59; C. Kostick, 'Women and the First Crusade: Prostitutes or Pilgrims?' in: C. Meek and C. Lawless ed., *Studies on Medieval and Early Modern Women 4: Victims or Viragos?* (Dublin 2005) 57-68; A.V. Murray, 'Sex, Death and the Problem of Single Women in the Armies of the First Crusade' in: R. Gertwagen and E. Jeffreys ed., *Shipping, Trade and Crusade in the Medieval Mediterranean: Studies in Honour of John Pryor* (Farnham 2012) 255-270.

[35] PT 124–5, GF 80.

[36] RA 269 (287).

[37] RA 173 (269).

[38] RA 270 (287).

tolerate. Around Christmas 1098 at a council of the Provençals a new political development took place. The knights, who up until this point had not sided with the radical ideas expressed by popular visionaries, now aligned themselves with Peter Bartholomew in insisting that the Count lead the way to Jerusalem. They failed to make the Count hand over the Lance and marched to Jerusalem with the Lord as their leader.[39] This mutiny of all but his most senior vassals forced his hand and Count Raymond therefore arranged a conference with the other princes to negotiate the terms on which the expedition would continue. This meeting took place at Chastel-Rouge, probably on 4 January 1099, but came to nothing.

   After this conference, Count Raymond showed no sign of resuming the march towards Jerusalem, indeed, he assigned a significant number of his knights and footmen to garrison Ma'arra. This drove an angry body of poor crusaders to revolt. They set about toppling the walls of the town, so that it would be useless as a base for Count Raymond's evident desire to create a principality for himself. Although the newly appointed bishop of Albara, acting for the Count, tried to halt the mutiny, he lacked the troops to guard all the length of the walls and soon the destructive task of the poor was complete. Furious, the Count gave in to the revolt and resumed the crusade.[40] This mutiny must have strained the relationship between count and visionary. While Peter Bartholomew was not directly associated with the revolt, the repeated message of his visions was that although the count was specially chosen by God, his failure to march to Jerusalem was a sin. Such a message can only have helped justify the action of those who defied the count and pushed over the walls of his town.

   During the march southwards, Count Raymond remained alert for any opportunity to obtain a sizeable town or city for himself, his envoys reported that Tripoli was a particularly lucrative city. The emir of Tripoli, however, bribed Count Raymond with a considerable quantity of gold and silver to leave his city alone. Count Raymond managed to divert the crusade to 'Arqah ('Akkār) where a siege began on 14 February, 1099. The operation was not without support in its early stages, but 'Arqah was not strategic to the expedition's progress and enthusiasm for the effort faltered.[41]

   On the night of 5 April 1099, during the now deeply unpopular siege, another vision occurred to Peter Bartholomew, one which he personally dictated to Raymond of Aguilers and so we have Peter's voice in the documentary record. Beginning by explaining the circumstances of the vision, Peter Bartholomew stated that he had been wondering why Christ had favoured another visionary, Stephen of Valence. That night Peter Bartholomew caught up to his rival with a vision of St Peter, St Andrew, another silent near-bald fleshy man and – crucially – Christ

[39] RA 183 (272).
[40] RA 183 (272).
[41] AA 383-385; William of Tyre, *Chronicon*, R.B.C. Huygens ed., *CC* 63 (Turnhout 1986) [hereafter WT], 366.

Himself. The Lord spoke to Peter Bartholomew before mounting a cross, supported by the three other saints. Then Christ introduced a set of instructions by drawing attention to the fact that he had five wounds while crucified (a nail in each hand and foot as well as a spear thrust). Having imbued the number five with a mystical quality in this way, Christ then explained that there were five ranks of person in the expedition.

The first rank were utterly dedicated to the expedition. Willing to die for Christ, they were guaranteed a seat at God's right hand side upon death. The second rank were solid and committed, providing a rear guard and a shelter in case of flight. The third rank, while not putting themselves in the way of danger supplied important assistance, such as by bringing stones and spears to those who fought, and they were spiritually worthy. The fourth rank, however, tended to their own affairs and did not believe Christ was the Son of God. Worse, the fifth rank were cowards who were actively undermining the efforts of the true followers of Christ through treachery: they were like Judas.

As Jay Rubenstein has analysed, this is not a conventional division of persons, either socially or militarily.[42] Rather, it is an assessment of the political strata of the expedition based on a person's adherence or otherwise to the goals of Christ as interpreted by Peter Bartholomew: in each category can be found persons of different social rank, military role and region. What unites them is their beliefs. One way to understand the vision is suggested by John France, who notes that since there were five armies at 'Arqah, we could read the five ranks as respectively the armies of: Count Raymond, Robert of Normandy, Robert of Flanders, Godfrey of Bouillon and Tancred.[43] This is not an obvious reading, even if we allow Tancred the status of the other senior princes. If it were the meaning of the vision, then Peter was abandoning any supporters of his who may have existed among the lower social orders of the Lotharingian and Norman contingents.

It is helpful, perhaps, to attempt a diagram of the support that existed for Peter Bartholomew at this time. Any such figure has to be understood to be an impressionistic one: historians have great difficulty establishing the numbers of crusaders and the relative proportions between the social groupings let alone in providing a tighter focus on their political and spiritual attitude to Peter Bartholomew.[44]

---

[42] Rubenstein, *Armies of Heaven*, 252-256.

[43] France, 'Two Types of Vision on the First Crusade', 17.

[44] For a summary of the various approaches to providing an estimate of numbers on the First Crusade, see: Kostick, *The Social Structure of the First Crusade*, 288-289.

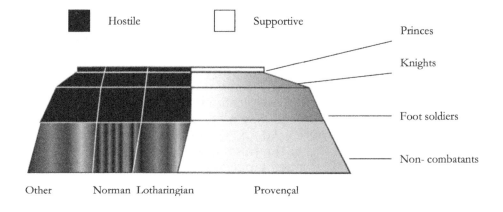

Fig. 1: Estimate of levels of support for Peter Bartholomew at the time of his ordeal.

The largest faction of crusaders at this time were those under the leadership of Count Raymond, who had attracted a significant body of dependents to his army. Despite a growing independence of policy from the count, Peter Bartholomew and the Holy Lance were an important asset in the count's efforts to establish hegemony over the entire army. Thus the visionary had a very sizeable Provençal base. But it should be noted that some, especially the soldiers who had formerly served with Adhémar, disagreed with Count Raymond over both the siege of 'Arqah and the longer term perspective of the expedition; these troops would soon burn their tents to force the count to leave the siege.[45] Hence the figure has some darker shading, even within the Provençal section. Similarly, within the regional sections that were hostile to the visionary, there is likely to have been support for Peter Bartholomew from the lower social orders. After all, he was advocating policies that were essential to their survival. The striations in the figure are indicative of the presence of this support.

In any event, this was a highly politicised vision, announced to a deeply divided army. And the vision itself was proof that the army was polarised between two committed and hostile factions, with a substantial middle ground.

The point of dividing the expedition into five ranks was made explicit through Peter Bartholomew's statements concerning Christ's orders to Count Raymond. The count should summon the whole army to arms and expose the cowards by deploying as if for battle or siege. Those who shirked from the muster proved themselves unbelievers. Their punishment? They should then be executed and their worldly goods given

[45] RA 298 (290).

to those of the first rank. In other words, Peter thought the time had come to launch a coup against his opponents and consolidate the influence of his loyal believers over the waverers.

The Lord also went on to give a command to the crusaders regarding justice, which was that they appoint judges according to family and kin. These judges should have the right to take the possessions of a defendant, giving half to the plaintiff and half to the authorities.[46] Thus, in the post-coup organisation of the army, a system of popular justice was to spring up: essentially to devolve decision making from the council of princes to the lower social orders of the army. There was clearly enormous resentment by the poor, not only that the princes were misdirecting affairs, but that they had the means to live well while everyone suffered. For example, it was noted by the army that despite the most difficult of circumstances a supply of wine and grapes abounded for those who had money.[47]

This vision at 'Arqah was to cost Peter Bartholomew his life. There had always been a contradiction in the policies of his visions between advocacy on behalf of the poor crusader and the promotion of Count Raymond as a divinely chosen figure to direct the crusade. Up until the siege of 'Arqah this contradiction had been resolved by Count Raymond, at times bitterly, being obliged to make concessions to the demands of the poor. Now, however, the greater part of the army – and not just the poor – wanted to leave 'Arqah and as Count Raymond was refusing to move, they were at boiling point. Another mutiny was developing. But unlike the revolt at Ma'arra, this time Peter Bartholomew placed himself openly against the mutineers. Although the latest vision did not explicitly refer to the ongoing siege, its martial spirit and the leading role given to Count Raymond meant that the message was understood to be one of urging the army to make a renewed effort to capture 'Arqah. Perhaps Peter hoped that the galvanising effect of the vision, like at Ma'arra, would lead to a decisive assault on the town. But at 'Arqah the idea of further sacrifices against the town's defences was unpalatable for all but Count Raymond's immediate followers.

At the same time as weakening his support with the poor, Peter Bartholomew had alarmed the opponents of the Holy Lance that their scoffing at the relic and dismissive attitude to it might have serious consequences. The visionary was attempting to galvanise a popular pogrom against the dissenters and for them it was now an urgent matter to strike back. Peter Bartholomew's enemies primarily consisted of the nobility of the other factions, especially the Normans, who had clashed with Count Raymond over control of Antioch. Raymond of Aguilers reported that the main line of attack on Peter Bartholomew was to belittle his lowly social status: 'they began to say they would never believe that God would speak to a man of this sort and overlook bishops and princes

---

[46] RA 280 (288).
[47] AA 411.

and reveal himself to a rustic man.'[48] By siding with the unpopular perspective of the count at 'Arqah, the visionary had made a fatal mistake. Sensing an opportunity to rid themselves of a dangerous popular agitator, it was the Normans who led the counter-cry that Peter Bartholomew was a charlatan.

The legitimacy of the Lance was challenged at a two-day council of the clergy, 6 and 7 April 1099.[49] Leading the attack on Peter was Arnulf of Chocques, the friend and chaplain of Count Robert of Normandy.[50] No more dangerous opponent remained among a clergy who had lost nearly all of their senior leaders. Arnulf of Chocques was skilled at logic and had taught the subject to Cecilia, daughter of William the Conqueror, at the Holy Trinity convent in Caen. In grammatical learning too, Arnulf was educated for a high position in the church. On the death of the crusading bishop Odo of Bayeux at Palermo, early in 1097, Arnulf inherited control of a great deal of the bishop's funds and valuable possessions. With this came a higher profile among the Christian army and Arnulf proved to be a very capable speaker and leader of Christian services.[51]

When Arnulf, therefore, made the case against the Holy Lance being an authentic relic, he did so with a powerful presentation. Surprisingly, however, the popular clergy rallied and threw Arnulf back on the defensive. Raymond of Aguilers – in a section of his history that John France has helpfully described as reading like a legal document drawn up for the trial[52] – reports the testimony of a number of southern French clergy in support of Peter Bartholomew. First came the priest Peter Desiderius, chaplain to Isoard I, count of Die (a senior noble in the company of Raymond of Toulouse), who at Antioch had come forward with a vision concerning the relics of St George.[53] In support of Peter Bartholomew, Peter Desiderius stated that he too had been visited by Adhémar and that the legate did indeed have the burns that Peter Bartholomew had spoken of. Another visionary to confirm the status of the Holy Lance as a relic was Ebrardus, a priest, who said that at the time Kerbogha had trapped the crusader army in Antioch, Saint Mark, the evangelist, brought him a message via a Christian Syrian. The message was that Christ was in Antioch and together with his disciples would assist in the coming battle. Moreover, it was foretold that the Christians destined to capture Jerusalem would not break out of Antioch until they found the Holy Lance. Ebrardus offered to cross an ordeal fire as proof of his testimony.[54]

---

[48] RA 280-281 (289): *Caeperunt (...) dicere quod nunquam crederent quod hujuscemodi homini loqueretur Deus, et dimitteret principes episcopes, et ostenderet se rustico homini: unde etiam de lancea Domini dubitabant.*

[49] H. Hagenmeyer, *Chronologie de la Première Croisade 1094-1100* (Hildesheim 1973) 224.

[50] WT 7.18 (366).

[51] C.W. David, *Robert Curthose, Duke of Normandy* (Cambridge, MS 1920), 217-220.

[52] France, 'Two Types of Vision on the First Crusade', 17.

[53] RA 111-113 (257). For Peter Desiderius see: Riley-Smith, *The First Crusaders*, 216; For Isoard I, count of Die see: RA 66 (2); Riley-Smith, *First Crusaders*, 213.

[54] RA 238–40 (282).

Next to speak at the council was another priest, Stephen of Valence, who repeated his story of Christ's appearance before him at Antioch, and said that although Christ did not specifically name the Lance, He promised aid by the fifth day: the day the Holy Lance was found. Stephen pointed out that he had offered before Adhémar to undergo the ordeal by fire in the presence of the crowd or jump from the highest tower of Antioch to prove himself. And he offered the same to the council.[55]

The bishop of Apt and Raymond of Aguilers himself were both keen to support the Lance, but hedged their testimony; the bishop by being uncertain if his vision of the Lance may have been a dream, and the chronicler through his wavering defence of the Lance.[56] Again, it strengthens the value of Raymond of Aguilers as a source that he was unwilling to invent or exaggerate in order to provide testimony from his own experience. Having once again described the finding of the Lance, Raymond gave only indirect evidence in support of the relic, reporting a vision told to him by a priest, Bertrand of Le Puy, a member of Adhémar's household. In a vision of Adhémar, the dead legate told Bertrand to believe in the Holy Lance even more than he did in the Lord's Passion.[57] Raymond of Aguilers was later confronted by Peter Bartholomew and in tears admitted to the visionary that in fact he did have reservations about the authenticity of the relic: Raymond had secretly desired to see the miracle of the Lance confirmed by ordeal.[58]

The council of crusading clergy was now deeply divided. Albert of Aachen's report of a schism among the Christian forces suggests the matter was the cause of a serious split.[59] Given how effectively the southern French clergy had rallied to the visionary, the attack on Peter Bartholomew had faltered. Arnulf of Chocques considered retreating, even if that meant having to perform penance for a false accusation, but in the end he held to his course.[60] And suddenly, in the middle of this crisis, Peter Bartholomew announced that he would voluntarily take the ordeal of fire with the Holy Lance in order to convince the doubters.[61] This brings us to the actual ordeal. In what state of mind is a person who volunteers to expose himself or herself to deadly fires? The obvious answer, and the most common one in regard to discussions of Peter Bartholomew, is to say it must be a person who has a devout spirituality and a sincere belief that he or she will be aided by miraculous and divine intervention. But given the statistic that in roughly half of all ordeals by fire (albeit a different type of ordeal, involving carrying or walking over hot iron) the accused was successful,[62] then to this answer can be added the following

---

[55] RA 240–3 (282).
[56] RA 240–3 (282).
[57] RA 243 (282).
[58] RA 284 (289).
[59] AA 377.
[60] RA 243 (282).
[61] RA 244 (282).
[62] Baker, *English Legal History*, 6.

idea: that depending on the opinion of those responsible for conducting the trial, the circumstances of the trial might not be too arduous. It is notable that Ebrardus and Stephen too, offered to undertake the ordeal. To the survivor of such a test would come enormous authority with the crusading army and when these two visionaries made their declarations, Peter must have felt a certain amount of pressure in regard to his status as the Lord's most favoured visionary. As we have seen, before his last vision Peter had admitted to brooding on Christ's appearance to Stephen of Valence.

There were medieval charlatans who exploited the popular desire for relics and miracles. Forgery was common, and it was a sin. But at the same time, when a medieval monk amended a monastic document in order to promote the holdings of his monastery he did not see this as forgery but rather a correction to make the document conform to the proper state of affairs. If anything, the monk was earning God's approval rather than the opposite. On the spectrum from sincere visionary to out-and-out rogue, it seems reasonable to place Peter Bartholomew somewhere in the middle. There can be little doubt that Peter himself planted in the ground the metal that he announced as the Holy Lance. But in doing so, he might well have adopted the same outlook as the monastic 'forger'. Peter Bartholomew was doing God's work: he was saving the expedition and the lives of the poor crusaders. In facing the trial by fire he could hope for divine assistance, but he did not have to depend on this to survive, especially if his supporters took charge of the arrangements. Offering to undergo the ordeal was a risk, but it was a realistic way forward for him personally and the crusade as a whole.

The date of the trial was set for 8 April 1099, Good Friday. Over the intervening four days Peter Bartholomew fasted, while the various factions of the crusading army made their preparations. The master of ceremonies for the trial was none other than Peter's companion and enthusiast for the Holy Lance, Raymond of Aguilers. At dawn on Good Friday the huge crowds assembled, the clergy barefoot. Two piles of dry olive branches had been created, about four feet in height, thirteen feet in length and with a space of one foot between them for Peter to walk along. Once the timber was lit and the flames began to soar over forty feet in height, Raymond of Aguilers proclaimed the nature of the test with the words that opened this article: if Peter Bartholomew were lying, then he and the Lance should be consumed by fire. The crowd around him knelt and declared 'Amen'. Then Peter Bartholomew came forward from his tent in Count Raymond's camp.[63]

The visionary was dressed in a simple tunic. He too bent, before Peter of Narbonne, to swear that he had seen Christ on the cross and that none of his reports were fabrications. It is worth pausing here to note that Peter of Narbonne was the bishop of Albara, raised to that position as Count Raymond's appointee. Also noteworthy is that Peter Bartholomew was standing by his last vision, with its call to action against unbelievers.

---

[63] RA 283 (289).

The stakes were high, with Peter Bartholomew making it clear that if he survived the day, he would not cease to agitate for a violent purge of his enemies. With the bishop handing Peter the Lance, the visionary walked confidently through the flames. Although he was delayed mysteriously on the path, he soon emerged triumphantly from the other side to shout 'Deus adjuva!'[64]

For Peter's supporters, this was the miracle they had wanted. A huge crowd rushed to the pyre to grab burning sticks to save as relics. Soon only the blackened ground remained. The gamble had worked. Or had it? Before Peter Bartholomew could relish his success, the mob – and at this point Raymond of Aguilers's language turns against the crowd – charged the visionary. Among those who wished only to venerate the man through whom God was working miracles were more sinister figures, armed with blades. Slashed three or four times in the legs, with his flesh cut away, and with his backbone shattered, Peter was mortally wounded. He would have died on the spot but for the belated intervention of Count Raymond's most powerful vassal, Raymond Pilet, who charged the crowd and battled his way through for the body.[65]

On 20 April 1099, Peter Bartholomew died of his wounds. According to Raymond of Aguilers, Peter's burns were of no consequence. Those who came to the dying man's tent to examine his face, head, hair and other parts were amazed that the visionary showed so little evidence of burns. He had failed the ordeal, however, for exactly the same reason as he very nearly passed it. His supporters successfully created a test that looked miraculous but was survivable. His enemies anticipated this and surprised the organisers of the ordeal with an unruly assault on the visionary. As I suspect was the case for very many medieval ordeals the result was manipulated, in this case, by two opposing political factions of a crusading army. And in the practical fashion of many such ordeals, it probably did provide a cruel but accurate verdict on the overall balance of public opinion.

---

[64] RA 284 (289).
[65] RA 252 (292).

Chapter 6   *Iuvenes* and the First Crusade (1096–99): Knights in Search of Glory?

In my approach to medieval history, I was enormously influenced by the writings of Georges Duby (1919–1996). Firstly, because he was a beautiful writer who knew how to draw you in to a moment in history, but also because he was quite brilliant at teasing out the implications of medieval documents for what they revealed about social structure and therefore about the drives and motives of other people than the kings and queens. Although Duby did not focus his attention on the crusades, he did offer a thought that has been extremely influential: that the emergence of central authority, quelling the opportunity for advancement by knights who did not own manors, created a pool of discontented, restless 'youths' and that this goes a long way to explain the appearance of the tournament and, at about the same time, the crusade.

This insight doesn't provide a full explanation for the crusade but when I used it as an analytical tool in my research into the First Crusade, I found that it helped me identify a particular group of knights who had all the characteristics of Duby's youths. It is this body of unrestrained warriors who give some crusades their explosive and particularly ruthless character.

The epitome of the medieval warrior, the hero of the *chanson*, the glorious competitor in the sports of the tournament, was the *iuvenis*. This 'youth' was a knight whose career was still unsettled. In what remains the most important study of the subject, Georges Duby wrote that 'youth' can be defined 'as the period in a man's life between his being dubbed a knight and his becoming a father.'[1] In other words, the condition of a *iuvenis* was not necessarily that he was young; what mattered was that, although knighted, he had yet to establish himself as the head of a family of his own.

      Such knights in search of reputation, family and career often grouped together in bands and, commenting on this, Duby drew an interesting conclusion with regard to the crusades. 'It is obvious that it was the bands of "youths", excluded by so many social prohibitions from the main body of settled men, fathers of families and heads of houses,

---

[1] Georges Duby, *The Chivalrous Society*, trans. C. Postan (Berkeley: University of California Press, 1977), 113. Originally published as 'Les "jeunes" dans la société aristocratique dans la France du Nord-Ouest au XIIe siècle,' *Annales: Économies, Sociétés, Civilisations* 19, 5 (1964): 835–46.

with their prolonged spells of turbulent behaviour making them an unstable fringe of society, who created and sustained the crusades.'[2] It is certainly overstating the case with regard to the First Crusade to say that *iuvenes* created the expedition and sustained it. Duby's observation does, however, raise an important question. The Latin term *iuvenis*, or collective substantive *iuventus*, is typically used to mean a young person, or body of young persons, not a subcategory of knights. It is therefore natural enough that as historians have encountered this term in the sources for the First Crusade they have assumed its common meaning. But is it always correct to make this assumption? Or were the sources drawing attention to knights on the First Crusade who were 'youths' in the sense of such unsettled, turbulent, glory-seeking warriors?

Robert the Monk

The historian of the First Crusade who had the most definite sense of the *iuvenes* being a body of militant knights in search of fame was Robert the Monk. Robert, apart from his testimony that he was present at the famous Council of Clermont, 18–28 November 1095, which launched the crusade, was not an eyewitness to the events he described.[3] He worked on his manuscript on the First Crusade, at the request of his abbot, from a monastery in the episcopate of Reims, probably writing in the year 1106.[4] Robert's task was to enrich a text in front of him, a history that was the work of an eyewitness, the anonymously written *Gesta Francorum*.

Robert was heavily dependent on the *Gesta Francorum* for the basic form of his history and for most of its content. His reworking of the *Gesta Francorum*, however, introduced new material and significant elaborations. Where the *Gesta Francorum* is some 20,000 words long, Robert's *Historia Iherosolimitana* comes to around 35, 000 words. There is a small amount of historical information in the text that is original to Robert. This might well be valuable eyewitness testimony from returning crusaders, but any such genuine material has to be reconstructed to free it from the distorting effect of the strong theological and literary lenses through which Robert viewed his source text.

For the purposes of investigating the appearance of *iuvenes* in Robert's work, it is important to try to assess the extent to which Robert was simply employing the term because it seemed an appropriate literary flourish for anyone at the forefront of battle, or whether he had a

---

[2] Ibid., 120.

[3] Robert the Monk, *Historia Iherosolimitana*, in *Recueil des historiens des croisades, Histo- riens occidentaux* [Hereafter *RHC Oc.*] 5 vols. (Paris: Académie des inscriptions et belles-lettres, 1841–95), 3: [hereafter RM], 725.

[4] G. Constable, 'The Place of the Magdeburg Charter of 1107/08 in the History of Eastern Germany and of the Crusades,' in *Vita Religiosa im Mittelalter. Festschrift für Kaspar Elm zum 70 Geburtstag,* ed. F. J. Felten and N. Jaspert (Berlin: Duncker & Humblot, 1999), 283–300. See also C. Sweetenham, *Robert the Monk's History of the First Crusade* (Aldershot: Ashgate, 2005), 7.

particular sociological idea of what a *iuvenis* was, and of which of the crusaders properly deserved the title.

A key passage in this regard is Robert's description of an Egyptian embassy sent by al-Afdal, the vizier of the boy Caliph, al-Mustali, which arrived at the crusader camp at the siege of Antioch early in March 1098. Robert wrote that the Christian army made a great effort to impress the legation. 'The tents were beautified with various kinds of ornaments; shields were attached to stakes in the ground on which the knights' game of quintain was to be played out the next day. There were not absent games of dice, chess and the rapid charges of horses, turning in a circle with taut reins, there were warlike charges and there were the shakings of spears by both sides, by which acts they demonstrated that those who performed such deeds did not fear. Indeed it was the *iuventus* who so participated but those who were elder and experienced sat together as one and discussed the matter with good sense and prudence.'[5]

The reference to *quintain* is significant. This was a sport of knights, in which the rider tilted at a target that could swing around on a counter-weighted arm. It was an activity that would be consistently associated with *iuvenes* throughout the medieval period. Even a hundred and fifty years later, the chronicler Matthew Paris assumed that *quintain* was the sport of *iuvenes*, as in his annal he wrote that in 1253 the London *iuvenes* tested their bravery and the pace of their horses at the exercise called *quintain*, a peacock having been established for a prize.[6] The description by Robert of the less prudent knights showing their prowess before the Egyptian delegation seems to be the earliest medieval writing to mention the exercise explicitly.[7] Thus the scene was not simply a literary topos, it probably reflects Robert's knowledge of the activities of *iuvenes* in France rather than his literary background.

Even supposing the details of the incident to be entirely fanciful on Robert's part, that is, that he was using his imagination to create a vivid scene, there still remains a clear sense that those described as *iuventus* here are not simply young. What defines them is very characteristic of the term in its social sense: they are fearless knights, skilled at riding and jousting. The passage also establishes that Robert saw these knights as a distinct group whose behaviour contrasted with that of the more experienced crusader. Whilst the report does not prove the presence of *iuvenes* on the First Crusade, much less their importance to sustaining

---

[5] RM 791: *Tentoria variis ornamentorum generibus venustantur; terrae infixis sudibus scuta apponuntur, quibus in crastinum Quintanae ludus, scilicet equestris, exerceretur. Aleae, scaci, veloces cursus equorum flexis in gyrum frenis non defuerunt, et militares impetus; hastarumque vibrationes in alterutrum ibi celebratae sunt. In quibus actibus monstrabatur quia nullo pavore treidabant qui talia operabantur. Talia quippe iuventus excolebat; sed aetate sensuque seniores in unum consederant, causaque consilii et prudentiae conferebant*

[6] Matthew Paris, *Chronica Maiora*, in *Rerum Britannicarum medii aevi Scriptores* (London: Her Majesty's Stationery Office, 1880), 5: a. 1253.

[7] C. F. Du Cange, *Glossarium mediae et infimae Latinitatis* (Paris: Librarie de sciences et des arts, 1938), 6: 614. See also L. Clare, *La quintaine, la Course de Bague et le Jeu des Têtes* (Paris: Éditions du CNRS, 1983), 37–41, 170–71; G. Duby, *William Marshall* (London: Faber, 1986), 70; J. Barker, *The Tournament in England 1100–1400* (Woodbridge: Boydell Press, 2003).

the expedition, it does demonstrate that Robert and his readers expected there to be such vainglorious knights in the Christian camp.

Shortly before this incident, on 6 March 1098, the Christian army had won an important victory against a sortie from the Turkish garrison of Antioch. The following day, wrote Robert, the Turks left the city at dawn and buried those bodies they could find. On hearing this, the *iuvenes* of Christ's army hastened to the cemetery, where they dug up the bodies and cut off the heads.[8] There is little information here to clarify who were meant by the term *iuvenes*, other than a certain sense of disapproval at their behaviour, indicated either by Robert or a later scribe, whose title for the section referred to the graves of the Turks being disgracefully destroyed by the Christians.

Antioch eventually fell due to the betrayal of Firuz, a commander of three towers along a stretch of the city wall. Disillusioned with Yaghi-Siyan, the Turkish ruler of the city, Firuz had entered into secret negotiations with Bohemond I of Taranto, a South-Italian Norman lord and the most famous of the crusading princes. According to a relatively late Muslim source, Firuz was bitter, having been punished for hoarding.[9] The chronicler Ralph of Caen, much closer to events, corroborates the spirit of this idea from the Christian perspective. He wrote that Firuz had kept back a certain amount of grain to feed his large family, but that, on learning of this, Yaghi-Siyan had it confiscated and redistributed, leaving Firuz feeling as though injury had been added to loss.[10]

After reaching agreement with Bohemond, Firuz allowed sixty men (*homines*) to climb the city wall on the morning of 3 June 1098, according to the *Gesta Francorum*.[11] Robert's version of the storming of Antioch was more detailed than that of his source; he reported that it was Fulcher of Chartres and sixty armed *iuvenes*, who first climbed the walls of the city.[12] The appearance of the name Fulcher was a divergence from the *Gesta Francorum* by Robert, but it is accurate in that the eyewitness Raymond of Aguilers also mentions Fulcher as being first on to the walls of Antioch.[13]

---

[8] RM 788.

[9] Kemal al-Din, *Chronique d 'Alep* in *RHC Oc.* 3: 581–82.

[10] Ralph of Caen, *Gesta Tancredi* in *RHC Oc.* 3: [hereafter RC], 651–52.

[11] *Gesta Francorum et aliorum Hierosolimitan*orum, ed. R. Hill (Oxford, Oxford University Press, 1962) [hereafter GF], 46.

[12] RM 800. The Fulcher of Chartres involved in this incident is not to be confused with the chronicler of the same name. See C. Sweetenham, *Robert the Monk's History*, 145 n. 24.

[13] Raymond of Aguilers, *Historia Francorum qui ceperunt Iherusalem*, ed. John France (unpublished Ph.D. thesis, University of Nottingham, 1967) [hereafter RA], 80 (252). I consider the edition by John France, based as it is on a sophisticated reconstruction of the archetype from all known manuscripts, superior to all other editions, but include reference in brackets to the more easily accessible *RHC* edition. I am grateful to John France for permission to quote from his thesis.

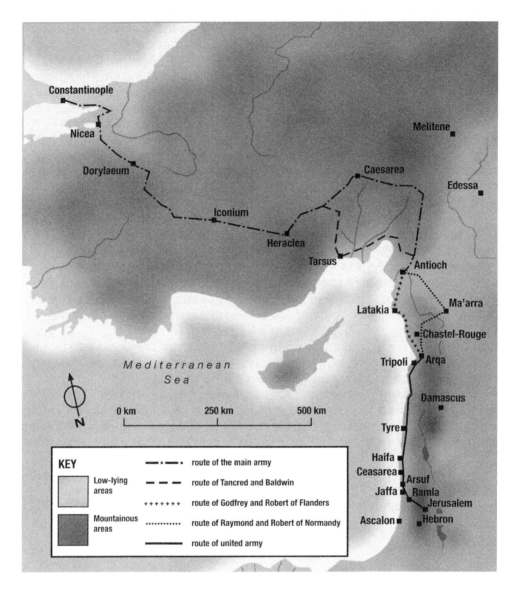

Map 1: The routes taken by the various factions of the First Crusade

At some point, possibly before the storming of the city, Fulcher had joined with other knights who had a reputation for bravery. By August 1098, when a plague broke out in Antioch, causing many knights to leave the city, Fulcher was in the company of Drogo of Nesle, Rainald of Toul and Gaston of Béziers.[14] These four knights were described as departing

---

[14] Albert of Aachen, *Historia Iherosolimitana,* ed. S. B. Edgington (Oxford: Oxford Uni- versity Press, 2007) [hereafter AA], v. 16 (356).

Antioch together, to seek service with the Lotharingian prince, Baldwin of Boulogne, who had managed to establish himself as lord of the city of Edessa. Drogo and Rainald, along with Clarembald of Vendeuil and Ivo of Grandmesnil, had earlier been singled out as the unanimous choice of the captains of the army when riders were required to investigate reports that Kerbogha, *atabeg* (governor) of Mosul, was arriving with a great army.[15]

Drogo seems to have been at the centre of a distinct group of celebrated warriors, certainly that is the impression given in another significant description of *iuvenes* in the work of Robert the Monk: his account of the critical battle against Kerbogha, on 28 June 1098. In his version of the conflict, Robert praised the famous feats of the illustrious *iuventus*[16] before going on to identify by name a particular grouping of *iuvenes* in the contingent led by Hugh the Great, count of Vermandois: 'because they saw that they were closing on [the enemy force], Everard [III] of Le Puiset, Payen of Beauvais, Drogo [of Nesle], Thomas [of Marle] and Clarembald [of Vendeuil], and the rest of the *iuventus* of Hugh the Great, did not hesitate to dash in amongst them.'[17]

Those here identified as *iuvenes* were significant nobles with something of a career behind them already, thus indicating Robert was not using the term *iuvenes* to make a statement about their age. As noted above, Drogo was subsequently associated with Fulcher of Chartres and again with Clarembald. But he was also strongly connected to Thomas of Marle. Thomas, Drogo and Clarembald had once been part of the contingent of Count Emicho of Flonheim, one of the few magnates associated with the People's Crusade of 1096. This army was notorious for its attacks on the Jew- ish communities of Speyer, Worms, Mainz and Cologne. The Lotharingian historian, Albert of Aachen, described them as an 'intolerable company.'[18]

Emicho's army had been dispersed as it entered Hungary, following its failure to take Wiesselburg in September 1096, but some of the knights continued with the expedition, and Robert was not the only historian to indicate that Thomas, Drogo and Clarembald subsequently attached themselves to Hugh the Great. They seem to have met as captives of the Byzantine Emperor, Alexios I Comnenus, who, reported Albert of Aachen, kept Drogo, Clarembald and Hugh in prison.[19]

---

[15] AA iv.13 (268). For Rainald of Toul, see J. Riley-Smith, *The First Crusaders, 1095–1131* (Cambridge: Cambridge University Press, 1997), 218.

[16] RM 831-2.

[17] RM 833: *Quod ut viderent qui eum vicinius subsequebantur, Edwardus scilicet de Puteolo, Paganus Belvacensis, Drogo et Thomas, et Clarenbaldus, ceteraque juventus Hugonis Magni, nil haesi- tantes in illos irruunt.* For these knights, see J. Riley-Smith, *The First Crusaders*, 203 (Clarembald), 205 (Everard), 205 (Payen). For Drogo of Nesle, see A. V. Murray, *The Crusader Kingdom of Je- rusalem* (Oxford: Unit for Prosopographical Research, 2000), 191. For Thomas of Marle, lord of Coucy, count of Amiens, see D. Barthélemy, *Les Deux Ages de la seigneurie banale: Pouvoir et société dans la terre des sires de Coucy (milieu Xe–milieu XIIIe siècle)*, (Paris: Publications de la Sorbonne, 1984). See also J. Riley-Smith, *First Crusaders*, 223.

[18] AA, i.28 (52): *intolerabilis societas.* For Emicho of Flonheim, see AA 51 n. 66.

[19] AA ii.7 (72).

Returning to an examination of the portrayal of crusading *iuvenes* in Robert the Monk, the next mention of the *iuventus* comes when the expedition attacked Ma'arra, a well-defended city that had been gathering Turkish forces for some time. With great risk a breakthrough was gained for the crusading forces when, on 11 December 1098, Gouflier, lord of Las Tours, was the first to climb a ladder onto the walls of the town. Robert described how when the famous *iuventus* saw Gouffier with a few men fighting on the top of the city walls, they climbed up forthwith and overwhelmed part of the defenders of the wall with the weight of their numbers.[20]

The last reference to the *iuvenes* by Robert occurred in his description of what turned out to be a critical moment in the direction of the crusade. Around Christmas 1098 a bitter conflict broke out between two of the most important crusading princes over the ownership of Antioch. By this stage in the crusade, Bohemond had proven to be an effective military and political leader, above all in the capture of Antioch. Count Raymond IV of Toulouse was the elderly leader of the very large Provençal contingent. Both held a different perspective on the future of Antioch now that it was back in Christian hands: Bohemond wanting to rule the city as an independent principality, Raymond as a fief of the Byzantine Empire. As a result of their conflict, the crusade had stalled entirely.

When a meeting of knights and princes at Chastel-Rouge, probably on 4 January 1099, proved unable to resolve the differences between the rival princes, the news of the failure triggered a mutiny of the lower social orders at Ma'arra. The 'poor' Christians (*pauperes*) dismantled the walls of the recently captured city, making it defenceless and obliging Count Raymond to continue the expedition.[21] The *Gesta Francorum* and Robert the Monk skip the events at Ma'arra, and follow the perspective not of the *pauperes*, but of those who remained at Chastel-Rouge. Robert wrote that many *iuvenes* were present who were on fire to complete the journey.[22] In Robert's eyes the *iuvenes* were a social grouping that were among the most fervent in wishing to press on to Jerusalem.

In Robert the Monk's *Historia Iherosolimitana*, then, it is clear that the historian had a strong sense that a *iuvenis* was a brave knight of illustrious background, although not an established prince; the *iuvenis* was inclined to be intemperate, but equally, he was brave to the point of recklessness; nor was there any doubting his skill in the military arts. Robert's application of this idea to his history of the First Crusade led him to portray certain knights as *iuvenes* and certain incidents as being the work of that grouping. Through his employment of the idea it is possible to dis- cern the beginnings of a pattern, one that suggests that a band of knights fulfilling Robert's criteria for being *iuvenes* coalesced as a

---

[20] RM 847.
[21] RA 180 (271).
[22] RM 837.

grouping on the First Crusade.This pattern becomes clearer by consideration of the other early crusading histories.

Gilo of Paris

The *Historia Vie Hierosolimitane* of Gilo of Paris is a poetic reworking of the *Gesta Francorum* that has a close connection with the narrative history of Robert the Monk. The exact relationship between the two has not been decisively estab- lished, but the generally accepted view is that they share a now missing common source.[23] Gilo was a Cluniac monk from Toucy in Auxerre who subsequently became cardinal-bishop of Tusculum.[24] His metrical history was written at some point before 1120, the suggestion of his most recent editors being that it was writ- ten in the first decade of the century.[25]

The *iuventus* first appear in Gilo's account of the winter of 1097–1098, at a point where the participants in the First Crusade were besieging Antioch. Gilo wrote that he ought to enumerate the deeds of the famous *iuventus* of *Gallia*, but no one could narrate so many bitter battles and narrow escapes, so much fasting and cold, so many anxieties.[26] On 5 April 1098, during the siege, a fort was built opposite the Gate of St George. A young southern Italian Norman prince, Tancred, the nephew of Bohemond and an important military commander in his own right, took charge of this fortification in return for a payment of four hundred marks. Of this event Gilo stated that a certain fortress was renovated and an old rampart was repaired where the *iuvenes* could keep their plunder.[27] The implication of this statement is that there was a distinct body of *iuvenes* willing to serve under Tancred at the fort and that they had sufficient plunder from raids and forays to require it as a holding place.

Like Robert, Gilo attributed to the *iuvenes* a major role in the capture of Antioch. The poet composed the following address by Bohemond to those assembled for the assault on the walls, betrayed to him by Firuz: 'And you, swift *iuvenes*, climb the walls at once.'[28] In Gilo's account Bohemond waited anxiously, while the *iuvenes* rushed into action, led by Fulcher of Chartres.[29] Fulcher here again was identified as the foremost of the *iuvenes* who responded to the appeal.

Gilo continued his description of the fall of Antioch to the crusaders by describing how once the gates of the city had been opened, the rest of

---

[23] C. W. Grocock and J. E. Siberry, eds., The *Historia Vie Hierosolimitane* of Gilo of Paris and a second anonymous author (Oxford: Clarendon Press of Oxford University Press, 1997) [hereafter GP] lx. Sweetman, *Robert the Monk's History*, 34.

[24] GP xviii. For further discussion of Gilo's career, see GP xix–xxii and R. Hüls, *Kardinäle, Klerus and Kirchen Roms* (Tübingen: Niemeyer, 1977), 142–43.

[25] GP xxiv.

[26] GP 102.

[27] GP 123.

[28] GP 162: *Vosque, citi iuuenes, muros superate repente.*

[29] GP 164–6.

the army was spurred to action, the horses were bridled and the *iuventus* clamoured for arms.[30] The very next day, some advance elements from Kerbogha's army arrived before Antioch. A rash sortie by Roger of Barneville, a knight who was famous both among Christians and Muslims,[31] eventually saw him chased back to the gates of the city where he was killed and beheaded in full sight of those on the walls. This was a particularly difficult moment for the *iuvenes* who were watching, wrote Gilo; the *iuventus* on the walls were assailed by confusion and shame.[32] Subsequently trapped by Kerbogha's army inside Antioch, the crusading army suffered from starvation, and the poet illustrated this by reporting that even a dying horse was devoured by the *iuventus*.[33]

In a manner very similar to Robert's account of the battle with Kerbogha, Gilo wrote of the vigorous role played in this conflict by the *iuvenes* in the contingent of Hugh the Great: 'Everard of Le Puiset and the impetuous *iuventus*, looked for a battle in the battle itself, and raised their swords... Then [Hugh the Great] said: "What you desire, *iuvenes*, is here! The iron field bristles with spears, let us turn to them and lay on with huge strength."'[34] In his description of the same battle Gilo added that after the death of Odo of Beaugency, standard-bearer to Hugh the Great, the *iuvenis* William of Benium immediately took his place, and raised the standard.[35] As will be seen, the association between *iuvenes* and the action of defending a standard was a recurrent one.

Gilo's next reference to the *iuventus* occurred in his description of a substantial raiding expedition led by a senior Provençal knight, Raymond Pilet. After some initial successes, Raymond Pilet's forces were defeated in an attempt to storm Ma'arra, on 27 July 1098, leading Gilo to sympathise with the plight of retreating *iuvenes*.[36] The united expedition was more successful on its approach to the city and Gilo wrote of the renewed siege of Ma'arra that the honourable *iuvenes* were awoken by the loud noise of the trumpets and ran to the walls.[37] When the city fell, on 11 December 1098, Gilo attributed the success of the assault to the destruction of a wall by the *iuvenes*, in so doing once again agreeing with Robert the Monk.[38] The final appearance of the *iuvenes* in Gilo of Paris was a reference to the expedition as it made its way towards Jerusalem,

---

[30] GP 168.
[31] AA iii.61 (234).
[32] GP 178.
[33] GP 180.
[34] GP 188: *Eurardus de Puteolo fervensque iuuentus,*
In bello querunt bellum, gladiosque leuabant ... Tunc ita fatur:
'Quod iuvenes optatis adest! Huc ferreus hastis Horret ager, uertamur ad hos, incumbite uastis Viribus!'
[35] GP 190. For Odo of Beaugency, see J. Riley-Smith, *The First Crusaders*, 205. Benium is given as Bény-sur-Mer by the editors of Gilo (GP 190), while Robert describes the same person as William of Belesme (RM 831), J. Riley-Smith lists him as William of Bohemia, *The First Crusaders*, 225.
[36] GP 198: *Tinnitum reddunt clipei galee que sonore,*
Obtenebrant oculos lapsi de uertice coni, Loricas odiunt iuuenes ad uerbera proni.
[37] GP 204.
[38] G 210.

in May 1099, where he reported that from al-Batrun, the *iuventus*, afflicted by the heat, followed the seashore.[39]

Clearly the poet shared with Robert an understanding of the main characteristics of the *iuvenes*. They were knights who sought battle and could be shamed by appeals to their desire for glory. When rewriting the *Gesta Francorum*, Gilo, like Robert, thought it appropriate to term those first onto the walls of Antioch as *iuvenes*, as well as those who fought in the contingent of Hugh the Great against Kerbogha and the knights who broke through at Ma'arra. In addition to echoing Robert's version of those scenes, Gilo indicated that among the knights associated with the Norman prince Tancred were a body of warriors whom he felt it was appropriate to regard as *iuvenes*.

Guibert of Nogent

Another early historian of the crusades who referred to *iuvenes* on the First Crusade was Guibert, abbott of Nogent. Like Robert and Gilo, Guibert was based in France and, in 1109, also composed his history with the *Gesta Francorum* before him as his main source. Written with the intention of providing many edifying passages for the reader, however, the *Dei gesta per Francos* has many commentaries, observations, reports of visions and miracles which means that, unlike the works of Robert and Gilo, it diverges considerably in structure and in content from the *Gesta Francorum*. Guibert also incorporated more historical material into the work than either of the other two northern French historians, both concerning the departure of the expedition, to which he was an eyewitness, and from the testimony of those who had returned from the expedition.

It was in writing about the departure of the expedition that Guibert first mentioned the *iuventus*, in verses composed to illustrate the perspective of the many non-combatants who joined the expedition. 'Everyone sang of warfare, but did not say that they would fight. They promised martyrdom, being about to give their necks to the sword, "You *iuvenes*," they said, "will draw swords with your hands, but we are permitted to deserve Christ by supporting this."'[40] The term *iuvenes* was here used to encapsulate the perspective of crusading combatants as opposed to that of the non-combatants of the expedition; it is good evidence that, for a contemporary, the image of a *iuvenis* was one considered to be appropriate to represent someone at the heart of the fighting body of the First Crusade.

Guibert described a three-fold hierarchy in the Lotharingian army of Duke Godfrey as it departed on the crusade: the senior princes, knights

---

[39] GP 232.

[40] Guibert of Nogent, *Gesta Dei per Francos*, ed. R. B. C. Huygens, Corpus Christiano- rum, Continuatio Mediaevalis, 127A (Turnhout: Brépols, 1996) [hereafter GN] 120:
Bella canunt omnes; nec se pugnare fatentur, Martirium spondent, gladiis vel colla daturos:
'Vos iuvenes', aiunt, 'manibus tractabitis enses At nos hic liceat Christum tolerando mereri.'

and a notable throng of very brave *iuvenes*.[41] This distinction is much less a literary one than that employed when the poor crusaders spoke to the combatants, and it probably reflected Guibert's own perception of the layers present among the warriors of the nobility, a class that he was very familiar with through his relatives and his experi- ences before becoming a monk.[42]

When Guibert turned to writing about Tancred, he stated that the Norman prince had earned and deserved the title of most sagacious *iuvenis*.[43] Tancred was a major figure in the events of the First Crusade: he took command of Bohemond's contingent in the absence of their lord in Greece; he led a sizeable Norman force into Cilicia, around 10 September 1097, and he led a group of Norman knights in the later stages of the crusade. It might seem inconsistent with the other examples given that so prominent a leader was termed a *iuvenis*, not just by Guibert but also, as will be seen below, by Albert of Aachen and Ralph of Caen. But until his establishment of a principality in Galilee, in late 1099, Tancred was an unmarried knight still in search of his fortune and position, acting largely under the direction of Bohemond.[44] It is perhaps in this regard that Guibert considered Tancred the epitome of a *iuvenis* during the expedition.

Guibert entitled Tancred a *iuvenis* in connection with his leading of the garrison of the castle that was built during the siege of Antioch opposite the Gate of St George. Here there is a connection with Gilo's report of the same initiative, with both authors indicating that the hazardous task of forming the garrison of this cas- tle was one associated with the *iuvenes*. A third author, Tancred's biographer, Ralph of Caen, also found the term *iuvenes* appropriate for some of those who joined with the Norman prince, for he wrote that, anticipating future successes, *iuvenes* from Bohemond's army had earlier transferred their allegiance to Tancred.[45]

The next use of the term *iuvenis* by Guibert was for a person who also does not seem to fit well with the definition provided by Duby. Guibert reported the death, during the siege of Antioch, around May 1098, of an excellent *iuvenis*, who had been constable for the King of France: Walo II of Chaumont-en-Vexin.[46] Walo was married to Humberge, the sister of Everard of Le Puiset. As noted above, Everard was identified by Robert and Gilo as a prominent *iuvenis* among the band that included Thomas of Marle and Drogo of Nesle. Unlike Tancred, Walo was married and already played a notable role at the French court. But he and Humberge, who accompanied him on the expedition, were without

---

[41] GN 129.
[42] Jay Rubenstein, *Guibert of Nogent: Portrait of a Medieval Mind* (New York: Routledge, 2002), 17–18.
[43] GN 194.
[44] R. L. Nicholson, *Tancred: a Study of his Career and Work in their Relation to the First Crusade and the Establishment of the Latin States in Syria and Palestine* (Chicago: Chicago University Press, 1940), 3–15.
[45] RC 610.
[46] GN 332. For Walo II of Chaumont-en-Vexin, see J. Riley-Smith, *The First Crusaders*, 224.

children. This, together with his departure from a settled position at the court of the Philip I of France, and his association with other turbulent and glory-seeking knights through his brother-in-law, seems to have prompted Guibert to describe Walo as a *iuvenis*.

Thereafter the term *iuvenis* does not appear in the *Gesta Dei per Francos* until Guibert's account of the storming of Jerusalem, on 15 July 1099. 'Several of the Frankish *iuvenes*, whom pious audacity had already made more pre-eminent, threw themselves forward ... and together they climbed to the top of the wall. I would identify them by name on this page, if I had not known that after their return they incurred the infamy of wickedness and crime.'[47]

A clue to the identity of the unnameable persons is to be found in Guibert of Nogent's autobiography. Here, Thomas of Marle looms large as a rebellious and sadistic lord in the 1110s, termed by Guibert the most wicked man of his generation,[48] making it likely that he and his troublesome associates were among those indicated by Guibert's use of the term *iuvenes* at this point.

Guibert may also have been familiar with the case of Raimbold Croton, who Ralph of Caen described as a *iuvenis*, and who was one of those who led the breakthrough into Jerusalem.[49] On his return to Chartres, Raimbold Croton became embroiled in a dispute with Bonneval abbey in the course of which he castrated a monk. As a result Raimbold was given fourteen years' penance by Bishop Ivo of Chartres.[50] Raimbold and Thomas were connected on the crusade by their association with Everard of Le Puiset. After 3 June 1098 the Christians had managed to penetrate into the city of Antioch but still had to defend a rampart against attacks from the citadel, which remained in Turkish hands. Those knights who were prominent in doing so were named by Albert of Aachen and the list included Ivo, Everard and Raimbold Croton.[51]

Even more interestingly, but less reliably, the *Chanson d 'Antioche*, an epic poem with considerable historical detail embedded in its dramatic account of the fall of Antioch, lists Raimbold Croton, Thomas of Marle, Everard of Le Puiset and Engelrand of Saint-Pol among those joining Fulcher of Chartres in the first group of knights to climb the walls of the city.[52] Regardless of the authenticity of that particular information, it is significant that the composer of the *chanson* considered these knights as being associates.

Jonathan Riley-Smith has briefly examined the later turbulent careers of these two members of the First Crusade, but it is worth noting

---

[47] GN 278: *Quique iuvenum Francicorum, quos pia jam dudum reddiderat illustriores audacia, sese proripiunt ... murorum pariter suprema conscendunt. Quos etiam nominatim huic insererem pagi- nae, nisi scirem post reditum tantorum eos flagitiorum ac scelerum infamiam incurrisse.*

[48] Guibert of Nogent, *Monodiae*, ed. E.–R. Labande (Paris: Les Belles Lettres, 1981), 3.VII. See also 3.XI, 3.XIV.

[49] RC 689.

[50] Ivo of Chartres, Letter 135 to Paschal II, *Patrologiae cursus completus. Series Latina* [hereafter *PL*] 162 col. 144D.

[51] AA iv.30 (294). For Raimbold Croton, see J. Riley-Smith, *First Crusaders*, 218.

[52] CA CCLIII.

that both these knights participated in the expedition in such a way as to earn the epithet *iuvenis*, suggesting a connection between the more rebellious of returnees and those whom the early historians considered *iuvenes*.[53] The knight who departed on the expedition motivated primarily by spiritual considerations is likely to have found favour from the Church on his return. Those, however, who primarily set out with a desire to prove themselves in battle, seem to have returned with a contempt for both secular and ecclesiastical authority, as, for example, was demonstrated by the actions of Raimbold Croton, but even more vividly in the career of the notorious Thomas of Marle.

Thomas returned from the First Crusade to live a life of abandon and insubordination. At least such was the view of the clerical authors who wrote about him. He laid waste the whole countryside in the vicinity of Laon, Reims and Amiens 'with the frenzy of a wolf ', wrote Abbot Suger of St Denis.[54] From his devil's pit, a den of robbers, Thomas became a 'common enemy of pilgrims and all humble folk,' wrote the Anglo-Norman monk, Orderic Vitalis, in a passage relating the words of King Louis VI.[55] Henry of Huntington seems to have been well informed about Thomas's career and described how his reputation was known throughout all Gaul. 'Human slaughter was his passion and glory.'[56] Thomas died on 9 November 1130 as a result of injuries sustained when he was captured by Raoul, Count of Vermandois, acting on behalf of the king of France.

There has long been a revision of the Enlightenment-inspired image of the knights of the First Crusade as violent and troublesome characters, in favour of a view that emphasises their piety and spiritual motives.[57] In the case of Thomas, and perhaps those of his associates also termed *iuvenes*, the eighteenth century depiction seems to be not so wide of the mark. While the Enlightenment historians and their followers attributed the source of crusader aggression to their desire for plunder, here it is presented as a characteristic arising from the *esprit de corps* of a particular layer of knights keen to demonstrate their military prowess.

There are a handful of other references to *iuvenes* in the history of Guibert of Nogent. In his description of the battle of Ascalon, on 12 August 1099, Guibert imagined the reaction of al-Afdal, Shah an-Shah, vizier of Egypt, on seeing the weary crusader forces: 'And he looked upon the ... *iuventa* weakened by long hunger, swords turned rusty, lances darkened, the slender military equipment of *milites*, their strength worn out; all those who seemed to be more distinguished than the rest

---

[53] J. Riley-Smith, *The First Crusaders*, 156.

[54] Abbot Suger of St Denis, *Vita Ludovici Regis VI, Qui Grossus Dictus*, PL 186, [Col.1304B]: *furore lupino devoraverat*.

[55] OV, 6, 258: *inimicum peregrinorum et omnium simplicium*.

[56] Henry of Huntingdon, *Historia Anglorum*, ed. D. Greenway (Oxford: Oxford Univer- sity Press, 1996), 602: *cedes humana uoluptas eius et gloria*.

[57] J. Riley-Smith, 'Crusading as an Act of Love' in *The Crusades*, edited by T. F. Madden (Oxford: Blackwell, 2002), 32–50.

rendered inactive by the bitterness of want.'[58] Here again, as in his account of the departing expedition, Guibert drew a tripartite picture of the crusader fighting forces: 'youths' (Guibert used the collective term *iuventa*), knights (*milites*) and princes. Finally, Guibert gave the choicest of the *iuvenes* a role in the vanguard of the army in the storming of Caesarea by Baldwin I, on 17 May 1101.[59]

Calling Walo and Tancred *iuvenes* in the *Dei gesta per Francos* suggests that Guibert did not use the term in a strict sense, like a legal definition. Rather he understood a *iuvenis* to be a knight with a certain quality, not necessarily 'youth' so much as valour. Despite a certain looseness in his employment of the term *iuvenes*, Guibert never went so far as to apply it to the very senior princes on the crusade: it was not simply a fanciful adjective for any champion. Overall Guibert's use of the term was not dissimilar to that of Robert and Gilo. He too employed the term for magnates who led the way in battle and in storming cities.

Thus far the discussion has focused on the works of those who sought to embellish the eyewitness text, the *Gesta Francorum*. Their writings demonstrate how French historians projected their own notions of what it was to be a *iuvenis* on to the knights of the First Crusade. To turn to other sources independent of the *Gesta Francorum* tradition, to find that they also made similar use of the term and that they applied it to the same individuals, considerably strengthens the possibility that there were indeed a body of knights on the First Crusade whose behaviour matched a widely understood notion of what it was to be a *iuvenis*.

Albert of Aachen

The *Historia Ierosoloymitana* of Albert of Aachen is a crucial text for this discussion. For a long time it was thought that Albert's history was a relatively late account, as it continues up to 1119. But modern scholarship has appreciated that the part concerned with the First Crusade was, in fact, written soon after the events it describes, probably in 1102.[60] As Albert based his history primarily on oral sources, 'the narration of those who were present',[61] his is a very valuable work, so much so, that John France has concluded that 'given the early date and the nature of his sources Albert's work deserves to be treated as an eyewitness account.'[62] Albert was a cleric at Aachen in Lotharingia. He had a great deal of information about and interest in the German contingents and therefore considerably supplements the overall picture of the crusade as portrayed by the French sources.

---

[58] GN 299: *At intuebatur... profligatam diutina fame iuventam, rubiginosis ensibus, lanceis nigrantibus, exilem destitutis militum viribus armaturam, cunctis qui pre ceteris videbantur insignes acri egestate torpentibus.*
[59] GN 347.
[60] P. Knoch, *Studien zu Albert von Aachen* (Stuttgart: Klett, 1966), 89; AA xxiv-v.
[61] AA i.1 (2): *relatione nota fierent ab hiis qui presentes affuissent.* See also AA iii.2 (138).
[62] John France, *Victory in the East: a Military History of the First Crusade* (Cambridge: Cambridge University Press, 1994), 381.

Two terms occur in Albert's work that were nearly always used to indicate someone from the same social grouping as a *iuvenis*, namely *adolescens* and *tyro*. There are two crusaders described by Albert as *adolescens*, both adult knights. The first is Gerard of Avesnes, a knight of Hainault who was given as a hostage to the Arabs of Arsuf by Duke Godfrey as part of an agreement that was subsequently broken. When Duke Godfrey besieged Arsuf, early in December 1099, Gerard was held spread-eagled on ropes outside of the battlements of the town. Undeterred, Duke Godfrey pressed the siege and Gerard was eventually pulled back up riddled with the arrows of his own companions.

Surprisingly, Gerard reappeared on 25 March 1100, released as a peace offering from the townspeople. Albert wrote that, 'when the duke saw and received the beloved *miles* and excellent *adolescens* Gerard unharmed, he rejoiced exceedingly.'[63] The fact that Gerard was then given a castle and great fiefs suggests both that he was not an *adolescens* in the sense of being immature and that his trials had earned him a change in status to becoming a lord, exactly the social progress striven for by the *iuventus*.

The other *adolescens* in Albert's work was the less fortunate Arnulf II of Oudenaarde, killed while searching for his horse on the return of a raiding expedition to Jerusalem in 1106. Arnulf was described at various times as a very noble *iuvenis*, a prince, an illustrious knight and *adolescens*.[64]

Another apparent synonym for *iuvenes* in the *Historia Ierosolimitana* was *tirones*. In classical times, the term had been used to describe a recruit, a soldier newly enlisted, without sufficient training. The *tirones* of the classical era were mostly 17 to 20 years of age.[65] By the medieval period the fact that there was a similarity of meaning of *iuvenis* and *tiro* is suggested by the noun *tirocinium*, which came to mean a joust or tournament, and the verb *tirocinare*, to be in training as a knight.[66] Moreover, Albert was not given to classical allusion and it is clear that those to whom he applied the term were fully trained knights. Those who were named and described as *tiros* were: Tancred; his brother William; Guy of Possesse; Rainald of Beauvais; Engelrand, son of count Hugh of Saint-Pol; Franco I and Sigemar of Maasmechelen on the river Meuse, blood relations; and Otto surnamed Altaspata, son of the sister of Albert of Biandrate.[67] A Venetian was termed *tiro* by Albert at the siege of Haifa,

---

[63] AA vii. 15 (506): *Dux itaque, viso et incolumi recepto Gerardo dilecto milite, et egregio adolescente, gavisus est vehementer.*

[64] AA ix.52 (714–17).

[65] A. Berger, 'Encyclopaedic Dictionary of Roman Law', *Transactions of the American Philosophical Society* 43,2 (1953): 737.

[66] J. F. Niermeyer, *Mediae Latinitatis Lexicon Minus* (Leiden: Brill, 2002) II: 1342.

[67] Tancred, AA ii.22 (94); William, AA ii.39 (130); Guy, AA ii.22 (96); Rainald, AA iii.35 (194); Engelrand, AA iii.48 (212); Franco and Sigemar, AA iv.35 (302); Otto, AA ix. 30 (674). For other references to these knights, see J. Riley-Smith, *The First Crusaders*, 210 (Guy); 225 (William); 218 (Rainald). For Sigemar, see A. V. Murray, *The Crusader Kingdom*, 228.

on 25 July 1100, when he was the only one of his com- panions not to abandon a siege machine.[68] Of these *tiros*, William and Engelrand were also termed *iuvenes* by Albert.[69] In fact, the description of William makes the close connection between *iuvenes* and *tirones* clear. 'William, most audacious *iuvenis*, and most beautiful *tiro*, brother of Tancred.'[70]

With regard to Albert's description of Rainald of Beauvais as a *tiro* there is a valuable agreement between the sources discussed so far. Albert invariably referred to Rainald in association with Walo II of Chaumont, who, as noted above, was termed a *iuvenis* by Guibert of Nogent and who was brother-in-law to the prominent *iuvenis* Everard of Le Puiset.[71] Furthermore, at the battle of Dorylaeum, on 1 July 1097, Rainald of Beauvais was mentioned as being in the company of both Walo and Thomas of Marle as well as two other knights described elsewhere as *iuvenes* by Albert of Aachen: Baldwin of Bourcq and Rothard, son of Godfrey.[72] Rainald was listed by Gilo of Paris as being among the group of knights who were attached to the contingent of Hugh the Great for the battle against Kerbogha, the same group (that which included Thomas of Marle and Drogo of Nesle) whom Robert the Monk included under the label *iuventus*.[73] Albert, who had twice as many divisions of crusaders marching from Antioch for the battle as Robert, listed Rainald in an *ad hoc* division that also included Thomas of Marle, Drogo of Nesle, Rothard and Baldwin of Bourcq.[74]

In order to reach Antioch, the crusaders had to cross the 'Iron Bridge',[75] which they reached on 19 October 1097, only to find it firmly defended. Robert of Normandy was the leader of the vanguard of the army at this point and with him were Roger Barneville and Everard of Le Puiset, who, as noted above, was several times termed a *iuvenis* by the French sources. In this instance Everard was described as being a *miles* praiseworthy in military affairs, and, with the other leaders, he directed the movement of the cavalry with banners.[76] Resistance from the Turkish garrison at the bridge was severe but once the Turks began to withdraw, some knights, 'out of a desire to begin battle' recklessly swam their horses across the river.[77] Albert named two knights here: Walo of Chaumont and Rainald of Beauvais, 'a most savage *tiro*'.[78]

Another important example of a grouping together of individuals elsewhere described as *iuevenes* is Albert's list of those were located

[68] AA vii.24 (518).

[69] William, AA ii.39 (130); Engelrand, AA v.30 (376).

[70] AA ii.39 (130): *Willelmus iuvenis audacissimus et tyro pulcherrimus, frater Tancradi.*

[71] AA ii. 23 (98); AA ii.42 (134); AA iii.35 (194), AA iv.47 (322).

[72] AA ii.42 (134). Rothard is otherwise unknown, as is his father Godfrey, not to be confused with Godfrey, Duke of Lotharingia.

[73] GP 190–2.

[74] AA iv.47 (322).

[75] A misnomer by the Latins, see WT 4,8 (243).

[76] AA iii.33 (191).

[77] AA iii.35 (195): *ex desiderio bellum committendi.*

[78] AA iii.35 (195): *tiro asperrimus.*

beside each other in the siege of Nicaea: Guy of Possesse, Thomas, Drogo, Baldwin of Bourcq and Engelrand of Saint-Pol.[79]

The interconnections and associations between the knights mentioned in all these incidents are quite striking. A coalescing of a certain type of crusading warrior seems to have taken place during the crusade. Having come to the attention of those who wrote about the crusade, both Albert and the French historians independently found the term *iuvenes* to be a suitable one for these knights. Was there something characteristic of the behaviour or social position of Thomas, Drogo and Everard et al., that led early Northern European historians of the crusade to see them in this light?

What this quality was cannot have been one that was strictly in keeping with the definition of Georges Duby: Walo was married, as was Thomas. But in both cases their domestic position was unsettled, with Thomas in conflict with his father, Enguerrand of Coucy, who had divorced Thomas's mother and, doubting the legitimacy of Thomas, strove to disinherit him.[80] One feature that does seem to have been important in the early crusading historians' use of the term *iuvenes* was that it was applied to those who were not lowly knights; these were knights who were potentially lords of castles or towns.

During the crusade itself, however, these nobles were not prominent enough figures to command a leadership role; rather they acted independently or else attached themselves to the senior princes. To judge by the fluidity of their associations these attachments seem not to have been tight ones, such as that created by vassalage. Clarembald, for example, seems to have set out on crusade under his own resources, been held in captivity with Hugh the Great, whom he fought under at Antioch, then travelled to Edessa to serve Baldwin of Boulogne.[81] Similarly, when Ralph of Caen reported that certain *iuvenes* left the following of Bohemond for that of Tancred, in the expectation of future success, the impression given is of a less formal relationship than that between vassal and lord.

With regard to the common qualities of behaviour that these knights might have displayed, Albert seems to have shared with the northern French writers a sense that the *iuvenis* was associated with indiscipline. Albert commented that while Bohemond prudently portrayed himself as loyal to the Byzantine Emperor, Alexios I Comnenus, Tancred's attempt to avoid having to take an oath to the Emperor by crossing the Bosporus in secret was an act of audacity.[82] There is also a suggestion of rashness in the action of the above-mentioned Arnulf of Aldenard for leaving the army in order to search unknown territory for his horse.[83] On

---

[79] AA ii.22 (96).

[80] J. Riley-Smith, *The First Crusaders*, 156–57. See also J. F. Benton, *Self and Society in Medieval France* (New York: Harper and Row, 1970), 184.

[81] AA i.28 (52); AA ii.7 (72); RM 833; AA v.16 (356).

[82] AA ii.19 (90).

[83] AA ix.52 (714).

a raid of Baldwin I's near Hebron, in November 1100, forty *iuvenes* were described as secretly forming a plan to hasten ahead in order to obtain money and booty.[84]

As with Robert, Gilo and Guibert, this negative aspect of the *iuvenes* is only one part of the picture, for Albert frequently praised them as a body and individually for their warlike prowess. *Iuvenis* was clearly not a negative term in the description of Rothold, son of Godfrey, 'a most famous *iuvenis*.'[85] A similar positive description was given for Baldwin of Le Bourcq, 'a splendid *iuvenis*,'[86] as well as for William and Engelrand above. When Engelrand died in Ma'arra, on 10 December 1098, he was described as 'an uncommonly daring *iuvenis*.'[87] Among the many favourable epithets for Tancred was the phrase, 'illustrious *tyro*.'[88] At the first battle of Ramla, on 6 September 1101, where he led the third division, Hugh of Saint-Omer was called 'a warlike *iuvenis*.'[89] Roger of Salerno, before he became prince of Antioch, in December 1112, was described as an 'illustrious *iuvenis* and knight.'[90] To be a *iuvenis* was not to detract from a knight's valour.

Although many of the knights named individually in his history were termed *iuvenis*, as a collective body influencing events the *iuventus* appear less frequently in Albert's work than in those of the other histories under discussion. Examples occur in descriptions of forces of the People's Crusade, but, given the large num- bers involved and the lack of magnates in such armies, in these instances the group described are probably simply those young in age. *Tyrones*, on the other hand, are more likely to be a collective body of those individuals whom Albert considered to be *iuvenes* in the term's more social meaning. *Tyrones* are described as participating in battle in the following of Hugh the Great and that of Duke Godfrey against the forces of Kerbogha;[91] as a body of scouts sent ahead when the First Crusade approached Ramla, 3 June 1099;[92] as the Latin garrison of the Armenian town of Melitene in 1100;[93] and as those picked to occupy siege towers at the unsuccessful siege of Tyre by King Baldwin I, in November 1111.[94]

Introducing the evidence from Albert of Aachen helps develop the impression that certain knights who shared a characteristic reputation for bravery and a will- ingness to be to the fore in battle banded together during the course of the crusade. That Albert was willing to apply the

---

[84] AA vii.41 (548).

[85] AA ii.23 (98): *Rothardus filius Gosfridi, iuvenis clarissimus.*

[86] AA iii.6 (148): *Baldwinus de Burch iuvenis preclarus.*

[87] AA v.30 (376): *iuuenis mire audacie.*

[88] AA ii.22 (94): *tyro illustris.*

[89] AA vii.65 (576): *iuuenis bellicosus.* For Hugh of Saint-Omer, also known as Hugh of Faquesmberques, see A. V. Murray, *The Crusader Kingdom*, 211–12.

[90] AA xii.29 (836): *illustrissimum iuuenem et militem.*

[91] AA iv.51 (328–30).

[92] AA v.42 (396).

[93] AA vii.29 (526).

[94] AA xii.6 (832).

terms *tyro* and *iuvenis* to these knights suggests that there was already, at the very start of the twelfth century, a shared understanding from France to Lotharingia of the vocabulary appropriate for distinguishing 'young' champions from the broader body of knights.

Ralph of Caen

A further useful source for shedding more light on this subject is the *Gesta Tancredi in expeditione Jerosolymitana* of Ralph of Caen. Ralph had served with Bohemond in 1107 before journeying to Syria, where he took service with Tancred. Shortly after Tancred's death, on 12 December 1112, Ralph wrote a history in the form of a panegyric to his former lord. The text is independent of the *Gesta Francorum* tradition and its value is enhanced by the fact that it was written in the knowledge that it would be read by participants in the First Crusade, and in particular by its editor, Arnulf, the chaplain to Robert I, duke of Normandy, who became patriarch of Jerusalem in 1099 and again from 1112 until his death in 1118.[95]

Ralph's first reference to the *iuventus* as a distinct social group occurs in a speech of Duke Robert II of Normandy rallying those who, including Bohemond, were described as wavering at the battle of Dorylaeum. Robert appealed to the *iuvenes* to charge with him into the middle of the enemy force and die. Admonished by these words, the *iuvenes* joined themselves to the leaders and were more ready for death than for flight.[96] Once battle was joined, Ralph described the *iuventus* as being intemperate and a dangerously undisciplined force. The minds of the *iuvenes* boiled over in passion but Bohemond forbade them to charge in case the rashness of a few threw the whole battle order into confusion.[97]

Ralph was yet another source who associated a following of *iuvenes* with the contingent of Hugh the Great, in this instance at the battle of Dorylaeum: in other words, a year earlier than the battle against Kerbogha in which they are grouped with Hugh by Robert and Gilo. The historian wrote that under Hugh's leadership the supporting *iuventus* ardently smote whatever came before them.[98]

According to Ralph, Tancred was accompanied by *iuvenes* during his expedition through Cilicia. At a battle outside Tarsus, c. 20 September 1097, the faithful *iuventus* were described as following Tancred in a charge.[99] Count Baldwin of Boulogne was able to attract some Norman *iuvenes* to his following, on or around 15 September 1097, by obtaining the services of their leader, Cono of Montaigu.[100]

---

[95] RC 604. See also B. S. Bachrach and D. S. Bachrach, eds., *The* Gesta Tancredi *of Ralph of Caen* (Aldershot: Ashgate, 2005), 2–4.

[96] RC 622.

[97] RC 623.

[98] RC 625.

[99] RC 631.

[100] RC 632–3.

As with the other sources under discussion, Ralph assigned to the *iuventus* the key role in the capture of Antioch on the morning of 3 June 1098. 'The flying winged *iuventus*, well girded with swords, flew by means of the ropes. Gouel of Chartres was the first, like an eagle calling forth its young to fly, and flying over them. This noble man since boyhood desired and thirsted for nothing more eagerly than praise.'[101] Gouel of Chartres has been understood to be that Fulcher of Chartres described by Robert and Gilo who led the *iuvenes* on to the walls of the city.[102] Ralph's version of the event supplements that of the French sources discussed here; they all shared a view that it was appropriate to term those willing to risk their lives in the climb as *iuvenes* and, if the sources are being consistent about who they applied the term to, it can be speculated that the *Chanson d'Antioche* might have been correct in including figures like Thomas of Marle and Everard of Le Puiset among the company who climbed up along with Fulcher to be first on to the walls of Antioch.

Ralph next mentioned the fiery *iuventus* as coming up to join the advance forces of the crusade, before the city of Jerusalem, probably on 7 June 1099.[103] On 15 July 1099 the crusaders stormed Jerusalem. Ralph's description of the day's events included phases of the struggle where the attackers became weary and disheartened. It was during the storming of the city that Ralph assigned the epithet *iuvenis* to Tancred, the hero of his poem.[104]

Ralph further wrote that the first on to the wall of Jerusalem was the brave knight and *iuvenis*, Raimbold Croton.[105] According to Ralph, Raimbold's lead was followed up by other *iuvenes*.[106] Ralph named another knight as leader of this party, Bernard of St. Valéry.[107] Ralph also praised Everard of Le Puiset for a battle inside the city, where a rally of the inhabitants threatened to turn back the Christian attack. Everard, however, engaged a thousand and moved the *iuventus* to follow him.[108] All in all, Ralph's account of the fall of Jerusalem fits very well with the conjecture that when Guibert of Nogent refused to name those *iuvenes* who played a prominent role in the taking of the city, the abbot was thinking of a grouping of knights that included Raimbold, Everard and Thomas of Marle.

Eyewitness sources

---

[101] RC 654–5: *juventus volucris pennata corpora accincti gladiis per funes volant: Gouel Car- notensis primus, 'sicut aquila provocans pullos suos ad volandum, et super eos volitans'* [Deut 32:2], *vir ille nobilis, et a puero nihil esuriens ut laudem neque sitiens, non propter vitam laudari, sed propter laudem vivere cupiebat.*

[102] C. Sweetenham, *Robert the Monk's History*, 145; J. Riley-Smith, *First Crusaders*, 206.

[103] RC 686.

[104] RC 688.

[105] RC 689.

[106] RC 693.

[107] RC 693. For other references to Bernard of St. Valéry, see J. Riley-Smith, *First Crusad- ers*, 202.

[108] RC 698.

If the historians who wrote in the aftermath of the First Crusade employed a vocabulary that distinguished those who they understood to be *iuvenes* from the other fighting forces of the Christian army, can the same be said of the eyewitness accounts? Essentially, there exist three major texts from crusaders: that of the *Gesta Francorum*; that of the historian and chaplain to Baldwin of Boulogne, Fulcher of Chartres, and that of the Provençal cleric who was raised to the priesthood during the expedition, Raymond of Aguilers.

The *Gesta Francorum* is a complicated text, sharing a great deal of material with another eyewitness account, that of the Poitevin priest, Peter Tudebode, but for the purposes of this discussion they can be considered as one as their variations do not bear on the question of *iuvenes*.[109] The text is relatively crude in its depiction of the social layers of the Christian army and typically the author simply writes of 'us' rather than differentiating among the various classes present. It also has an Italian bias in its language.[110] It is therefore perhaps not too surprising that there is no mention of *iuvenes* in this text. It is, however, curious that one of those knights who were first on to the walls of Antioch is described in the *Gesta Francorum* as a *serviens* and that this term, which encompassed a very wide range of contemporary meanings, was elsewhere used in the *Gesta Francorum* in a passage where Gilo of Paris preferred the term *iuvenes*.[111]

Rather more disappointing is Fulcher of Chartres's *Historia Hierosolymitana*. Fulcher's terse, straightforward, style also does not favour a sophisticated examination of social structure. But he had a considerably richer social vocabulary than that present in the *Gesta Francorum* and it is in Fulcher's occasional digressions from the historical narrative that the historian's strong theological framework can be discerned along with a certain amount of social commentary. The term *iuvenes* and its equivalents, however, were not employed by Fulcher.

Lastly, the *Historia Francorum qui ceperunt Iherusalem* of Raymond of Aguilers had a generally archaic social language and a very distinct theological perspective that encouraged the historian to be attentive to the lower social orders, whom he understood to be especially meritorious in the eyes of God, precisely because of the hardship that they had to endure during the expedition. There are four references to *iuvenes* in Raymond's history that seem to be references to a certain type of combatant rather than those young in age.

The first possible mention of such a *iuvenis* occurs in Raymond's description of a skirmish during the siege of Antioch, on 29 December 1097, in which the standard bearer of the papal legate, bishop Adhémar of Le Puy, was killed, and his standard captured. Raymond wrote that there also perished at that time a certain most noble *iuvenis*, Bernard

[109] For a discussion of the relationship between the two texts, see J. Rubenstein, *What is the* Gesta Francorum, and who was Peter Tudebode?' *Revue Mabillon* 16 (2005): 179–204.

[110] J. G. Gavigan, 'The Syntax of the *Gesta Francorum*,' *Language* 19, III (1943): 11.

[111] GF 46; 43, compare with GP 123.

Ato, viscount of Béziers.[112] As with Gilo's reference to William of Benium's raising of the banner of Hugh the Great, there seems to be a connection between defending the standard and being a *iuvenis* and it is this military context and the phrase *nobilissimus iuvenis* that suggest that Raymond meant something other than simply the adjective 'youth' here.

A further very striking example of a *iuvenis* who was also a standard bearer occurred in the next reference to the *iuventus* given by Raymond of Aguilers, namely his account of a vision of St George. Raymond wrote that when the priest and visionary Peter Desiderius discovered the relics of an unknown saint, the crusading clergy decided to leave them behind, but in the night which followed a certain *iuvenis*, about fifteen years old, most beautiful, was present with him as he kept vigil.[113] In seeking the identity of this *iuvenis*, Peter Desiderius was asked by the vision to name the standard bearer of the army and learned that he was in the presence of St George.

The fact that Raymond reported the age of the saint as fifteen means that the term *iuvenis* might have simply meant 'youth' here. On the other hand, the cult of St George was to grow, considerably accelerated by the success of the First Crusade, until by the fifteenth century he was the personification of chivalry. From Raymond's theological perspective the embodiment of the highest ideal of a crusading warrior and standard-bearer of the whole expedition was St George, whose prowess was assisting the Christian army. Raymond's employment of the term *iuvenis* for the warrior saint might have been to intentionally evoke some of the qualities associated with the term in its social sense: bravery, eagerness for battle, willingness to take the most dangerous place by carrying the standard. Another eyewitness, the anonymous author of the *Gesta Francorum,* provided evidence that on the crusade it was popularly believed that St George was offering military assistance to the Christians, in his description of the battle against Kerbogha, where St George was described as being among the resplendent saints who rode into battle with the crusading forces.[114]

The third mention of a *iuvenis* in Raymond of Aguiler's history occurs with regard to a detachment of knights under Count Galdmar Carpenel of Dargoire, who were sent from the siege of Jerusalem, on 18 June 1099, to make contact with six Christian vessels that had arrived at Jaffa. This expedition ran into a troop of Arab and Turkish riders, dispersing them after some losses, including three or four knights of the following of Geldemar and Achard of Montmerle, a most noble *iuvenis*, and renowned knight.[115] This last example is an important one for

---

[112] RA 40–1 (244). For Bernard Ato, see J. Riley-Smith, *The First Crusaders,* 201. The standard bearer mentioned here was not the better-known Heraclius I of Polignac who bore Adhémar's standard at the battle against Kerbogha, for whom see J. Riley-Smith, *The First Crusaders,* 211.

[113] RA 291–3 (290).

[114] GF 69. For further discussion of St George and the First Crusade, see C. Erdmann, *The Origin of the Idea of Crusade,* trans. M. W. Baldwin and W. Goffart (Princeton: Princeton University Press, 1977), pp. 6, 54, 87, 135, 273–81.

[115] RA 318–9 (294).

demonstrating that the term *iuvenis* could be used by Raymond of Aguilers in a different sense than that of a young person, for he would have known Achard as a mature man. Albert of Aachen described Achard as being 'white-haired'.[116] The former castellan of Montmerle had mortgaged his patrimony to the monastery of Cluny in return for 2,000 *solidi* and four mules in order to join the crusade and his donation charter included a clause making provision for the possibility that he might stay in the Levant.[117] While the later stories that sprang up about Achard, such as those in the *La Gran Conquista de Ultramar*, were clearly legendary, it is significant that local traditions indicated that he already had something of a career and reputation for bravery before departing on the First Crusade.[118] Again, also, the context is an appropriate one for a *iuvenis* in the social sense of the term. Achard was *nobilissimus* and died bravely, fighting against the odds.

The last possible reference to *iuvenes* in the work of Raymond of Aguilers occurs with regard to the storming of Jerusalem, on 15 July 1099. Although Raymond did not describe them as being first on to the wall, he described a *iuvenis* as playing a key role at the point where the breakthrough occurred: this *iuvenis* devised arrows, firing at the coverings which protected ramparts that the Saracens had made to face the wooden tower of Duke Godfrey of Lotharingia and Count Eustace of Boulogne.[119]

Conclusion

Lacking decisive examples from the eyewitness accounts, there has to remain a certain element of speculation about the role of *iuvenes* in the First Crusade. Certainly there seems to have existed a distinct stratum of the nobility to whom later authors found it appropriate to apply the language of 'youth'. A band of a particular sort of knight appears to have formed during the crusade, at the core of which were Thomas of Marle, Rainald of Beauvais, Drogo of Nesle, Clarembald of Vendeuil and Everard of Le Puiset. What they had in common was an illustrious, if not quite princely, background, an unsettled career and a reputation for bravery. Their behaviour was characteristic of those who from the latter half of the Twelfth Century, perhaps more precisely, fitted Georges Duby's definition of the 'young'.

It might well have been this faction that Guibert of Nogent had in mind when he wrote that Hugh the Great was 'supported by certain *proceres* so that if, by right of battles, the Gentiles were conquered and it came to pass that they occupied [the land] they planned to make him

---

[116] AA ii.23 (100).

[117] *Recueil des chartes de l'abbaye de Cluny*, ed. A. Bernard and A. Bruel (Paris: Imprimerie Nationale, 1876–1903), 5: 51–53.

[118] See C. Sweetenham, *Robert the Monk's History*, 193, n. 3.

[119] RA 343 (300).

king.'[120] Following the victory over Kerbogha, however, Hugh was sent as a messenger to Alexios but did not return, causing his potential supporters to disperse. Some of this band sought work with Baldwin of Edessa in the plague-filled summer months at Antioch in 1098. They also seem to have been to the fore in pushing the expedition on to Jerusalem. After completing the pilgrimage, Thomas and Raimbold Croton returned to France where they pursued very violent and troublesome careers.

The most important turning points of the expedition were the battle at Dorylaeum; the capture of Antioch; the battle against Kerbogha; the decision to leave Ma'arra and push on to Jerusalem and the storming of Jerusalem. From the descrip- tions of these early historians of the crusade a picture emerges that shows these knights and others termed *iuvenes* coming to the fore at each of these moments, seeking glory in being the first into battle and the first on the walls in the storming of cities. They were a small layer of crusaders, but distinct enough to catch the eye of the historians and to be identified with a vocabulary that contemporary readers would have understood not so much as meaning young knights, but as champions out to prove their worth.

---

[120] GN 131: *Huic quidam procerum innitebantur; et si quid bellorum jure evictis gentilibus: eos obtinere contingeret, ipsum sibi regem praeficere meditaban.*

Chapter 7   William of Tyre, Livy, and the Vocabulary of Class

Most of my research in medieval history is focused on social structure. But before being able to put together a persuasive account of the different social groupings involved in a particular event I have to understand with as much accuracy as possible what the authors of the sources I'm using meant by the terms they employed to identify knights, burghers, peasants, lords, serfs, etc. So, helped considerably by my supervisor and mentor I.S. Robinson, I've spent as much time engaged in the history of ideas as with political and military history and, in particular, the history of sociological concepts.

One early discovery I made was with regard to the very notion of 'class' in medieval society. For much of the early medieval period, the way in which the clerics who composed the sources we use wrote about society was to refer to *ordo*, orders of people. For much of the medieval period, the key orders were: those who pray; those who work; and those who fight. This division by function into a fundamentally tri-partite society seems to have arisen with the Germanic migrations across the Roman empire, replacing a Roman understanding of society that was more hierarchical and related to wealth.

That the concept of a 'first class' of person and a 'second class', etc. returned to Europe towards the end of the twelfth century was perhaps driven by the economic changes of that century and in particular the growth of urban centres. But it seemed to me that a very particular moment saw its revival: the need of the Kingdom of Jerusalem to raise emergency taxes in proportion to a citizen's ability to pay. The chancellor of the day, William of Tyre, was also a classical scholar, one of the intellectuals whose learning and erudition has led modern historians to talk about a twelfth century renaissance.

Having noticed William's innovative use of the idea of class I was able to test for the originality of the idea with a technique that is commonplace now but was only just available to historians in 2001: via a search of comprehensive databases. Before the twenty-first century, the tracing of an idea across time and space could only be carried out with confidence by an expert steeped in years of reading and familiarity with a vast range of sources. By 2001, with the scanning of the major databases of classical and medieval sources, even a first year postgraduate with poor Latin could search (CD-Roms, the online versions coming through c.2004) centuries of literature for the patterns of use of concepts like 'class'.

Thanks to this new research technique, I have a great deal of confidence in the result: that a major development in the concepts used to analyse society took place in the 1180s when William of Tyre reintroduced a concept of class that had been neglected for nearly a millennia.

The most valuable source for the history of the early crusades and the Kingdom of Jerusalem is undoubtedly William of Tyre's *A History of Deeds Done Beyond The Sea*. A work of great scholarship and careful detail, it is particularly important in that William was Chancellor of the Kingdom of Jerusalem from 1174 and Archbishop of Tyre from 1175 to his death c. 1185 and so was closely placed to the political decision making of the period. William was also a careful and highly educated scholar; although born in Jerusalem, he spent twenty years among the leading intellectuals of France and Italy and, after pursuing an avid interest in the liberal arts, devoted himself to civil law and the teachings of the masters at Bologna.[1] In this respect William is far more than a narrator of crusading history, for which he would be highly regarded; he is also an important figure in the intellectual advances of the twelfth century. A close examination of William's vocabulary of social order shows that in his work he advanced the evolution of twelfth-century social concepts and also shed some light on the social structure of the Kingdom of Jerusalem.

The *History* was commissioned by King Amalric of Jerusalem in 1167 and took its final form after redrafting by William in 1184, and it is clear that in his work William reveals a very rich vocabulary to describe social classes (see appendix). William actually uses the term *classis* to mean a social category of person. Current scholarship in history, sociology, and political theory would consider it anachronistic to talk about class in the twelfth century. Indeed, the use of *classis* as a term for social category must have been extremely rare as even such eminent scholars of lexicographers as Charles Dufresne Du Cange and Jan Frederik Niermeyer do not note it.

Insofar as medieval writers before William discussed society, they referred to *ordines*, the orders of society. In the early part of the eleventh century even the most advanced discussion of the subject of class had not progressed beyond the work of Adalbero, Bishop of Laon, and Gerard, Bishop of Cambrai, writing c. 1025, who had articulated the famous tripartite division of society according to function—those who pray, those who fight, and those who labour.[2]

William uses the term *ordo* to mean order in the theological sense and *ordines* to indicate social order, but equally often he uses the term

---

[1] William of Tyre, *Chronicon*, ed. R. B. C. Huygens, *Corpus Christianorum*, Vols. LXIII and LXIII A (Turnholt, 1986), 19.2.

[2] See G. Duby, *The Three Orders, Feudal Society Imagined* (Chicago, 1978).

classis for the same purpose. For example, in describing the character of Baldwin III, he writes that '[Baldwin] acquired so great favour to himself from the commoners and the greater people that he was more popular with both classes [*classis*] than his predecessors.'[3] After the defeat of King Louis VII at Mount Cadmus, 7 January 1148, during the Second Crusade, William describes how the women fearfully cast about during for the return of fathers, lords, husbands, and sons: 'and while they did not find what they sought they spent the night kept awake by the burden of their cares ... nevertheless there returned in the night some of each of these classes [*classis*].'[4]

Classis also appears in the phrase *secundae classis homines*, a phrase used three times to indicate a category of middle-class person. In describing the distant origins of the Hospitallers he says that it was a time when 'there also flocked [to Jerusalem] some of the other nations, both nobles and the second class of men.'[5] At the fall of Balbis (3 November 1168) King Amalric's troops, 'scarcely spared the old people and children, and were not any more merciful to the second class of persons.'[6] For his campaign beginning December 1170 the king's formidable opponent Saladin 'increased his army with commoners and the second class of people.'[7] It is interesting to note that in these last two examples the term is referring to Muslim society, which William must have considered as socially diverse as his own. The existence and activity of a middle class of person as subjects of his history required William to use similar phrases throughout his work such as *mediae manus hominum, secundae manus homines,* and *inferioris manus homines*. That these terms are interchangeable is explicit in the protest against Count Baldwin at Tarsus (c. 20 September 1097) where Baldwin is described as being criticized for leaving 300 Norman knights outside the city, the criticism coming '... from those also who were inside, men of lesser status having sympathised with their brethren.'[8] Shortly afterward, for stylistic purposes (so that William can avoid repetition), the term *inferioris manus homines* is exchanged for *secundae classis homines*: 'the second rank took up arms against Lord Baldwin and the greater men ... when they clashed the enraged people rushed against their superiors with righteous indignation.'[9]

[3] WT 16.2.24: *Unde tantam sibi plebis et patrum conciliaverat gratiam, ut predecessorum suorum quolibet amplius utrique classi haberetur acceptus.*

[4] WT 16.26.19: *et domestica iactura non premeret: hic patrem, ille dominum; illa filium, hec maritum cuncta lustrando perquirit; dumque non inveniunt quod querunt, noctem percurrunt pondere curarum pervigilem, quidquid absentibus potest accidere deterius suspicantes. Reversi sunt tamen nocte illa de utraque classe nonnulli.*

[5] WT 18.5.32: *Confluebant etiam per illa periculosa tempora nonnulli ex aliis gentibus, tam nobiles quam secunde classis homines.*

[6] WT 20.6.18: *vix senibus parcitur et pueris, et secunde sorti non plenius indulgetur.*

[7] WT 20.19.4: *ampliatoque ex plebeis et secunde classis hominibus militum numero.*

[8] WT 3.23 (22).24: *pro quibus etiam qui interius erant, inferioris manus homines, compatientes fratribus, cum preces porrigerent.*

[9] WT 3.24 (23).8: *secunda classis contra dominum Balduinum et maiores arma corripiunt..... Unde facto impetu, in primates suos iusta indignatione commotus irruit populus.*

Other examples of William referring to the deeds of a middle class are common. For example, after the fall of Nicea (19 June 1097) there was discontent among the *secunde manus homines*, in particular that the city had surrendered to Emperor Alexius I Comnenus rather than been sacked: 'the people and the men of second rank who had sweated most diligently to this end in the siege of the aforesaid city of the world had laboured in order that they could recoup the losses of their property with the many types of wealth found within the city.'[10]

A threefold division of the army of the First Crusade is given in the description of their common experience of suffering at Antioch (June 1098): 'pitiful calamity and famine had enveloped not only commoners and the middle ranks of people but also only too rudely intruded upon greater princes.'[11] At the battle of the Mount of Pilgrims, where Baswaj of Damascus defeated Count Pons of Tripoli (c. March 1137), 'there fell in the same battle very many nobles of the city but also a great crowd of men of middle rank.'[12]

The term *secundae classis homines* is a formulation that appears to be created by William of Tyre as it does not seem to occur in the writings of any other Latin author before William. A certain amount of confidence can be put in such propositions by modern scholars thanks to the existence of powerful databases which allow researchers to survey a vast corpus of works in minutes: a task which would have taken our predecessors months and which could never have hoped to achieve the same degree of thoroughness. In particular this study used the *Patrologia Latina* for Latin works from Tertullian in 200 AD to the death of Pope Innocent III in 1216 and the *Pandora* database for Latin works predating 200 AD. It is therefore possible to conclude that in this case William seems to have found it necessary to arrive at a new term to allow him to describe events accurately.

If not from medieval authors, was there any precedent that stimulated William to arrive at his distinct usage of the term *classis*? Throughout his work it is clear that William was familiar with a number of classical writers, quoting them in spirit and occasionally in detail. In particular in the preface to Book 23 of his *History*, the historian makes the following point:

> For those who have the heart [to read it] we will
> continue in that design which we once had begun and
> those who pray constantly that our efforts which
> should be to depict the whole status of the Kingdom

---

[10] WT 3.13 (12).9: *Verum populus et secunde manus homines, qui ad hoc in predicte urbis obsidione studiosius desudaverant, ut de spoliis captivorum civium, et de substantia multiplici infra urbem reperta rerum suarum dispendia que pertulerant resarcire possent.*

[11] WT 6.7.43: *Nec solum plebeios et medie manus homines huius tam miserabilis inedie calamitas involverat, verum et maioribus nimis importune se ingesserat principibus.*

[12] WT William of Tyre, *Chronicon* 14.23.12: *Cecidit in eodem prelio nobilium predicte urbis, sed et medie manus hominum, maxima multitudo.*

of Jerusalem for posterity whether prosperous or adverse, putting forward the example of the most accomplished of historical writers, Titus Livy, who recorded with his writing not only prosperous but also evil times.[13]

Livy is the key to William's adoption of the term *classis*. Of all the Roman writers it is Livy who uses the term *classis* to the greatest extent and gives it a very specific definition. Livy wrote that Servius Tullius (King 578-34 BC) instituted the census in order to raise funds for the Roman army from people of differing social status according to their means: 'Then he assigned classes and centuries and this order from the census, for beautiful peace or war.'[14] Each of the categories created by Servius Tullius was described by Livy as a class. For example, those who were rated with the value of 100,000 bronze coins or more 'were all named the first class.'[15] The second class had between 100,000 and 75,000 bronze coins, the third class 50,000 and so on.[16]

It seems that William inherited Livy's vocabulary for the different social orders. This proposition is strengthened by two other considerations. First, it is likely that William himself was from the second class of citizen, his brother featuring as a burgess on a Jerusalem charter, and so he would have had a certain sensitivity to the position of this class.[17] Second, William was chancellor at a time when King Baldwin IV called a general assembly of all the barons of the realm (February 1183) at Jerusalem, to take measures to raise funds to deal with the threat posed by Saladin's reunification of the Muslim world. The result of the council was a special emergency tax, a census, the full document of which is inserted into William's history. It is more than likely he had a significant role in the formulation of the census, given that it assigns him the prime role in the protection of the revenues that are taken from the northern half of the Kingdom. In a similar manner to the measures Livy attributes to Servius Tullius, the census of 1183 is based on the assessment of wealth, not land ownership, and it has the same spirit of setting out the nature of the payment in such a way as to ensure 'that the richer do not to give more lightly nor the poorer be overburdened' as the 1183 census

---

[13] WT 23.P.32: *Sed quibus cordi est, ut in eo, quod semel cepimus, nos continuemus proposito, quique orant instantius ut regni Ierosolimorum statusomnis, tam prosper quam adversus, posteritati, nostra significetur opera, stimulos addunt, proponentes historiographorum disertissimos, Titum videlicet Romanorum non solum prospera, sed etiam adversa mandasse litteris.*

[14] Livy, *Ab Urbe Condita*, ed. B. O. Foster (Cambridge, 1976), 1.42.5: *tum classes centuriasque et hunc ordinem ex censu discripsit, vel paci decorum vel bello.*

[15] Livy, *Ab Urbe Condita*, 1.43.1: *Ex iis, qui centum millium aeris aut maiorem censum haberent octoginta confecit centurias, quadragenas seniorum ac iuniorum; prima classis omnes appellati.*

[16] Livy, *Ab Urbe Condita*, 1.42.

[17] P.W. Edbury and J.G. Rowe, *William of Tyre Historian of the Latin East* (Cambridge, 1988), 14.

puts it, or 'in proportion to the money they hold' as Livy describes it in not dissimilar language.[18]

Stylistically the census has a far more bureaucratic and repetitive tone than William's *History*. Its use of the social term *vavassor* suggests that an Italian influenced author had some involvement with the actual draft of the census as William does not use the term in his own work.

As several nineteenth-century historians have noted, this census is remark- able for being non-feudal.[19] The payments it sets out are based on the value of moveable goods and income rather than the obligations owed based on the land ownership relation of lord and vassal. This innovation was quickly copied, spreading to England and France within five years.[20] That the idea of taxing wealth rather than property should begin in the Latin Kingdom of Jerusalem is not in fact that surprising. The wealth being generated by trade through the coastal ports of the Kingdom was disproportionately high compared to that from the soil, which in this distant realm of near constant border warfare suffered from a chronic shortage of agricultural labour. Given the perilous position of the Kingdom in the face of the military crisis, it was necessary to be as effective as possible in raising cash, and that meant looking in a fresh way at the sources of wealth in the kingdom. The fact that the chancellor of the time was familiar with a similar Roman mechanism for covering the costs of the army is probably not a coincidence.

In their biography of William of Tyre, Edbury and Roe suggest that the historian did not make a special study of Livy, saying that 'although there are a number of echoes of phrases from their works scattered in the *Historia*, neither Cicero nor Livy is referred to or quoted directly elsewhere, and it may be suspected that William was not as familiar with these authors as he would have liked his readers to believe.'[21] The reason they give for doubting William's own testimony is that they claim that in the historian's use of classical sources 'lines are quoted without attribution, in such a way as to suggest that they formed part of his general knowledge rather than that he had a close familiarity with the authors' works.'[22] It is correct to say that William utilizes classical (and biblical) images and phrases without attribution, as is the case for most twelfth-century authors, but this favours a view that his concern is not to display his erudition but to find appropriate language to communicate the events he is describing.

The following investigation suggests that even if he did not have a copy of Livy's history at hand, William had in fact paid very close

---

[18] WT 2.24(23).73: *ne ditiores levius transeant, vel graventur pauperiores*; Livy, *Ab Urbe Condita*, 1.42.5: *Censum enim instituit, rem saluberrimam tanto futuro imperio, ex quo belli pacisque munia non viritim, ut ante, sed pro habitu pecuniarum fierent.*

[19] See J.L. La Monte, *Feudal Monarchy in the Latin Kingdom of Jerusalem 1100 to 1291* (Cambridge, 1932), 180-83.

[20] See F.A. Cazel Jr., 'The tax of 1185 in aid of the Holy Land', *Speculum,* 30 (1955), 385- 92.

[21] P.W. Edbury and J.G. Rowe, *William of Tyre*, 37.

[22] *Ibid.*, 33.

attention to Livy's writings, especially those concerned with the defence of Rome.

William's own claim that he was inspired by the example of Livy cannot be lightly dismissed. In general, William was more focused on explaining events than with providing classical embellishments to the reader in order to show off his own intellectual worth. In any case, we have a decisive phrase that occurs in the Preface of Livy's *History* and the preface to book 23 of William's. William adopts wholesale Livy's comment that 'it has come to these times, in which we can tolerate neither our vices nor of their cure. In William the Latin reads: *Iam enim ad ea tempora, quibus nec nostra vicia nec eorum remedia pati possumus, preventum est*,[23] and in Livy: *donec ad haec tempora, quibus nec vitia nostra nec remdia pati possumus, preventum est*.[24] That William uses this phrase in this preface, written in a pessimistic context, and therefore part of the redraft of 1184 suggests that he had access to Livy, although it is possible that he retained this evocative phrase from his period of study some thirty years earlier. Given the sporadic survival of the various chapters of Livy, it is noteworthy that this sentence appears shortly before the description of the census of Servius Tullius.[25]

Further connections between William's vocabulary and that of Livy can be established through detailed textual comparison. Although insufficient as they are not quite unique to both authors, there are a number of uncommon phrases that both historians share which supplement the more conclusive comment about William's times. Thus, the innocuous looking phrase *communicato inter se consilio* is in fact unique to Livy among classical writers, and in the whole range of works published in the *Patrologia Latina* series it is used only by two other medieval authors prior to William in works which are unlikely to have been known to the historian.[26] Similarly, when William talks of men rushing to their ruin having been elated by success, he uses *successu elatus*, a phrase used twice by Livy, no other classical author, and very few medieval writers before William.[27] Two other terms, while not being classical phrases unique to Livy, have probably come to William from Livy. Other than Livy,[28] Annius Florus[29] is the only other classical writer to use the image of *ancipiti Marte* to describe the untrustworthy outcome of battle. William makes use of the image, the only other proceeding medieval author to do so being the relatively obscure Pacatus

---

[23] WT 23.P.

[24] Livy, *Ab Urbe Condita*, P.1.9.

[25] On the scattered distribution of the parts of Livy see below, n.38.

[26] WT 11.10.24; Livy, *Ab Urbe Condita*, 8.25.9. The phrase appears only in Seher, Abbot of Chaumouzey, *De primordiis Calmosiacensis Monasterii* PL 162 Col 1143D and Wibald of Stablo, *Epistola CXLV*, PL 189 Col 1247C.

[27] WT 18.13.33: *plures enim acti prosperis et successibus elati solent in preceps ruere*; Livy, *Ab Urbe Condita*, 28.6.8, 42.66.3. Other authors are Rufinus of Aquileia; Freculph of Lisieux; Richard of St-Rémy; Herman of Reichenau; and Sigebert of Gembloux.

[28] WT 7.29.2.

[29] Lucius Anneus Florus, *Epitome* 2.13.285.

Drepanius.[30] Livy, Cicero, Peter Damien, Theobald, Archbishop of Canterbury (1138-61), and William share the use of the phrase *praeter opinionem omnium*.[31] Again, it is possible that these phrases lingered in William's vocabulary from his years in Paris and Bologna, but it is more likely that, given the circumstances of the census of 1183 and his desire to redraft the history in a time of adversity, William turned to Livy and so inherited some of his vocabulary.

It is relevant to consider the distribution of Livy in twelfth century Europe. The full history was broken into its various decades in the early middle ages and not reassembled until Petrarch (1304-1374) made his partial compilation. Library catalogues show that various parts of Livy's *Ab Urbe Condita* existed in the Cathedral School of Bamberg and Verona and the monasteries of Cluny, Corbie, Limoges, Murbach, and Pomposa.[32] Wipo, the chaplain of Emperor Conrad II, wrote in 1046 to Henry III that 'while the Italian youth sweated over the study of history, the German schools neglect it,'[33] yet as early as 970 Widukind, monk of Corbie, had used Livy in his *Res gestae Saxonicae*, and Livy was a school text in eleventh-century Germany.[34] The Norman historians William of Poitiers (c. 1020–87) and William of Malmesbury (c. 1090–c. 1143) knew Livy,[35] as did the polemicist Sigebert of Gembloux (c. 1035–1112), who utilized Livy in establishing the chronology of his extremely widely disseminated world chronicle.[36] John of Salisbury, who was a student in Paris (1141–45) around the time William of Tyre left Jerusalem to develop his own studies, refers to Livy in his *Policraticus*.[37] Munk Olsen's catalogue of surviving manuscripts from the eleventh and twelfth centuries shows that the works of the Roman historian were very widely distributed, albeit in a partial form, with copies of the preface and first decade surviving with a noticeably greater frequency than any other section.[38]

Perhaps the most helpful assessment of the distribution of Livy in William's day is that of his exact contemporary, the statesman and theologian Peter of Blois (c. 1130–c. 1203), who studied in Paris and Bologna while William was also present. Peter wrote that 'besides all the other books that are famous in the schools, it profited me to frequently examine Trogus Pompeius, Josephus, Suetonius, Hegesippius, Q. Curtius,

---

[30] WT 13.7.1; Pacatus Drepanius, *Panegyricus,* PL 13 Col 0499A.

[31] Livy, *Ab Urbe Condita,* 38.16.14; Cicero, *Planc.* 49.5; Peter Damien, Sermon V.II, PL 144, Col. 0527D; Theobald, *Letter to the General Chapter of Arrouaise,* in *The Letter of John of Salisbury (1153-61),* ed. C. N. L. Brooke (Edinburgh, 1955) 166; WT 10.3.21.

[32] J.S. Beddie, 'The Ancient Classics in the Medieval Libraries', *Speculum,* 5 (1930), 3-20; R.R. Bolgar (ed.), *Classical Influences on European Culture (AD 500 – 1500)* (Cambridge, 1971), and see S.P. Oakley, *A commentary on Livy books VI – X* (Oxford, 1997), 156.

[33] In E. Matthews Sanford, 'The Study of Ancient History in the Middle Ages', *JHI,* 5 (1944), 21-43.

[34] B. Doer, 'Livy and the Germans', *Livy,* ed. T. A. Dorey (London, 1971), 104.

[35] On William of Poitiers see Antonia Gransden, *Historical Writing in England* (London, 1974), 100. William of Malmesbury, *Gesta Regum,* PL 179, Col 1414A.

[36] E. Matthews Sanford, 'The Study of Ancient History in the Middle Ages', *JHI,* 5 (1944), 24.

[37] John of Salisbury, *Policraticus,* PL 199, Col 0495C.

[38] B. Munk Olsen, *L'Étude Des Auteurs Classiques Latins Aux XIe Et XIIe Siècles* (Paris, 1985), 1-16.

Cornelius Tacitus, Titus Livy, who all in the histories which they recorded interwove much material for the edification of morals and the advancement of liberal knowledge.'[39] In other words it was possible, although untypical, for a scholar of the period to study Livy.

William's use of the term *classis* reflected the fact that new social orders had come into being by the end of the twelfth century, social orders that were not adequately covered by existing tax laws or social theorists. By reaching back to the Roman writers for a vocabulary in order to write about these social orders, William cloaked the rise of a new social structure in the mantle of tradition. However, in thus attaching the ancient term to the new conditions, he modernized it and brought it forward another step in its evolution into the modern English term 'class'.

Other social terms are of interest in William's vocabulary, if not on the same scale of significance. *Gregarius* is also a classical term, and while rare in the works of medievalists, it was far from unique to William. Historians of the First and Second Crusades use it with disproportionate frequency.[40] *Gregarius* is a term employed by William in the conventional classical sense of the rank and file soldier but also in a more technical sense to denote soldiers, both noble and non-noble, who draw pay. The crucial example for this latter use of the term is that of Renaud de Chatillon, who is described as *miles quasi gregarius*[41] on his being the surprising selection of Lady Constance of Antioch for her husband.

Although Renaud de Chatillon was a prominent knight and an important leader at the capture of Ascalon (23 November 1152), he was not of the highest status, being merely a paid, rather than property-owning, knight. William twice makes it clear that Renaud was a *stipendium miles*, first when explaining the popular amazement at his fortune in marrying the heiress and second when qualifying the list of prominent knights at the capture of Ascalon.[42] The importance of the social distinction between paid and unpaid knight is also clear in William's description of the offer by Thoros, ruler of Edessa (February 1098) to pay Count Baldwin of Bouillon for his services. Baldwin entirely rejects that he

[39] Peter of Blois Ep. 101. PL 207 Col 0314B: *Praeter caeteros etiam libros, qui celebres sunt in scholis, profuit mihi frequenter inspicere Trogum Pompeium, Josephum, Suetonium, Hegesippum, Q. Curtium, Corn. Tacitum, Titum Livium, qui omnes in historiis quas referunt, multa ad morum aedificationem, et ad profectum scientiae liberalis interserunt.* See Sanford, 'The Study of Ancient History in the Middle Ages'.

[40] That is, Guibert of Nogent, Albert of Aachen, William of Malmesbury, Odo of Deuil, Orderic Vitalis, and John of Salisbury.

[41] WT 17.26.8: *Festinavit igitur predictus Rainaldus ad exercitum et verbum domino regi communicans, sumpta eius conventia Antiochiam rediens predictam duxit in uxorem principissam, non sine multorum admiratione quod tam praeclara, potens et illustris femina et tam excellentis uxor viri, militi quasi gregario nubere dignaretur.* And 17.21.40: *De principibus autem laicis: Hugo de Ibelin, Philippus Neapolitanus, Henfredus de Torono, Symon Tyberiadensis, Gerardus Sydoniensis, Guido Beritensis, Mauricius de Monte Regali, Rainaldus de Castellione, Galterus de Sancto Aldemaro, qui duo stipendia apud dominum regem merebant.*

[42] WT 17.26.1: *Dumque hec circa Ascalonam in castris geruntur, domina Constantia, domini Raimundi Antiocheni principis vidua, licet multos inclitos et nobiles viros, eius matrimonium appetentes, more femineo repulisset, Rainaldum de Castellione, quendam stipendiarium militem, sibi occulte in maritum elegit.*

should be paid 'like anyone among the *gregarius*.'[43] This technical meaning makes sense of an incident of 1160, when Najim al-Din of Damascus prevented a raid by Baldwin III with the offer of 4,000 pieces of gold and the release of six *gregarii milites.* The point of the incident is to show the wisdom of Najim al-Din and the lengths he was willing to go to in order to achieve peace at a time of weakness for Damascus. If William was using the term for its conventional meaning, it does not really suit the purpose, as the release of six footsoldiers would not have been particularly noteworthy. It is far more likely that the *gregarii* here are paid knights, perhaps even of the status of Renaud de Châtillon before his marriage.[44] Again, it does not quite make sense directly to substitute commoner in the case of a certain Rohard, about whom William says that while he was a man with the splendid title of guardian of the citadel at Jerusalem, he was in fact a *gregarius homo.*[45] In general, while retaining the term *gregarius* for common soldier, William also uses it in a technical sense which draws attention to the existence by the mid-twelfth century of a layer of lesser, paid knights. It is worth noting in this connection that the lack of royal demesne in the Latin Kingdom of Jerusalem meant that, as a matter of policy, the monarchy preferred to hire forces for pay than levy troops on the basis of the ownership of fiefs.

William had a sophisticated vocabulary for terms covering the lower social orders, which again befits a chancellor interested in matters of tax. He uses a number of standard terms for commoners, which he shares with the Vulgate and his contemporaries, terms such as *plebs, vulgus,* and *pauperes,* and *populares.* At the same time, however, his use of terms for the lower orders is in fact quite nuanced and context dependent. Within the very broad terms for the lower class there is significant differentiation, perhaps the most important being that between the free and unfree poor. He reserves the term *servi* for the farmers of Egypt, whom William recognizes as being bound to the land in more servile conditions than for agricultural workers elsewhere in the region.[46]

His explanation for this is an interesting example of the legal understanding of social relations in the twelfth century. William explains that the Egyptian lords hold the *servi* in extreme terms because the people once sold the entire country, first the possessions and then their persons, to the biblical figure Joseph (Genesis 47, 19-26).[47]

---

[43] WT 4.3.11: *Quod dominus Balduinus omnino respuens, ut tanquam gregarius aliquis apud eum stipendia mereret, ad reditum se parabat.*

[44] WT 18.27.28: *et multiplicatis sibi data pecunia intercessoribus, impetrat postulatam, datis insuper sex gregariis militibus, quos in vinculis detinebat.*

[45] WT 21.4.15: *Hic ut videretur aliorum quodammodo lenire invidiam, arte quadam, sed nimium manifesta, ad colorem quesitum alium quemdam Rohardum nomine, arcis Ierosolymitane custodem, gregarium hominem et minus sufficientem, subornaverat tanquam is preesset, Milo vero ejus mandatis obsequeretur. Erat autem versa vici nimis: nomen magis splendidum quam solidum gestabat, ille autem sub hoc colore de regni negociis pro sua voluntate tractabat.*

[46] WT 19.20.23: [with regard to Joseph] *unde et servili nexu et extrema conditione ei tenentur adnexa.*

[47] WT 9.20.18: *Emit ergo prius possessiones, deinde personas. Unde est quod artiore vinculo tenentur Egyptii domino suo et amplius sunt ei obligati quam aliarum habitatores regionum magistratibus suis quippe qui et eos*

By contrast the crusading settlers even from the lowest social orders were free in the sense that they never sold their persons and retained the right to relocate themselves. This is the conclusion that J. Prawer draws from the charters concerning the colonization of Beit-Jibrin, built in 1136, whose charters were renewed in 1158 and 1177. These charters show that the settlers had the right to leave. Tenures there were hereditary and could be sold, the obligation on the producers being the payment on rent. The rent was not a fixed one based on the amount of land cultivated, but, more favourably to the farmers, was *terraticum*, a portion of the crops.[48] Similarly with Castle Imbert (Akhzib), colonized by royal initiative 1146-53. There the inhabitants received houses as hereditary possessions without rent or duty. Each farmer obtained a plot of land for tillage and a further allocation in order to cultivate vines or a garden. Rent to the king was a quarter of the crop, and although these conditions were extremely favourable, the king also obtained revenues from his control of baking and bathing.[49]

The relatively free status of the colonists almost certainly arose because of the circumstances of the conquest and the conditions of the First Crusade. After a sense of betrayal overtook the footsoldiers and *pauperes* on the surrender of Nicea (19 June 1097) to Emperor Alexis I Comnenus, it became the rule for conquered property that it would remain in the possession of those who left their mark upon it, regardless of their rank.[50] This rule, which was particularly insisted upon by the poor before the conquest of Jerusalem, provides a further material motivation for the ruthless annihilation of the non-Christian population of Jerusalem upon its fall to the Crusade (15 July 1099). Whatever status the poorest crusader had once held before leaving on the pilgrimage, as colonists in a region short of Christian farmers, they were not to be compared with the *servi* of Egypt and their masters.

Confirmation of the free status of the Christian peasantry of the Kingdom of Jerusalem is indicated by the vocabulary of William of Tyre. When describing a settlement near Daron, William makes a very interesting comment. He explains that 'certain cultivators of the fields from the neighbouring places had gathered together and certain of them giving help through mediation they had built there a church and a suburb near the fortress of Daron, where the men of less substance could prosper more easily than in the city.'[51] The social terms here are *agrorum cultores* for those who initially gathered together and *tenuiores homines*

---

et eorum possessiones precio interveniente comparavit, unde et servili nexu et extrema conditione ei tenentur adnexi.

[48] J. Prawer, *Crusader Institutions,* 124.

[49] *Ibid.* pp. 140–1

[50] WT 8.20.43: *clipeos vel quodlibet armorum genus in introitu defigentes, ut esset signum accedentibus ne gressum ibi figerent, sed loca preterirent quasi iam ab aliis occupata.* A tradition also noted and briefly discussed in J. Prawer, *Crusader Institutions,* 253-54.

[51] WT 20.19.54: *Convenerant autem aliqui ex locis finitimis agrorum cultores et negociationibus quidam operam dantes, edificaverant ibi suburbium et ecclesiam non longe a presidio, facti illius loci habitatores: erat enim locus commodus et ubi tenuiores homines facilius proficerent quam in urbibus.*

for the class of people who prospered more easily. Both are unusual terms. The former occurs more times in William's work than in all the writers of the *Patrologia* put together, and the latter is unique to his *History*. Why did William not use more conventional terms, such as *rusticus* or *agricola*? Almost certainly because the situation he was describing was itself unconventional. The colonists are described as gathering and erecting a church and dwellings on their own initiative. So while they are clearly of the lower, labouring social orders, they seem to be free from lordship and indeed prospering as a result. Even in his deployment of more standard social terms, William can be shown to be a very careful commentator, unusually alert to social differentiation. As a result, his work allows for a more sophisticated understanding of the social structure of his world than can be derived from more typical twelfth- century writing. For example, *plebs* is an extremely frequent term in the social vocabulary of medieval writers, including William. It is generally applied sweepingly to the non-noble classes. For example, when King Amalric took over the direction of Antioch in 1164, William describes him as 'ruling over nobles and commoners [*plebs*] with great gentleness and far-seeing moderation.'[52] Elsewhere, however, William makes it clear that the term includes a variety of types. For example, the army led by Eustace Grenier against the Egyptians c. 1123 is described as having *plebs omnimoda*: all kinds of commoner.[53] The kinds of distinction that William is referring to can be seen in context. *Plebs* is used for (Muslim) farmers at the fall of Sidon (19 December 1111) as the terms of the surrender of the city permit the *plebs* to devote themselves to agriculture under good conditions.[54] But it also covers a crowd of fierce pilgrims, such as the *plebs indomita* (untamed commoners) on the First Crusade who, unbidden by the lords, steal into the undefended city of Marrat (November 1098).[55] *Plebs* can also be an urban class of commoner with potentially dangerous political aspirations. When John II Comnenus arrived at Antioch (September 1135), trapping the Latin nobility between their desire of independence and their need for an alliance with the Emperor, they skilfully manipulate the *plebs* into anger against Greek rule before turning to the Emperor and warning him of an impending riot should he continue his plans for the direct rule of the city.[56]

An even broader term whose nuances can easily be overlooked is *populus*, the people. Very often it is the term used by William to cover the whole of society. So, for example, for the trial by fire of the peasant

---

[52] WT 19.11.12: *nobiles et plebeios multa mansuetudine providoque moderamine regens.*

[53] WT 12.21.35: *Nostri porro populi promiscui et plebis omnimode, dicebantur esse quasi septem millia.*

[54] WT 11.14.71: *et missa legatione petunt, ut nobilibus concedatur exitus, plebi vero, sicuti et prius, agriculture operam dare liceat bonis conditionibus.*

[55] WT 7.9.45: *nostri equites et maiorum manus negocium, ut summo mane redirent in id ipsum, tota nocte circa urbem, ne hostibus pateret exitus, custodierunt vigilias. At vero plebs indomita longis fatigata laboribus et diutinae famis acerbitate vexata, videns quod hostium nemo compareret in menibus, quod civitas sine strepitu tota quiesceret, absque maiorum conscientia in urbem ingressa est.*

[56] WT 15.3.59: 'ne tumultu plebis intercurrente executioni petitionum vestrarum future prestetur impedimentum.'

visionary Peter Bartholomew (7 April 1099) 'the entire *populus* assembled, from the least even unto the greatest.'[57] Similarly 'in the year of the Incarnation of the Lord 1104, in the month of May, the same lord king [Baldwin I] having summoned his men and all his people, from the least even unto the greatest, hastened to besiege that same city [Acre] about which we have spoken above.'[58] But this wide usage can obscure a more technical, legal use of the term which seems to denote those citizens who, in addition to the nobility, are entitled to a say in public affairs. They are a category of persons listed in the great assembly at Nabalus in late 1166 to raise an emergency tax. Present were bishops, prelates, princes, and the people.[59] Similarly, those witnessing the raising of the status of the church of Bethlehem to that of a Cathedral were the 'rejoicing clergy, the princes, and the people.'[60] When the term *populus* is used to include the lower social orders, William often qualifies it with an adjective. For example, the crowds whose threats dispersed the clergy during the election of Ralph as Patriarch in 1136 are described as *furentis et vociferantis populi*, 'furious and noisy.'[61] The same incident shows that the term *populus* can have a specifically secular meaning since 'Ralph was elected by the *populus* alone without the knowledge of the brethren and the bishops.'[62] *Populus* is also used interchangeably with *plebs* in a few instances.

The point of this examination of the language of William of Tyre is primarily to gain further evidence of the social conditions of the Latin Kingdom of Jerusalem and also to indicate an important stage in the evolution of sociological vocabulary, particularly that of the notion of class. But this close examination of the social language of William of Tyre also allows comment to be made on a very old controversy. William is the only source for a famous letter from Daimbert, Patriarch of Jerusalem, sent to Bohemond, Prince of Antioch, on the death of Godfrey, ruler of the Kingdom (18 July 1100). The letter is much discussed because in it Daimbert puts forward the view that the church should rule the entire city of Jerusalem. William claims that he is inserting a copy of this letter into his *History*, but for over a hundred years historians have been arguing over whether this letter was genuine or not. While the most unconvinced think that it is fraudulent, even the most sympathetic to the validity of

---

[57] WT 7.18.22: *convenit universus populus a majore usque ad minimum...*

[58] WT 10.27 (28).1: *Anno itaque ab incarnatione Domini M^{o}C^{o}IIII, mense Maio, idem dominus rex, iterum convocatis viribus et populo universo a minimo usque ad maximum, eamdem de qua supradiximus Ptolomaidam obsidere contendit...*

[59] WT 19.13.23: *curiam apud Neapolim convocat generalem, ubi praesentibus domino patriarcha, archiepiscopis, episcopis et aliis ecclesiarum prelatis, principibus et populo necessitates regni docet ex ordine, omnium suppliciter implorans auxilium.*

[60] WT 11.12.23: *Cui ego Balduinus ab exsultante clero, principibus et populo primus rex Francorum.*

[61] WT 14.10.17: *timentes furentis et vociferantis populi indiscretos impetus.*

[62] WT 14.10.13: *absque fratrum et coepiscoporum conscientiasolo populi, ut dicitur, suffragio electus est.*

the letter see it as an 'elaboration'[63] or 'suspect.'[64] Yet William's inclusion of other documents is not put under such scrutiny, largely because they are less controversial, and indeed other charters included by William in his *History* are demonstrably authentic.[65] Nor are William's motives explained if he is inventing or distorting the letter, because for all that he himself is an advocate of Church rights, after having investigated the question, William's own conclusion was that, dating back to an agreement of 1063 between Constantin X of Byzantium and the Caliph of Egypt, the Church in fact ruled over only a particular quarter of the city.[66]

An examination of the language of this document indicates that the vocabulary is not that of William of Tyre and is thus not an invention or an elaboration on his part. In describing how the city was seized by supporters of an opposing faction, Daimbert writes, 'even after this happened, however, some baseborn men of the common people took over the tower and the entire city.'[67] The terminology used for baseborn men is *viri ignobilies*. This term is not used in the *History* other than in this letter, suggesting it is that of the patriarch. Similarly the method of address, *filius charissimus*, is unique to this letter, as is the description of the Patriarchate as *omnis Ecclesia singularis*.[68] Again, the use of the description *totus Christianitas* is confined to this document.[69] Furthermore the verb *monstrare* (to point out) occurs only at this point, as do the adjectives *rationabilis* and *irrationabilis*.[70] To maintain that William invented the letter in the face of this distinctively different vocabulary, his lack of motive, and his use of other documents in the history is no longer plausible.

A sophisticated gradation of the social structure of the Kingdom of Jerusalem in the second half of the twelfth century is revealed in the vocabulary of William of Tyre. His careful and varied use of a number of terms for differing social classes, and indeed the revitalizing of Livy's category of *classis* for his overall framework, shows an extraordinarily attentive scholar at work, one who far surpasses his contemporaries in his awareness of social distinctions and whose desire to set out an accurate account of his times led him to advance sociological concepts.

---

[63] E.A. Babcock and A.C. Krey (trans.), *A History of Deeds Done Beyond the Sea, by William Archbishop of Tyre* (New York, 1943), I, 418.

[64] J. Prawer, *Crusader Institutions*, p. 297.

[65] For example, the treaty between Venice and Baldwin II for the siege of Tyre (16 February 1124).

[66] J. Prawer, *Crusader Institutions*, 297-98.

[67] WT 10.4.88: *viri ignobiles ac de plebe adhuc eandem turrim cum tota urbe occupantes tenent.*

[68] WT 10.4.1: *Scis, fili karissime, quoniam me ignorantem et invitum, bone tamen ac sancte intentionis affectu, in eam quae omnium ecclesiarum singularis est mater et gentium domina.*

[69] WT 10.4.37: *Hoc ipso autem mortuo viri ignobiles ac de plebe, adhuc eamdem turrim cum tota urbe occupantes tenent, adventum Balduini, ad ruinam ecclesie et totius Christianitatis interitum prestolantes.*

[70] WT 10.4.59 [of Baldwin I]: *monstrans ei quoniam inrationabile est tot pro eadem ecclesia labores sustinuisse totque pericula ut illa libera fieret, si nunc vilis et abiecta servire cogatur illis, quibus dominari et preesse materno iure debet.*

Appendix of Terms Denoting Social Classes in William of Tyre

agrorum cultores – Peasants, literally, cultivators of the fields *artifices* – Craftsmen

burgenses – Burghers

classis – Class (of persons)

coloni – Serfs

consules – Consuls (of the Genoese)

cultores – Inhabitants

domestici – Household slaves

equestres – Knights

gregarius – Common soldier or paid soldier (including knights)

inferus – A person of lower position

inferioris manus homines – Men of lesser might

ingenui – Freeborn

maiores – Greater people. Often contrasted to *minores*

mancipia – Slaves

manubiae – Moveable plunder. Half the time that William uses this term it is a catch-all term which includes human captives

mediae manus hominum – Men of middle strength

milites – Knights

minores – Lesser people. Often is contrasted to *maiores*

nobiles – Nobles

ordo – Social order, class

patres – Patricians (akin to *maiores*)

pauperes – The poor

plebs – The common people (see also *plebs inferior* – The lesser
        commoners and *plebs indomita* – The untamed commoners)

populares – The commoners, associated with *plebs* and *vulgus*

populus – The people – but exactly which category of person is included
        depends on context

proceres – Magnates

secundae classis homines – A social order lower than the nobility, but
        above the commoners

secundae manus homines – Second rank of men

seniores populi – Elders of the people

servi – Slaves

servientes – Sergeants, but used only of the Templars

tenuiores homines – Men of lesser substance, literally "thinner people"

turba – The mob

vir magnificus – Great magnate *viri prudentes* – Wise men

vulgus – The common people

Chapter 8 God's Bounty, *Pauperes*, and the Crusades of 1096 and 1147

While working on my PhD about the social structure of the First Crusade a simple question occurred to me: were there environmental reasons for so many people joining these crusades. Specifically, was some kind of hardship driving peasants and serfs from their lands in northern Europe, pushing them into the extremely hazardous enterprise that was the crusades? A simple enough question but not one explored in any depth, partly because the predominant way of thinking about the crusades at the time was in terms of the religious motivation of the crusaders. Partly too, because the tree ring and ice-core data that would have led to a quick result was not so openly available as it is now (to a certain extent it was being horded or chronologies with errors were unquestioned, rendering them inexact).

Nowadays I would go straight to my good friend and colleague Francis Ludlow, with whom I've been fortunate enough to have a wonderfully fruitful collaboration in researching environmental history. Back in the late 1990s, however, I had to find a methodology for answering the question. I decided to survey the entire 200-year-period 1000-1200 as recorded in the annals and chronicles of the 38 volumes of the *Monumenta Germaniae Historica Scriptores* series and make a note of each mention of plague and famine. That way I'd get an approximate sense of when the peak periods for these events was and then could see if there was a match between these peaks and the dates of the crusades. And there was, a very striking one for the first two crusades.

This backdrop of severe hardship gives a context to the preaching of the first two crusades and makes sense of their appeal to the poorest in society. In fact, when you understand the first two crusades as much as incidences of mass emigration as pilgrimage, the dynamics of the events of these crusades make a lot more sense.

'Cease, therefore, your discords, let your quarrels fall silent, your wars become quiescent, and let the disagreements of all controversy be put to sleep. Start the journey to the Holy Sepulchre, get that land off the criminal race and make it subject to you, that land the possession of which had been given by God to

the sons of Israel, which - as the Scripture says
- is *flowing with milk and honey.*'[1]

Robert the Monk was present at the famous council of Clermont in
1095, at which Pope Urban II launched the First Crusade by announcing
that there would be a major expedition against the pagans to assist the
Christians of the East. According to Robert, Urban reminded his listeners
of *Exodus* and the journey of the Children of Israel from Egypt; a journey
in which God's bounty several times saved Moses and his followers from
famine and thirst. The report of another eyewitness at Clermont, Baldric
(or Baudri) of Dol, reinforces the likelihood that *Exodus* was in the
thoughts of those who listened to Urban. Shortly after the announcement
that Adhémar, bishop of Le Puy, had volunteered to go on the expedition,
the Provençal count, Raymond of Toulouse made it clear he was willing to
join the crusade and share the responsibility for it with Adhémar. Baldric's
version of the message of Raymond's envoys to the assembly included
the lines: 'Behold! God be thanked, two men voluntarily offered to
proceed with the Christians on their journey. Behold! Religious and
secular power, the clerical *ordo* and the laity, harmonise in order to lead
the army of God. Bishop and count, we imagine ourselves like another
Moses and Aaron.'[2] Again, then, we have a conscious echoing of the epic
undertaking by Moses.

How literally did the audience for this message interpret the
references to a land of milk and honey? How much did they anticipate
that like the Children of Israel, they could depend upon God's bounty to
sustain them for this extraordinary journey? When the crusading message
spread through northern Europe, did listeners believe that the logistical
difficulties of such an ambitious journey could be overcome by divine aid
given that the enterprise was such a Holy one? Those princes who
responded to the appeal of the crusade took a very pragmatic and
practical approach to the questions of supply. Robert of Normandy, for
example, raised the funds he needed by mortgaging his duchy for 10,000
silver marks. Duke Godfrey of Lotharingia sold the county of Verdun, the
towns of Stenay and Mouzay, his personal lands at Baisy and Genappe
and the castle of Bouillon for a great sum of coin to meet his needs.[3] But

---

[1] Robert the Monk, *Historia Iherosolimitana*, *Recueil des historiens des croisades,
Historiens occidentaux* 1 – 5 (Académie des inscriptions et belles-lettres: Paris 1844 –
95), 3, 717 – 882, here 728: '*Cessent igitur inter vos odia [vos discordiae], conticescant
jurgia, bella quiescant et totius controversiae dissensiones sopiantur. Viam sancti
Sepulcri incipite, terram illam nefariae genti auferte, eamque vobis subjicite, terra illa
filiis Israel a Deo in possessionem data fuit, sicut Scriptura dicit, quae lacte et melle
fluit.*' Referring to *Exodus* 3:8, 17; 13: 5; 33:3.
[2] Baldric of Dol, *Historia Hierosolymitana*, *Recueil des historiens des croisades, Historiens
occidentaux* 1 – 5 (Académie des inscriptions et belles-lettres: Paris 1844 – 95), 4, 1 –
111, here 16: '*Ecce, Deo gratias, jam Christianis ituris, duo ultronei processere viri; ecce
sacerdotium et regnum; clericalis ordo et laicalis ad exercitum Dei conducendum
concordant. Episcopus et comes, Moysen et Aaron nobis reimaginantur.*'
[3] A. V. Murray, *The Crusader Kingdom of Jerusalem, A Dynastic History 1099-1125*
(Oxford, 2000), pp. 38 – 42.

how did the poorest sections of society and those least able to sustain themselves for a two-thousand-mile march think that they would obtain the food they needed? Did they really believe that God's bounty would be directly provided to them like manna from heaven?

Obtaining an insight into the mentality of the lower social orders in this era is a tricky business, given that we have no direct testimony from serfs, peasants, free farmers or the urban poor, instead we have to rely on those of the clergy who took an interest in the outlook of the poor. In the case of both the First Crusade and the Second Crusade there were, however, at least some clergy who not only believed that those with the least wealth were the most deserving of God's bounty, but it was the efforts of the poor above all that earned divine approval for the First Crusade. An important example of a crusader and a writer with just such a perspective was Raymond of Aguilers, a canon of the cathedral church of St. Mary of Le Puy, in the Auvergne region of France. Raymond joined the First Crusade (1096 – 99), probably in the company of Bishop Adhémar of Le Puy, the papal legate.[4] He was raised to the priesthood during the course of the expedition and subsequently joined the chaplaincy of Count Raymond IV of Toulouse.[5]

The key term used by Raymond to encompass the lower social orders was *pauperes*. Loosely, this meant 'the poor', but quite apart from the fact that, as Karl Leyser has observed, at this time *pauperes* could also mean 'defenceless',[6] in the context of the crusade it could be used for all of Christ's followers, including combatants. This is evident in the history of the First Crusade written by Raymond of Aguilers soon after the events it describes. Many of Raymond's uses of the term *pauperes* were relatively straightforward, such as where they are juxtaposed to the *divites*, the rich.[7] But Raymond was writing in a framework that saw the mighty pagan powers being confronted by a Christian force that, although in appearance lowly and weak, was powerful through the assistance of God. From this theological point of view the entire movement could be considered to be one of *pauperes* and Raymond had no difficulty describing Christian warriors on horseback as *pauperes*;[8] in this sense Raymond of Aguiler's use of *pauperes* anticipates a similar use of the term by the scholar and civil servant, Peter of Blois (c. 1180), and Innocent III (r.1198 – 1216).[9]

---

[4] ; J. France, *A Critical Edition of the* Historia Francorum *of Raymond of Aguilers* (unpublished PhD. thesis: University of Nottingham, 1967), hereafter RA, pp. 11 – 12, 17 (237, 238). I am grateful to J. France for permission to quote from his thesis. References to the more easily accessible *RHC* edition are in brackets.

[5] RA 202 (276); RA 100 (255).

[6] K. Leyser, *Communications and Power in Medieval Europe: the Gregorian Revolution and beyond*, trans. T. Reuter, (London, 1994), p. 82 n. 26.

[7] RA 46 (245).

[8] RA 68 – 69 (249).

[9] See C. Morris, *The Papal Monarchy: The Western Church from 1050 – 1250* (Oxford, 1989), pp. 316 –50; I. S. Robinson, *The Papacy 1073-1198 Continuity and Innovation* (Cambridge, 1990), pp. 365 - 6.

With these nuances of the term in mind, what then, can we determine about the *pauperes* of the First Crusade and their beliefs in regard to God's bounty? One piece of evidence that emerges very directly from the sources is that *pauperes* responded to the appeal to join the crusade in enormous numbers. Very soon after the Council of Clermont, the pope himself was anxious to dampen down an unexpected enthusiasm for the crusade among non-combatants. Urban wrote a letter to the clergy and people of Bologna, 19 September 1096, in which he tried to restrain women, children and clergy from joining the Christian armies.[10] Ekkehard, later abbot of Aura (1108 – 1125), was an eyewitness to the departure of people in Bavaria on the expedition and observed of the very first contingents that along with a great many legions of knights were as many troops of footsoldiers and crowds of those who worked the land, women and children.[11] Ekkehard also noted that some of the commoners as well as persons of higher rank admitted to having taken the vow through misfortune.[12] Furthermore, a great part of them proceeded laden with wives and children and all their household goods.[13]

Guibert of Nogent, an eyewitness to the departure of crusaders from northern France, observed the recruiting activity of the itinerant preacher, Peter the Hermit, and the social composition of Peter's army amused him. Guivert noted exactly the same phenomena as Ekkehard: that entire families of *pauperes* with carts full of their belongings joined the various contingents. Guibert wrote that after the council of Clermont: 'the spirit of the *pauperes* was inflamed with great desire for this [expedition] so that none of them made any account of their small wealth, or properly saw to the sale of homes, vineyards and fields.'[14] This passage is evidently a description of property-owning farmers, turning their fixed assets into ready wealth for the journey, even at much reduced prices. Guibert referred to the same body of people again, with additional detail: 'There you would have seen remarkable things, clearly most apt to be a joke; you saw certain *pauperes*, whose oxen had been fitted to a two-wheel cart and iron-clad as though they were horses, so as to carry in the cart a few possessions together with small children.'[15] Independently but with a similar turn of phrase, the northern French

---

[10] Urban II, *Letter to the clergy and people of Bologna* in H. Hagenmeyer ed., *Epistulae et Chartae ad Historiam Primi Belli Sacri Spectantes Quae Supersunt Aevo Aequales ac Genuinae: Die Kreuzzugsbriefe aus den Jahren 1088 – 1100* (Innsbruck, 1901), p. 137 - 8.

[11] Ekkehard of Aura, *Frutolfs und Ekkehards Chroniken und die Anonyme Kaiserchronik*, ed. F-J Schmale and I. Schamle-Ott (Darmstadt, 1972), p. 140, hereafter EA.

[12] *Ibid.*

[13] *Ibid.*

[14] Guibert of Nogent, *Gesta Dei per Francos*, ed. R. B. C. Huygens, CC LXXVIIa, (Turnhout, 1996), hereafter GN p. 119: ... *pauperum animositas tantis ad hoc ipsum desideriis aspiravit ut eorum nemo de censuum parvitate tractaret, de domorum, vinearum et agrorum congruenti distractione curaret.*

[15] *Ibid.*, p. 120: *Videres mirum quiddam, et plane joco aptissimum, pauperes videlicet quosdam bobus biroto applicitis, eisdemque in modum equorum ferratis, substantiolas cum parvulis in carruca convehere.*

historian and the Bavarian chronicler found it noteworthy that peasant families participated in the crusade. Guibert also provided clear evidence that people from the very lowest layers of the eleventh-century social spectrum responded to the idea of the crusade. He noted that the meanest most common men (*homines extremae vulgaritatis*) appropriated the idea of the expedition for themselves.[16]

The use of the term *pauperes* in these passages seems to cover a broad grouping of the lower social orders, from relatively wealthy farmers - owners of a team of oxen - through to those from the very bottom of society: serfs and even slaves. Christopher Tyerman's very impressive survey across the history of the crusades as to the various social groupings who took the cross doubts that serfs participated in such expeditions. Because, he argues, the serf had no freedom of action or choice, the serf could not participate in the movement independently of their master. Also their lack of resources meant that 'it does seem to have been the case that ... serfs did not become crusaders.'[17] But this precludes the possibility that some serfs took advantage of the crusading message to leave their homes without permission from their lords, hoping to survive on charity and the distribution of captured booty. Tyerman is right, though, to raise the question of how such very lowly crusaders expected to sustain themselves? Perhaps from the charity of the Christian communities they passed? But there still remained over a thousand miles to walk through lands owned by those hostile to them.

A critical passage with regard to the Second Crusade provides evidence that insubordinate serfs did indeed leave their fields for the expedition and that their solution to the problem of supply was indeed to rely upon their faith in God and manna from Heaven. Gerhoch, provost of Reichersberg, was an eyewitness to the departure of the German contingent of the Second Crusade in 1147. He explicitly noted that there was among the army, 'no lack ... of peasants and serfs (*servi*), the ploughs and services due to their lords having been abandoned without the knowledge or against the will of their lords. Having little or nothing of gold or silver, inadvisably having begun that very long expedition, hoping in such a Holy business that like long before in such an ancient time happened to the people of Israel, that nourishment would either rain down from heaven or to be everywhere provided by God.'[18]

---

[16] *Ibid.*, p. 300.
[17] C. Tyerman, 'Who Went on the Crusades?' in B. Z. Kedar ed., *The Horns of Hattīn* (Jerusalem, 1992), pp. 14 – 26, here p. 24.
[18] Gerhohi, *De Investigatione Antichristi Liber I· Monumenta Germaniae Historica Libelli de Lite Imperatorum et pontificum, Saeculis XI et XII conscripti* 3 (Hannoverae, 1897), p. 374: *non rusticanorum ac servorum, dominorum* [375] *suorum relictis aratris ac servitiis, ignorantibus quoque nonnulli vel invitis dominis, parum aut nichil arui vel argenti habentes inconsulte expeditionem illam longissimam arripuerant, sperantes in tam sancto negotio sicut olim antiquo illi Israhelitarum populo, vel pluente desuper celo vel undecunque celitus ac divinitus amminiversitates eundem exercitum in eadem sancta via, ut estimabant, comprehenderunt.*

Other sources suggest that a similar participation by serfs took place with regard to the First Crusade. The anonymous author of the *Historia Peregrinorum euntium Jerusolymam* reported that so great a commotion of men and women took place in all the regions of the world wishing to join the Holy journey that 'the father did not dare restrain the son, nor the wife the husband, and the *dominus* did not dare to restrain the *servus*.' Because of the fear and love of God, everyone was free to join the journey.[19] Marwan Nader assumes *servus* here stands for a serf,[20] which is entirely possible, but even if its alternative meaning of 'servant' was meant by the compiler of the history, the point still stands, that the usual bonds of authority could be undermined by the appeal of the crusade. Similarly, the Annals of Augsburg say that along with warriors, bishops, abbots, monks, clerics and men of diverse professions, 'serfs and women' (*coloni et mulieres*) joined the movement.[21] For 1096 Cosmas of Prague wrote that so many people departed for Jerusalem that there remained very few *coloni* in the *urbes* and *villae* of Germany and Eastern France.[22]

From a modern perspective it seems the height of folly for those with nothing, nor with the arms to procure plunder, to embark on the crusades. But there were many contemporaries, especially those imbued with the kind of theology expressed by Raymond of Aguilers, who wore their poverty as a badge of pride. It was their poverty that made them worthy for the divine aid that they anticipated would meet their needs on the journey. This spiritual self-belief and enthusiasm for the crusade was interconnected with very harsh conditions in the homelands of the *pauperes*. If we look at the state of western Europe at the time of the first two crusades it becomes clearer why the appeal of moving to a land of milk and honey might displace thousands of poor people from the land to search of a better life.

---

[19] *Historia Peregrinorum euntium Jerusolymam, Recueil des historiens des croisades, Historiens occidentaux 1 – 5* (Académie des inscriptions et belles-lettres: Paris 1844 – 95), 3, 167 – 229, here 174: *Pater non audebat prohibere filium, nec uxor prohibere virum, et dominus non audebat prohibere servum.*
[20] M. Nader, *Burgesses and the burgess law in the Latin Kingdom of Jerusalem and Cyprus (1099 – 1325)* (Aldershot, 2006), p. 20.
[21] *Annales Augustani, Monumenta Germaniae Historica Scriptores, Scriptores in Folio* [hereafter *MGH SS*], 32 (1826 – 1934), 3, 134.
[22] *Cosmae Chron. Boemorum, MGH SS* 11, 103.

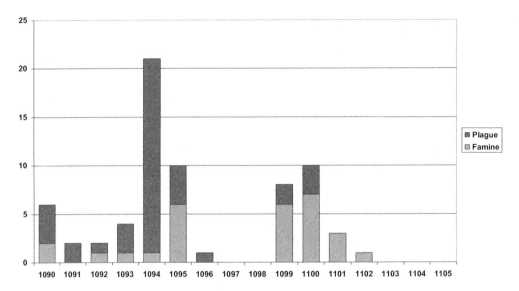

Figure 2: Famine and Plague at the time of the First Crusade

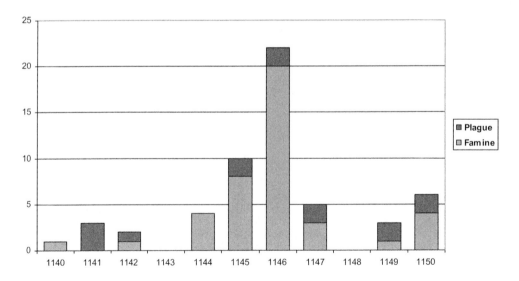

Figure 3: Famine and Plague at the time of the Second Crusade

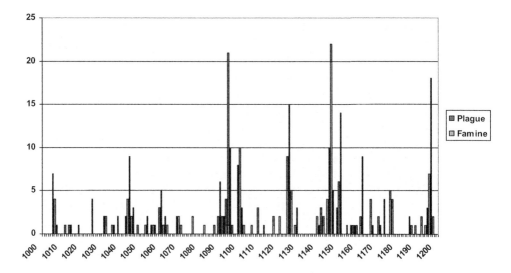

Figure 4: Famine and Plague in perspective

These graphs show how many references exist to plagues and famine in a large collection of annals of the twelfth century. So, for example, in 1091 not one annalist mentioned the presence of famine and only two noted a plague. In 1092 one annalist recorded a famine, one an outbreak of plague. In 1093 we have mention of famine by one annalist and plague by two. But in 1094 – the year before the First Crusade was launched - we have a shocking upsurge of mentions of plague, twenty in all, with one annalist mentioning famine. But as a result of the plague, famine increased, we have six entries to that effect in 1095 as well as plague in four. Absolute economic data for this era is extremely difficult to obtain as we lack marriage, birth and death records. Even the basic demographic details, let alone agricultural and manufacturing information, are only available in the broadest sense. There is a strong consensus among economic historians that in general this was an era of population increase, with growing numbers of towns, with an expansion of the land under cultivation and improvements in the productivity of agriculture.[23] But at the same time, this growth was faltering and human existence precarious in the face of periodic outbreaks of plague, or famine, or both. There is a way to study this *relative* hardship of one year compared to

---

[23] N. J. Pounds, *An Economic History of Medieval Europe* (Longman: London and New York, Second Edition: 1994 [1974]); M. M. Postan, E. Miller, H. J. Habakkuk, et. al. *The Cambridge Economic History of Europe: Trade and Industry in the Middle Ages* (Cambridge University Press, 1987), pp. 204 – 239; L. T. White, *Medieval Technology and Social Change* (Oxford University Press, 1964).

another and obtain a sense of the years that would have been particularly difficult, which is to survey the western European annals and note the number of references to plagues and famine. The annals used in the compilation of the charts presented here are those published in the 38 volumes of the *Monumenta Germaniae Historica Scriptores* series. By making a note of each time an annalist described the appearance of plague or famine it proved possible to create these charts and therefore get a good sense of the periods of economic and social distress across the twelfth century.

There were problems in assembling the data. Often an annalist would incorporate an earlier work wholesale, for example the many annalists who began their own works as continuations of the widely circulated annals of Sigebert of Gembloux or Ekkehard of Aura. Thus information from the entries in the *Annals of Rosenfeld* or the *Annals of Würzburg* has not been used here, as at this point both were copies of the *Annals of Hildesheim*. Assisted by the works of Cruschmann (who in 1900 was the first to discuss the background of famine against which the early crusades took place), W. Wattenbach, and F-J Schmale such repetitions can be eliminated, so the each entry, as much as possible, represents a unique observation.[24] The other distortion to the data that is worth bearing in mind is that there was an increase in the numbers of annals being written across Europe in the twelfth century, so we might expect an increase in the number of entries concerning famine and plague, even if the frequency of incidents of hardship remained about constant. Despite these reservations, the graphs show something very striking and conclusive. There were years of extreme hardship and dislocation at exactly the times when the First and Second crusades were being preached.

In fact, the period around the First Crusade described above stands out as a particularly difficult one, only that around 1145 - shortly before Bernard of Clairvaux began to promote the Second Crusade - is worse. The *Annals of the Four Masters* are not included here, as they are not in the *MGH Scriptores* series, but they reported that in Ireland up to a quarter of the population died of famine in 1095.[25] By 1097, however, the crisis was over. It has plausibly been suggested that the 'plague' mentioned in these reports refer to an outbreak of ergot poisoning among the rye crop, which would fit the pattern of a sharp outbreak of mortality that disappeared by the time of the following harvest. In addition, ergotism also fits the description of Ekkehard - an eyewitness - who graphically portrayed the effects of a plague that caused limbs to wither through an invisible fire.[26]

---

[24] F. Curschmann, *Hungersnöte im Mittelalter* (Leipzig, 1900), F. Wattenbach & F.- J. Schmale, *Deutschlands Geschichtsquellen im Mittelalter. Vom Tode Kaiser Heinrichs V. bis zum Ende des Interregnum*, (Darmstadt 1976).
[25] *Annals of the Four Masters*, ed. J. O'Donovan (Dublin, 1856), p. 949.
[26] EA 140: *Tactus quisquam igne invisibili quacumque corporis parte tam diu sensibili, immo incomparabili tormento etiam inremediabiliter ardebat, quosque vel spiritum cum cruciatu vel cruciatum cum ipso tacto membro amitteret. Testantur hoc hactenus*

The impression given by these graphs is of a correlation between the times when preaching the crusade obtained a massive popular response among the *pauperes* and times of extreme economic difficulty. This connection is confirmed for the First Crusade by the historical sources. According to the brief entry in the *Annals of St Blaisen*, it was the plague that created the movement to Jerusalem.[27] Similarly, in addition to the previously cited comment by Ekkehard that many took the vow through misfortune, he reported in his chronicle that it was easy to persuade the *Francigenae* to go to the orient because for some years previously *Gallia* had been afflicted by civil disorder (*seditio*), famine and an excessive mortality.[28] Guibert of Nogent reported that the preaching of the crusade took place at a time of famine, which had the consequence that the *inopum greges* learned to feed often on the roots of wild plants.[29] The famine reduced the wealth of all and was even threatening to the *potentes*.[30] Guibert condemned those magnates who stored food for profit during a year of famine, writing that they considered the anguish of the starving *vulgus* to be of little importance.[31]

The exact manner in which the upsurge of hardship connected with the mentality of the *pauperes* and the crusading message is impossible to determine. When Ekkehard reported that the crusaders were easily persuaded to depart because of hardship, he explained that 'certain prophets' carried out this agitation.[32] Presumably these were figures like Peter the Hermit, the itinerant and popular leader of the 'People's Crusade' that departed in advance of the main princely contingents of the First Crusade.[33] But what was Peter's message to the 'poor' about their difficult circumstances that was so well received? A clue is provided by the fact that that immediately after making his report Ekkehard adds that in the same year extraordinary events occurred, such as a woman giving year to a boy who could talk after a two year pregnancy and lambs being born with two heads.[34] Other contemporaries observed contingents of the lower social orders following women who held a cross that had fallen from heaven; there were followers of a woman who had a divinely inspired

---

nonnulli manibus vel pedibus hac pena truncati. For Ergot poisoning, high temperatures and gangrenous limbs, see M. McMullen and C. Stoltenow, *Ergot* (Fargo, 2002). See also J. Sumption, *Pilgrimage* (paperback edition: London, 2002), p. 75; J. Riley-Smith, *The First Crusaders*, p. 16.

[27] *Annales Sancti Blasii, MGH SS* 17, 277.

[28] EA 140.

[29] GN 118.

[30] *Ibid.*

[31] *Ibid.*, p. 119.

[32] EA 140.

[33] For Peter the Hermit see J. Flori, *Pierre l'Ermite et la Première Croisade* (Paris, 1999); see also H. Hagenmeyer, *Peter der Eremite* (Leipzig, 1879); E. O. Blake and C. Morris. 'A hermit goes to war: Peter and the origins of the First Crusade,' *Studies in Church History* 22 (1984), pp 79 – 107 and M. D. Coupe, 'Peter the Hermit – A reassessment,' *Nottingham Medieval Studies* 31 (1987), pp. 37 – 45.

[34] EA 141.

goose; and there were even crusaders who followed a she-goat.[35] In other words the sense of dislocation seems to have of fuelled an eagerness among some to grasp at the miraculous as a sign that they should join the movement to Jerusalem. And the fact that the first section of Peter's army left Cologne shortly after Easter, 12 April, 1096, long before the harvest implies an urgency that – unlike for the princes who left in the autumn - placed the question of supply in God's hands.[36]

Attempting to reconstruct the mentality of the lower social orders in the twelfth century is extremely challenging, given the lack of direct testimony from the historical sources. Nevertheless, some monastic authors were sufficiently attentive to the deeds of farmers and serfs at the time of the departure of the First and Second Crusades that we have historical evidence to reinforce the picture created by compiling data on famines and plagues. The statement from Gerhoch that serfs abandoned their fields in the expectation that nourishment would rain down from heaven is particularly important in demonstrating that some of the poor crusaders did indeed take seriously the idea that the miraculous manifestation of God's bounty would sustain them on the journey. Given the background of a dramatic upsurge of plague in 1096 and famine in 1146, it is perhaps not so hard to believe that people with little or no wealth could be attracted by the papal message that the time had come to emulate the sons of Israel and march to a land flowing with milk and honey.

---

[35] Baldric of Dol, *Historia Hierosolymitana*, RHC Oc. 4, 1 – 111, here p. 17; Albert of Aachen, *Historia Iherosolimitana* ed. S. B. Edgington (Oxford, 2007), p. 58.
[36] F. Duncalf, 'The Peasants' Crusade,' *American Historical Review*, 26 (1920/1), pp. 440 – 453, argues in favour of good logistical planning by Peter and his followers, but see C. Kostick, *The Social Structure of the First Crusade* (Brill, Leiden), pp. 95 – 103.

Chapter 9   Social Unrest and the Failure of Conrad III's March Through Anatolia, 1147

Following on from my insight into the push factors behind peasant and serf participation on the crusades – that they were suffering from famine and epidemics and that therefore escape to Jerusalem sounded particularly attractive – I pitched for and won a grant to stay on at TCD and research the Second Crusade from the same standpoint as I had the First. It would be reasonable to describe that standpoint as Marxist in that my hypothesis was that the Second Crusade would also prove, under close scrutiny, to be riven by class tensions.

What I found went far beyond my expectations. The Second Crusade was a disaster for the Christian army because it fell apart along social lines. The poor, perhaps inspired by events on the First Crusade, even went so far to repudiate Conrad III as their king and elected 'a certain Bernard' in his stead. I'm all for revolutions, but this one did not end well...

> When afterwards the king returned to Constantinople, he brought back with him only a few of the great army that he had previously possessed.[1]

The career of Conrad III as king of Germany (1138–53) has not been considered a successful one, particularly in regard to the difficulties he experienced in managing a chronic rivalry between the two most powerful dynasties: the Staufens (Conrad's own family) and the Welfs.[2] A critical moment in Conrad's fortunes came at the end of 1146 when he had to decide whether to place himself at the head of a gathering momentum for a great crusade—the second of its kind—which Pope Eugenius III had launched a year previously with the active support of the king of France. Despite the risk, both personal and political, at Christmas in 1146 Conrad chose to take the cross, perhaps influenced in this by the fact that a bitter opponent, Welf VI, had also agreed to participate.[3] Setting out on the

---

[1] *Annales Palidenses, Monumenta Germaniae Historica Scriptores, Scriptores* in Folio, 32 (1826–1934) [hereafter *MGH SS*], 16. 83: *Postea rex Constantinopolin repetens, paucos admodum de grandi exercitu quem prius habuerat secum reduxit.*

[2] Wilhelm Bernhardi, *Jahrbücher der Deutschen Geschichte. Konrad III* (Leipzig, 1883), whose assessment of the reign of Conrad III has not been challenged by more recent studies, see D. Luscombe and J. Riley-Smith (eds), *New Cambridge Medieval History*, vol. 4 (Cambridge, 2003), vol. 4, pt 1, pp. 415–16.

[3] G. Waitz and B. Simson (eds), *Ottonis et Rahewini Gesta Frederici I. Imperatoris* (Monumenta Germaniae Historica Scriptores rerum Germanicarum in usum scholarum, vol. 46, Hanover and Leipzig, 3rd edn, 1912,

crusade in the spring of 1147, Conrad III commanded an enormous army and for a brief while seemed to have embarked on a course of action destined to secure him the praise of the Church and enhanced authority over the German nobility. Yet by the winter of 1147 Conrad III was in Constantinople, wounded, sick and without the greater part of his army, which had been lost in Asia Minor. What had gone wrong?

Modern discussion of the failure of Conrad III's army in Anatolia has mainly concentrated on the question of logistical supply,[4] and there is no doubt that lack of food and water played a considerable part in weakening the crusading forces. But ever since the late nineteenth-century study by Bernhard Kugler, *Studien zur Geschichte des Zweiten Kreuzzugs* (Stuttgart, 1866), there has been a school of thought that has emphasized the lack of discipline and internal dissent among the German army. A recent PhD study of Conrad's expedition by Jason Roche makes the claim that Kugler's case rests on a brazen and tendentious use of Byzantine sources. This Greek material, argues Roche, is unreliable as it should be understood as *topoi* from a tradition that emphasizes barbarian unruliness in order to emphasize the effectiveness of the rule of the Byzantine emperor.[5] But whether or not the Byzantine sources should be read as *topoi*—and we will return to the question below—there are important Latin sources, including ones written by authors resident in the kingdom of Germany who had spoken to returned crusaders, that support the contention that social unrest within the ranks of Conrad's army played an important part in his defeat. In particular, the annalists of Würzburg and Pöldhe take this view of events. Because neither has been fully translated into English, substantial excerpts from them will be quoted in due course. But what the two annalists depict can be stated at the outset: Conrad III failed to bring his vast crusading army through Anatolia, essentially because it was too turbulent and mutinous for him to control.

The fact that the German crusading army of 1147 had more than a hint of insubordination in its makeup was evident from the moment people began to gather to join the expedition. The first impact of the appeal for crusade in Germany was a wave of attacks on the Jewish communities of the Rhineland. A rogue Cistercian monk, Radulph, inspired popular uprisings against the Jewish populations in Cologne, Mainz, Worms, Speyer and Strassburg, the survivors fleeing to the protection of the royal army at Nuremberg.[6] The agitation of Radulph was so effective that when Bernard, the abbot of Clairvaux and official organizer of the crusade, came in person to attempt to halt the movement, the Christian population of the towns refused to accept that their preacher should be

---

hereafter OF), p. 60: *de nobilissimis regni optimatibus*. Reprinted in F.J. Schmale (ed.), *Gesta Frederici seu rectius Chronica* (Darmstadt, 1965).

[4] See J. Roche, 'Conrad III and the Second Crusade: Retreat from Dorylaion?', *Crusades*, 5 (2006), pp. 85–97, based on a chapter of *Conrad III and the Second Crusade in the Byzantine Empire and Anatolia, 1147* (unpublished PhD thesis: University of Saint Andrews, 2008); J. Phillips, *The Second Crusade: Extending the Frontiers of Christendom* (New Haven, 2007), pp. 178–79.

[5] Roche, 'Conrad III and the Second Crusade', pp. 5–7.

[6] OF, p. 58.

recalled and were willing to defy the authorities on his behalf.[7] Radulf, however, was persuaded by his superior to return to his monastery without resistance. Bernard's objection to Radulf 's agitation was not that it was stirring up the entire population, from top to bottom, but that it had a mistaken focus on the Jewish community. The abbot's own efforts to gather support for the crusade had just as much of an appeal to a popular element among the urban poor. A contemporary, Bishop Herman of Constance, later recalled that at Freiburg the poor had been quick to respond to the crusading message, while the rich had hesitated: 'Bernard ordered a prayer to be made for the rich, so that God should remove the veil from their hearts; because why should they be slow in taking up the cross when the poor were in agreement with it?'[8] After meeting Conrad III in the autumn of 1146 at Frankfurt am Main, Bernard preached the crusade at Freiburg, Basle, Schaffhausen and Constance. Even allowing for considerable exaggeration in the interests of self-congratulation, Bernard's claim that his preaching left seven women for each remaining man in the towns and castles is testimony to the scale of the popular response.[9] It would have helped generate popular support for the crusading message that—as in the First Crusade—the preaching of an expedition to Jerusalem took place against a background of severe economic dislocation. The year 1146 was the worst year for famine in a generation.[10]

On Christmas Day, 1146, Bernard met Conrad III again at Speyer, and two days later, the German king agreed that he would lead the Germans on crusade in person. At a general council in Bavaria, in February 1147, Conrad mustered some of his most loyal supporters for the expedition. At least four bishops took the cross: Henry of Regensburg, Reginbert of Passau, Bishop Ortlieb of Basel and the king's half brother Otto of Freising. Another half-brother, Henry XI 'Jasomirgott', duke of Bavaria, agreed to accompany Conrad, as did Conrad's nephew, Duke Frederick of Swabia (later Emperor Frederick I) and these very senior princes were joined by 'countless men from the ranks of counts, nobles and knights'.[11] But an unexpected incident also took place at the council. A huge crowd of brigands and thieves arrived to join the expedition, 'so great that no sane person could doubt that a change, as sudden as it was unexpected, had happened by the hand of God'.[12] Bernard had made a particular appeal to those currently outside the law to use the crusade as

[7] OF, p. 59.

[8] *Sancti Bernardi abbatis Clarae-Vallensis vita et res gestae, Liber sextus seu miracula a sancto Bernardo per Germaniam, Belgium, Galliamquapatrata, anno 1146*, in J.P.Migne (ed.), *Patrologiae cursus completus. SeriesLatina*, 221 (Paris, 1844–66), p. 185, col. 375A: *pro divitibus jussit fieri orationem, ut auferret Deus velamen de cordibus ipsorum; quia, pauperibus accedentibus, ipsi crucem suscipere cunctarentur?*

[9] Bernard of Clairvaux, *Epistola* 247.2, in J. Leclercq, H.M. Rochais and C.H. Talbot (eds,) *Sancti Bernardi opera* (9 vols, Rome, 1957–1977), vol. 8, p. 141.

[10] F. Curschmann, *Hungersnöte im Mittelalter* (Leipzig, 1900), pp. 123–43.

[11] OF, pp. 60, 89.

[12] *bid.: ut nullus sani capitis hanc tam subitam quam insolitam mutationem ex dextra excelsi provenire non cognosceret cognoscendo attonita mente non obstupesceret.*

an opportunity to reconcile themselves with authority, writing—and presumably preaching—that the crusade was an opportunity for salvation for murderers, robbers, adulterers, perjurers and those guilty of other crimes.[13] In the case of the First Crusade, crowds of common people under the leadership of an itinerant preacher, Peter the Hermit, had departed four months ahead of the official, papally approved, princely contingents. The 'People's Crusade' had met with near utter destruction at Civitot on 21 October 1096 at the hands of Qilij Arslān I, the young sultan of Rūm, and the lesson was not lost on those commoners and outlaws who wished to join the Second Crusade. In fact, by arriving without summons at the royal assembly, this unexpected throng was simply following the advice of Bernard, who in the same letter that appealed to those beyond the law to redeem themselves through crusading, had also warned those willing to go on the journey of the fate of Peter the Hermit's contingent on the earlier crusade.[14]

Having accepted Bernard's message both of redemption and of the importance of marching under experienced military leaders, these outlaws turned up to bring a large accretion of forces to Conrad's army, but the ties between king and such followers were not strong ones. Even a more conventional royal army of the era would have been difficult to manage, requiring the king to consult carefully with his most senior nobles, particularly given the presence of former rivals for the crown. In this case any difficulties Conrad might have had with managing his senior vassals were compounded by the accretion of bands of soldiers with even weaker ties to his command. Already, as popular contingents of crusaders independently marshalled themselves to join with Conrad, they had demonstrated utter contempt for royal and episcopal authority. This was evident in a renewed outbreak of attacks and extortions against the Jewish community early in 1147.

In Würzburg, the annalist believed such disobedient actions by troops of crusaders were widespread and described one such army, whose behaviour he witnessed, 'so that by the certainty of this one example I may better convince with regard to the others'.[15] The author of the Würzburg annals is unknown but he was a cleric or monk of Würzburg, and he was close enough to Bishop Siegfried (1146–50) to be able to report the details of the Bishop's discomfort in the face of a contingent of crusaders (see below). The annalist had clearly spoken to returned crusaders before writing his account, something which is most evident in his pity for those who had been imprisoned for some time and who returned to Würzburg after undergoing mutilations that ensured they would never fight again.[16] Although outraged by the behaviour of the departing crusaders, elsewhere in his account the annalist indicates that

---

[13] Bernard of Clairvaux, Epistola 363, in Sancti Bernardi opera, vol. 8, p. 315.
[14] Ibid.
[15] Annales Herbipolenses, MGH SS 16. 3.
[16] Ibid. p. 5.

he was positively disposed towards the German king.[17] G.H. Pertz, who edited the annals for the *Monumenta Germaniae Historica Scriptores* series, drew attention to the fact that the author referred to the events he was describing as being some time in the past and reasonably suggests the account was written down more towards the end than the middle of the twelfth century.[18]

There are two passages worth quoting at length for the insight that they give into the nature of the German crusading army. First, the annalist described the crusaders as having a variety of motives and he made it clear that their forces contained criminals:

> Some men lusting for novelties went to discover new lands; others whom poverty dominated, whose resources were narrow at home, went not only against the enemies of the cross of Christ but also against the friends of the Christian name, where it seemed opportune to fight for the relief of their poverty; others, who were oppressed by debts or who thought of abandoning service owed to their lords, also those whom awaited the punishment of wicked offences, pretended to have a zeal for God. They hastened rather for the sake of suppressing the inconvenience of such great anxieties. A very small number, however, were found who had not bowed their knees to Baal, whom a holy and wholesome intention directed, whom the love of the divine majesty warmly kindled to the holy of holies, even to the shedding of their blood. But we leave these things to God, who is the inspector of hearts [Proverbs 24.12], to be more fully examined, adding this alone: that the Lord knows who are his.[19]

Second, the annalist described the activities of one of the popular crusading armies, that which was present in Würzburg at Easter 1147. He wrote that, having slaughtered the local Jewish population without

---

[17] *Ibid.* pp. 4–7.

[18] *Ibid.* p. 1.

[19] *Ibid.*: *Alii namque, rerum novarum cupidi, ibant pro novitate terrarum consideranda; alii quibus egestas imperabat, qui- bus etiam res angusta domi fuerat, non solum contra inimicos crucis Christi, sed etiam contra quoslibet christiani nominis amicos, ubi oportunum videretur dimicaturi pro paupertate relevanda; alii qui premebantur ere alieno, vel qui debita dominorum cogitabant relinquere servitia, vel etiam quos flagitiorum suorum merita expectabant supplitia, simulantes se zelum Dei habere, festinabant potius pro incommoditate tantarum sollicitudinum reprimenda. Vix autem pauci inventi sunt qui non incurvarent genu ante Baal, quos videlicet sancta et salubris intentio dirigeret, quos amor divine maiestatis usque ad sanguinis effusionem pro sanctis sanctorum decertare vehementer accenderet. Sed hec interim plenius discutienda ei relinquimus, qui cordium inspector est Deus, illud solummodo aditientes, quia novit Dominus qui sunt eius.*

consideration of age or gender, the crusaders insisted that the Bishop of Würzburg declare that a certain man called Theoderic—who had been found dismembered in the nearby river and ditches—be declared a saint. Theoderic's murder had been blamed on Jews and the discovery of the body was the pretext for the outbreak of the pogrom. As a result of the agitation against the bishop his life was in danger.

> Siegfried, the religious bishop of the same city, together with the clergy, was hesitant in the face of their im- portunity and error. The citizens and pilgrims raised up so great a persecution of the bishop and the clergy that they forced the bishop into the safety of the towers, wishing to stone him. The canons in no way dared either to ascend the choir nor to chant matins on that most sacred night of the Lord's supper [Holy Thursday, 17 April 1147] for fear of persecution. When Easter Week then occurred the pilgrims began on their intended expedition and thus at last the disturbances in the city were suppressed and things became quiet.[20]

This incident indicates an extraordinary autonomy from royal and episcopal authority on the part of this body of crusaders. As such contingents, and those mustered directly by the king, gathered together in order to set off with Conrad from Regensburg at the end of May, it was evident to eyewitnesses that this crusading army was an unusual one, both in its size and in its social makeup. Otto of Freising wrote that, having boarded ship at Regensburg, they travelled along the Danube with 'so great a multitude that the river seemed hardly wide enough for those who were sailing and the fields hardly wide enough for those on foot'.[21]

The same image struck the polemicist and Gregorian reformer, Gerhoh, provost of Reichersberg. In the course of his De Investigatione Antichristi (1162), in which he was demonstrating that a series of calamities indicated that the time of the antichrist was drawing near, Gerhoh recalled witnessing the departure of the German forces of the Second Crusade.

> There was not a city that did not send forth multitudes or a village or town that did not at

---

[20] Ibid. p. 4: religioso eiusdem civitatis episcopo Sifrido una cum clero importunitati eorum immo errori reluctante: tantam in episcopum et clerum persecutionem suscitaverunt, ut episcopum lapidibus obruere volentes ad turrium presidia compellerent, canonici in ipsa sacratissima nocte cene Domini timore persequutorum nec chorum ascen- dere nec matutinas canere ullatenus auderent. Superveniente dehinc ebdomada resurrectionis dominice, peregrini iter propositum arripiunt; et sic tandem compressis in civitate motibus omnia quieverunt.

[21] OF, p. 64: Tantam autem post se multitudinem traxit, ut et flumina ad navigandum camporumque latitudo ad am- bulandum vix sufficere videretur.

least send a few. Bishops together with magnates were each setting out with his own squadrons, carrying shields, swords, armour and other instruments of war with abundant preparation of finances and of tents that they convoyed with carts and innumerable horses. The highway and that of the neighbouring plains could scarcely contain the innumerable carts and horses; the breadth of the Danube could hardly hold the multitude of boats. For so infinite was the army that from the times when nations began to exist I should have thought that never had so great a multitude of knights and foot soldiers been concentrated together. No markets of goods were lack- ing for the sale of the necessities, nor were there any fields that lacked carts or horses for conveying food. No lack either of peasants and serfs, the ploughs and services due to their lords having been abandoned without the knowledge or against the will of their lords. Having little or nothing of gold or silver, inadvisably having begun that very long expedition, hoping in such a holy business that like long before in such an ancient time happened to the people of Israel, that nourishment would either rain down from heaven or be everywhere provided by God.[22]

The army, it is clear, was accompanied right from the outset by great numbers of non-combatants, many of whom had no means of providing for themselves. In this regard it had similarities with the crowds who set out on the First Crusade. Gerhoh also drew attention to the presence of runaway peasants and serfs, who used the call of the crusade

---

[22] Gerhohi, *De Investigatione Antichristi, MGH Historica Libelli de Lite Imperatorum et pontificum, Saeculis XI et XII conscripti 3 (Hanover, 1897)*, I. 374–5: *Non fuit civitas, que multitudines, non villa seu vicus, que non saltim paucos emitteret, episcopi cum magnates singuli cum suis turmis incedebant, scuta, gladios et loricas aliaque belli vasa secum perferentes cum capiosa preperatione sumptuum ac tabernaculorum, que plaustris et equis innumeris subvehebant. Vix terrestris via simul et campi contigui per terram gradientes, vix Danubii decursus navium multitudines capiebat. Tam enim erat infinitus exercitus, quod, ex quo gentes esse ceperunt, numquam tantam hominum, equi- tum simul et peditum, multitudinem in unum congregatam estimarverim. Nulla earum necessitatibus venalium rerum fora, vix ulli campi cui plaustra et equi victualibus perferendis deerant, non rusticanorum ac servorum, domi- norum suorum relictis aratris ac servitiis, ignorantibus quoque nonnulli vel invitis dominis, parum aut nichil arui vel argenti habentes inconsulte expeditionem illam longissimam arripuerant, sperantes in tam sancto negotio sicut olim antiquo illi Israhelitarum populo, vel pluente desuper celo vel undecunque celitus ac divinitus amminiversitates eundem exercitum in eadem sancta via, ut estimabant, comprehenderunt.*

to escape their obligations to their lords. In other words, not only were there many poor crusaders present on the journey, but there were insubordinate people who had already defied the lords to whom they had previously been bound. There are also—albeit fleeting—indications of the diversity of the social makeup of the army in the near contemporary Weingarten *History of the Welfs*, which referred to men of all condition joining the crusade,[23] and in the *Annals of Würzburg*, which wrote of both sexes of mankind rushing indiscriminately, 'the men with the women, the poor with the rich, the princes and the magnates of the kingdoms with their kings, the clerks and monks with the bishops and abbots'.[24] The presence of absconding serfs and peasants with a royal army could not have been desirable from Conrad's perspective, but he did not act against them, rather the German king found himself in the unenviable position of leading a force over which he had even less control than one drawn solely from the vassals of his senior nobles. In particular, Conrad was to experience persistent problems with those unable to provide for themselves engaging in depredations at the expense of the Byzantine lands.

The depiction of German troops disobeying their king and looting Byzantine towns is a major theme in the writings of John Kinnamos, imperial secretary to the Byzantine emperor Manuel I Comnenus at the time of the Second Crusade. Kinnamos set down his history around 1180. Accepting the observation by Jason Roche that Kinnamos was working within a literary tradition that took for granted the superiority of Byzantine culture over that of its 'barbarian' neighbours and that the Greek historian's aim was to show Manuel in the best possible light in comparison with Conrad,[25] it is nevertheless significant that the particular incidents described to achieve this effect were those which demonstrated that the German King could not control his own people. Kinnamos wrote of the German army that:

> When they entered the plains that succeed to
> the difficulties of the regions in Dacia, they
> began to manifest their evil intent: they applied
> unjust force on those who were offering them
> goods for sale in the market. If one resisted
> their seizure, they made him a victim of their
> sword. King Conrad was entirely heedless of
> what was happening: he either paid no attention
> to the accusers, or if he paid attention, he
> ascribed everything to the folly of the
> multitude.[26]

---

[23] *Historia Welforum Weingartensis MGH SS* 21. 468: 'allis cuiusqumque conditionis hominibus.'
[24] *Annales Herbipolenes, MGH SS* 16. 4.
[25] Roche, 'Conrad III and the Second Crusade', pp. 29–31.
[26] John Kinnamos, *The Deeds of John and Manuel Comnenus*, trans. C.M. Brand (New York, 1976), p. 61.

In describing how relations deteriorated to the point of a possible major conflict between Greek and German forces, Kinnamos put the following words into the mouth of the German King, as supposedly expressed in a letter to the Greek Emperor: do not impute to us the causes of the damage lately wrought by the commonality of our army in your land, nor be wroth on that account, since we ourselves have not been causes of such things, but the mob's impulse, recklessly hastening onwards, was capable of doing this of its own will.[27]

Again, Kinnamos in describing the German troops depicted them as much more of a mob of commoners than the disciplined military force the Byzantines had expected. In a further purported letter from Conrad to Manuel, Kinnamos had the German king say, 'nor will it be possible for us to chastise the mob's irreverence. How [could we]? We have allowed them absolutely to be swept along by their own volition'.[28] And Kinnamos reported that Manuel described Conrad's army as 'a common herd and largely unwarlike'.[29]

Whether these letters actually existed or not, and allowing for exaggeration by Kinnamos to suit his purpose, modern historians have not disputed that violent incidents took place as German troops seized goods from the Byzantine towns they passed. Nor would it be plausible to do so, as the Greek historian was writing for the benefit of those who would have had memories of the passage of the German army through Constantinople. While the depiction of Conrad might have emphasized the German king's inability to command, the context out of which Kinnamos was fashioning his account was that of the Byzantine memory of the German army as being turbulent and prone to damaging imperial property.

One particular incident described by Kinnamos demonstrated that for the Greek historian it was not only the commoners among the German army who caused their king difficulties by their unsanctioned actions. Near Adrianople, Conrad's nephew Frederick avenged the death by fire of one of his comrades by burning out of hand the monastery where the incident happened.[30] Again, even allowing for the subsequent exaggeration of the importance of this incident by Kinnamos, it seems that Conrad had difficulty controlling not just the crowds of commoners but also the most senior nobles.

Moreover, it was not only unsympathetic Byzantine observers who held the view that the German army was outside the control of Conrad. Odo of Deuil, a monk from St Denis, was in the French army of King Louis VII that was marching about a month behind the German contingent. During the crusade Odo was chaplain to the French king and he later replaced the very important figure of Suger, regent of France, as abbot of St Denis. Odo wrote his *De profectione Ludovici VII in Orientem* to

---

[27] *Ibid*. p. 64.
[28] *Ibid*. p. 78.
[29] *Ibid*. p. 79.
[30] *Ibid*. p. 71.

highlight the saintly character of his king and to ensure that future French expeditions would be able to benefit from the experience of those on the Second Crusade.[31] The French historian also had an idiosyncratic notion of the *libra vita*, the 'book of life' mentioned in the letter of Paul to the Philippians and in the Apocalypse.[32] He seems to have treated his history as a part of the *libra vita* and was careful about who did and who did not deserve to have their names recorded.[33] So, notably, Odo refused to name Manuel Comnenus, the Byzantine emperor, who he thought had betrayed the crusaders.[34]

King Conrad, on the other hand, was treated with some sympathy in Odo's history. This was a fellow Latin Christian ruler who had suffered from Greek perfidy and even though Odo drew attention to the fact that St Denis objected to Conrad's occupation of Esslingen in Swabia and Castle Estusin (Königsberg) in Alsace,[35] this did not undermine the fact that Conrad was entitled to respect for his royal authority and for attempting to implement the common goals of the Latin Christians. The German army as a whole, on the other hand, was treated in a very different manner to their king and Odo was clearly furious with the German soldiery for making the journey of the French army all the more difficult by having aroused the hostility of Byzantine citizens to the passage of the crusaders.

As a case study, Odo recounted an incident at Philippopolis, early in September 1147, where in a tavern an entertainer with a snake alarmed some German soldiers, who then seized him and tore him to pieces. The subsequent uproar led to fighting that was all the more difficult to defuse because the Germans were agitated by wine.[36] Again, when some of the French army had pushed on ahead of the main body of troops they encountered German crusaders at a market, who refused the French the right to buy anything until they were done. This confrontation again led to a clash of arms.[37] Odo summarized the situation by reporting that the Germans caused disturbances as they proceeded that caused the Greeks to flee the French king.[38] Moreover, when German foot soldiers lagged behind the main army because they were drunk, the Byzantines killed them, leaving corpses and the danger of pollution for the French to contend with.[39]

Can we take these incidents in Odo's history as confirming the substance of John Kinnamos's allegations of unruliness in the German forces? John France believes so, pointing out that in presenting these examples, Odo was not trying to demonstrate the superiority of the

---

[31] Odo of Deuil, *De profectione Ludovici VII in Orientem*, ed. V.G. Berry (New York, 1948, hereafter OD).
[32] Paul to Philippians, 4.3, Apocalypse 13.8.
[33] e.g. OD, pp. 10, 12, 20.
[34] OD, p. 10.
[35] OD, p. 102.
[36] OD, p. 42.
[37] OD, pp. 42–44.
[38] OD, p. 44.
[39] OD, p. 46.

discipline of Louis's army, as there are several incidents recorded in the *De profectione Ludovici VII in Orientem* that express Odo's equal frustration with the indiscipline of the French army.[40] Odo wrote, for example, that despite the fact that King Louis frequently punished offenders, he could not check the folly of the multitude who 'either [due to] scarcity of wood or with the arrogant drunkenness of fools' burned many Greek houses and olive trees.[41] The historian also wrote of how King Louis had drawn up decrees for ensuring peace on the expedition but because they were not observed Odo did not bother to set them down.[42] Jason Roche disagrees with John France, believing that although Odo was not overtly favouring the French army over the German one, in a more subtle way he was excusing the insubordinate actions of the French by depicting their looting as being a necessity whereas the German looting was portrayed as being unjustified and the cause of the French difficulties.

> The Germans who advanced ahead of the French army are portrayed as wanton despoilers, and this, Odo argues, subsequently caused the French to be provisioned inadequately. Accordingly, Odo maintains that the French were compelled to pillage because of the previous actions of German crusaders. We are thus left with an impression that the French army perpetrated justified acts of violence, whereas the Germans were merely an indisciplined rabble.[43]

This justification of French looting is hard to find in Odo, especially given the example above in which Odo explicitly allowed for the possibility that the French crowds engaged in depredations that were the result of drunkenness rather than necessity. In any case, whether favouring the French army or not, Odo's history gives us depictions of events that support the contention that Conrad's army in Byzantine territory did not behave in the peaceful fashion that the king would have wished for. Furthermore the English scholar John of Salisbury provided evidence that this issue was the essence of the problem as far as some contemporaries saw it. John undertook a number of missions to the Papal See around the time of the Crusade and was in a position to obtain feedback from the papal curia as to their view of the failure of the expedition. His brief comment that 'Conrad's army was destroyed through the rashness

---

[40] J. France, 'Logistics and the Second Crusade' in J.H. Pryor (ed.), *Logistics of Warfare in the Age of the Crusades* (Ashgate, 2006), pp. 77–93, here pp. 82–83.
[41] OD, p. 66: *vel penuria nemorum vel insolentia et ebrietate stultorum.*
[42] OD, p. 20.
[43] Roche, 'Conrad III and the Second Crusade', p. 34.

(*temeritas*) of the Germans', is therefore noteworthy with its strong suggestion of indiscipline among the crusaders.[44]

In the case of the First Crusade, the fact that the commoners were at times politically active probably saved their lives. Certainly they impelled the movement forwards to Jerusalem at critical times when it looked like the expedition might falter.[45] In the case of the Second Crusade, however, the opposition of commoners to the nobles seems to have been disastrous as the army came to grief in Anatolia after an encounter with the forces of Mas'ud I, Sultan of Rūm. Before we can look at what happened to this enormous but undisciplined crusading army, a basic chronology has to be established. It is a curious fact that modern historians seem to be introducing a level of confusion to the subject. According to Jonathan Philips in his 2008 monograph on the Second Crusade, the German army left Nicea on 25 October 1147.[46] This cannot be correct because, as we will see, some ten or eleven days after leaving the border city, Conrad encountered the Turkish army on 26 October. Another 2008 publication on the crusades has the date of the critical battle as 25 October 1147. Norman Housley states this in *Fighting the Cross*, perhaps following Stephen Runciman's narrative at this point in his work;[47] while the editor of the 2006 Routledge *Companion to the Crusades* says that this battle took place in November.[48] For greater precision on the subject we have to turn to the solidly reliable scholarship of the late nineteenth-century German historians, and in particular the work of Wilhelm Bernhardi.[49]

Bernhardi drew attention to the statement made by Odo of Deuil that on the day the decisive turning point took place there was a partial solar eclipse. Odo was travelling some ten days behind the German army in the company of King Louis VII of France as the royal chaplain. He wrote of the day of the destruction of the German army:

> On that day the sun saw a crime which it could not endure, but, lest it might seem that the crime should be equal to the betrayal of the Lord, half of the sun served the world and half hid itself. When the army there- fore proceeded—having parted from the king—it saw the sun appear like a half loaf of bread for most of the day. The army feared lest he [Louis] who shone above all others with faith, burned with love and attained the heights of hope, had been

[44] John of Salisbury, *Historia Pontifcalis*, ed. M. Chibnall (Oxford, 1986) p. 12: *Sed exercitus Conradi temeritate Teutonum confectus est.*

[45] C. Kostick, *The Social Structure of the First Crusade* (Leiden, 2008), pp. 138–49.

[46] Philips, *The Second Crusade*, p. 178.

[47] N. Housley, *Fighting for the Cross* (New Haven, 2008), p. 94; S. Runciman, *The Crusades* (3 vols; 2nd edn, London, 1990 [51–54]), vol. 2, p. 268.

[48] P. Lock, *The Routledge Companion to the Crusades* (Abingdon, 2006), p. 48.

[49] Bernhardi, *Konrad III*.

deprived of some part of his light by the treachery of the Greeks. But another thing happened, equally to be lamented; for the German emperor was betrayed by his guides and secretly abandoned in the narrow places in the mountains and was forced to withdraw after many thousands of his men had been struck by Turkish missiles, as we shall tell afterwards. Because we learned later what it signi- fied, we have rightly expounded the heavenly phenomena, saying that our king and the German king were one; since they shone with the light of one faith and that the sun half shone and half hid the rays of its disc because the Germans retreated while the king kept his course with customary vigour.[50]

Modern astronomers have confirmed the date of this eclipse as 26 October 1147,[51] as do the medieval annals of central Europe. The Gembloux continuation of Sigebert's well-known chronicle, written c.1148, recorded that 'an eclipse of the sun took place about the third hour of the day, on the seventh kalends of November [26 October]. And the sun did not regain its whole light until it was surrounded by a misty cover'.[52] The *Annals of Egmond aan Zee* (North Holland), again based on Sigebert but independent from 1112, record that 'In the year 1147 the sun was obscured from the third hour of the day to the sixth in the month of October'.[53] The *Annals of Engelberg*, Switzerland, written c.1175, continue annals brought from St Blaisen in 1147: 'In that same year there was an eclipse of the sun on the seventh kalends November at the third hour of the day on the twenty-eighth of the moon'.[54] The *Annals of St*

---

[50] OD, pp. 82–4: *Illo die sol vidit scelus quod ferre non potuit, sed ne videretur illud acquare proditioni Dominicae, servivit mundo dimidius et dimidius se abscondit. Cum igitur exercitus dimisso rege procederet et solem in forma dimidii panis magna diei parte conspiceret, verebatur ne ille qui super alios fide lucebat, dilectione fervebat, spe su- perna tenebat proditione Graecorum aliqua portione sui luminis privaretur. Sed aliud accidit aeque dolendum; im- perator enim Alemannorum, a duce suo proditus et in concavis montibus clam relictus, multis suorum iaculis Turcorum confossis milibus retrocedere compulsus est, sicut postea referemus. Quod postquam didicimus quid sig- nificaret, caeleste prodigium rectius exposuimus, dicentes nostrum regem et Alemannum esse unum solem, quo- niam unius fidei lumine coruscabant, et hunc lucere dimidium et dimidii circuli radios abscondisse, quando, rege fervoure solito tenente cursum, Alemanni retrocedebant.*

[51] T.R. Oppolzer, *Canon der Finsternisse Kaiserlich-Königlichen Hof- und Staatsdruckerei* (Wein, 1887); F.R. Stephenson and L.V. Morrison, 'Long-Term Fluctuations in the Earth's Rotation: 700 BC to AD 1990', *Philosophical Transactions: Physical Sciences and Engineering*, 351, 1695 (15 Apr. 1995), pp. 165–202; and R.R. Newton, *Medieval Chronicles and the Rotation of the Earth* (Baltimore and London 1972).

[52] *Gemblacensis. MGH SS* 6. 389: *Eclypsis solis facta est circa tertiam horam diei, 7. Kal. Novembris. Necdum quoque ad purum redintegrato solari lumine, sed adhuc circumfuso eclyptica caligine.*

[53] 53 *Annales Egmundani, MGH SS* 16. 456: *sol obscuratus est tercia hora diei usque ad sextam mense Octobri.*

[54] *Annales Engelbergenses, MGH SS* 17. 279: *Eodem anno eclipsis solis contigit 7. Kal. Novemb. hora diei 3. luna 28.*

Jacob in Liège, written c.1174 and conscious that the eclipse occurred on the same day as the defeat of the German army, state: 'on the seventh kalends November, on the first feria, an eclipse of the sun from nearly the third hour of the day until the full sixth hour; the reddening of the sun is to show how much Christian blood will be shed',[55] and the *Annals of Würzburg* say, 'there was an eclipse of the sun in the year of this expedition, namely 1147, on the seventh kalends November, sixth hour, the twenty-eighth of the moon, on the Lord's Day in the feast of St Amand'.[56]

Note that the last entry has the time of the eclipse as at the sixth hour, rather than the third. The astronomer R.R. Newton made the point that this suggests the author was present on the crusade, since the time accords with a perspective on the eclipse appropriate to someone east of Constantinople. While elsewhere in the text the annalist indicated he was not present in person on the Crusade, the fact that the Würzburg Annals have a time for the eclipse that conforms to an eastern perspective does lend weight to the argument that returned crusaders informed his version of events.[57]

So, thanks to the eclipse, we are confident of our date of 26 October 1147 for the battle. What happened to Conrad's army after its departure from Nicea? Probably the best contemporary overview of events is the brief summary in the report by the Damascene historian Ibn Al-Qalānisī who wrote that when news of the crusade reached the Muslim world

> the governors of the neighbouring lands and of the Islamic territories in the proximity began to make preparations for warding them off and to muster their forces for engaging in the Holy War with them. They repaired to their outlets and mountainous defiles which hindered them from crossing and debouching on the land of Islam and assiduously launched raids upon their fringes. Death and slaughter commingled with the Franks until a vast number of them perished and their sufferings from lack of foodstuffs, forage and supplies or the costliness of them if they were to be had at all, destroyed multitudes of them by hunger and disease.[58]

---

[55] *Annales S. Iacobi Leodiensis, MGH SS* 16. 641: *7. Kalendas Novembris in dominica solis deliquium a tertia pene*
hora diei usque in plenam sextam erubescente sole videre tantum sanguinem christianorum qui fundendus erat.
[56] *Annales Herbipolenses, MGH SS* 16. 6: *Eclypsis solis facta est hoc ipso expeditionis anno, videlicet 1147, 7. Kal. Nov. hora 6, luna 28, die dominica in festo sancti Amandi confessoris.*
[57] R.R. Newton, *Medieval Chronicles and the Rotation of the Earth* p. 418.
[58] Ibn al-Qalānisī, *The Damascus Chronicle of the Crusades*, trans. H.A.R. Gibb (New York, 2002), p. 281.

The Christian accounts, such as they are, broadly agree with this overview, albeit with a different emphasis. Conrad himself wrote along similar lines in a letter to Abbot Wibald of Corvey written early in 1148.

> After we had arrived at Nicea with a numerous and untouched army, we wanted to complete our expedition in good time. So we set off towards Iconium on the direct route, accompanied by guides to show us the way, and carrying with us as many supplies as we could. But however, after ten days on the road, and with a similar march still left, the supplies began to run short for everyone, particularly for the cavalry, while the Turks unceasingly harried and inflicted death upon the crowd of people on foot, who were unable to keep up. Pitying the fate of the suffering people, who were dying both from famine and from the arrows fired by the enemy, and on the request of all the princes and barons, we led the army away from that wasteland towards the sea, so as to regroup; prefer- ring to keep it unharmed for greater things [in future] rather than to win a bloody victory over the archers.[59]

As with the Damascene chronicler, hunger and constant harassment by Turkish forces explain the retreat of the German army. But Conrad in this letter was making light of the events of 26 October 1147, when the German army suffered what could more accurately been described as a military defeat, one in which the king himself was wounded. For more specific details of what happened it is necessary to turn to the German annals that carried more detailed reports of this disaster.

The *Annals of Magdeburg* appear to have material concerning the Second Crusade that was written within a few years of the events they describe.[60] With regard to Conrad's retreat from Anatolia they state that

---

[59] Friedrich Hausman (ed.), *Conradi III et filii eius Heinrici Diplomata* (MGH Diplomatum Regum et Imperatorum Germaniae, 9, Vienna and Cologne, 1969), document 195, pp. 349–57, here pp. 354–55, Conrad to Abbot Wibald of Korvey, Jan./Feb. 1148. *Mandamus itaque fidelitati tuę, quod cum Nyceam integro et copioso exercitu perve- nissemus, mature expeditionem consummare volentes, per compendium notis vie ducibus hoc ostendentibus ver- sus Iconium proficisci cepimus, illus usque necessaria portantes, quantum valuimus. Et ecce, decem dierum itinere [itieneris-B] iam peracto totidem adhuc nobis residuo victualia omnibus fere, equitaturis maxime defecerant, cum Turci pedestre vulgus, quod exercitum sequi nequibat, invadere et cedere non cessabant. Nos vicem populi dificien- tis et tam sua morte quam sagittis hostium pereuntis dolentes rogatu principum omnium et baronum ad mare de terra illa deserta exercitum, ut refocilaretur, reduximus, malentes incolumem ad maiora servare quam tam cruenta victoria de sagittariis triumphare. Cum vero ad mare venissemus et castra metati fuissemus* [Trans. G.A. Loud.].

[60] See S.B. Edgington, 'Albert of Aachen, St Bernard and the Second Crusade', in J. Phillips and M. Hoch (eds), *The Second Crusade: Scope and Consequences* (Manchester, 2001), pp. 54–70, here p. 59.

Having been enticed by the King of Greece through a deserted and pathless region, almost the whole multitude died of eighteen days of famine and thirst, in addition to having been beset by Pagans they call Turks. They were easily destroyed by arrows in as much as they were already overcome by toil, famine and thirst. Here Bernard, Count of Plötzkau died. The king, however, far away from this slaughter, at length with the few men who could escape the frequent attacks of the barbarians, returned to Constantinople.[61]

Here the significance of the army's lack of resources is evident and in this short report is the first indication of serious fighting having taken place with the mention of the death of Count Bernard. Note also that the Magdeburg annalist placed Conrad at some distance from the destruction of the count.

Turning again to the Würzburg annalist, who gave a number of indications that he had talked to returning crusaders before setting down his account, we have the longest description of these events but one that is rather neglected by modern historians.

The whole multitude of knights and armed men set out with the king from Nicea. With Focas— whom the Greek king had assigned them—going ahead as a guide, they moved towards Iconium. Advancing into an extremely vast wilderness, when the sources of food they had prepared for themselves had failed and they discovered nothing that was suitable for use as food, their spirit, as it is written, pined away in their calamity [Psalm 106.26]. Advancing, nevertheless, in the hope of aid rather than in the assurance of their strength, now those men, now these, failed because of hunger. They perished without pause, whether man or beast. What more is there to say? At last, on the fortieth day after they had departed Nicea, full of many distressful labours, they entered the desert in the region of Iconium. And it was not

[61] *Annales Magdeburgensis, MGH SS* 16. 188: *a rege Grecorum per loca deserta et avia abducti, 18 dierum fame ac siti pene omnis multitudo interiit, insuper a paganis qui dicuntur Turci circumventi, facile sine congressione, utpote laboure fame sitique confecti, sagittis interimebantur, ubi et Bernhart comes de Plozeke occubuit. Rex autem, qui longe abierat ab hac cede, tandem cum paucis, qui secum barbaros sepe invadentes evadere potuerunt, Constantinopolim rediit.*

enough that nothing that it would be possible to eat could be found for so many days. Even worse, waters that had hitherto been found as the sole consolation of life now failed. And thus sorrow was added to sorrow and so their slow progress was extended up to the fourth day.

Meanwhile, the kings of the Saracens, having been terrified by the rumour which had gone before them, assembled in aid of the king of Iconium, and after holding counsel, they seized the narrow places and, unanimously ready for battle, with mutual exhortation they determined to live or die for the fatherland. After they had sent scouts to meet them, as is the custom, those who had been sent out, returning with the greatest haste, informed them of the weakness of the Christian army, the starvation also and the exhaustion of both men or horses.

Now the sun was setting, already the fourth day was coming to an end. Behold, there were those who reported to King Conrad and the princes that there was drinkable water at the foot of a high mountain. At their report the king was immediately filled with joy and hurried secretly with his men to the mountain which was more or less four miles from the camp in order that he might see if it were so. And while they were delaying there, first Duke Welf, next Henry, duke of Austria, then Duke Frederick—who later took up the helm of the kingdom—and last of all the bishops, counts and all the more healthy men, hastened after him in search of water. For they had suffered from thirst rather than by hunger because in the desert so great an abundance of savage beasts had offered themselves that sometimes the entire army fed itself abundantly on them. Therefore, as was aforesaid, the princes with the greater part of the nobles slipped away gradually from the camp at night, while all the rest of the multitude retained hope of the former returning and that they themselves could refresh their spirits. Meanwhile, unexpectedly in the dead of night, from silence a clamour arose in the camp. The wicked mob of Saracens was shown to be present, betrayed by the arrows and javelins.

While each of [the Christians] tried to take care of their lives, therefore, and by some means or other to withdraw themselves by flight from the swift swords on their necks, the barbarous multitude flung them- selves suddenly into the camp of the Christians. They struck the wretched limbs of the pilgrims—who were so weak it was an effort to breathe—with arrows and outstretched swords.

Here and here the worshippers of Christ were slaughtered by the worshippers of idols and there was not one who could resist being cut down: no rest for the weary, no relief for the dying. Those who were present were destroyed to complete extinction; nothing from the opposite side except the horrid voice of the people of those who exhorted each other with dog-like grins: 'pilgrims to the slaughter!' And so until at last the sun grew hot on the fifth day, the Christians wandering all over were captured and cut down like sheep.[62]

---

[62] *Annales Herbipolenses*, MGH SS 16. 5–6: *Omnis vero multitudo equitum et armatorum regem comitata ab urbe Nicea profecta est, et precedente Foca, quem rex Gretie ductorem eis constituerat, Yconium tendebat. Ingressi igitur solitudinem longissimam, cum nichil eorum que usui ciborum apta viderentur invenirent, tandem defitienti- bus cibariis que sibi preparaverant, anima eorum, ut scriptum est, paulatim in malis thabescebat. Progrediebantur tamen spe potius adiuti quam virium robore; et modo illis modo istis fame defitientibus, moriebantur tam hom- ines quam iumenta sine intermissione. Quid plura? Quadragesima demum die postquam a Nicea profecti sunt, multis repleti labouribus et erumpnis, desertum Yconio vicinum intraverunt. Nec satis erat, nichil rerum quibus vesci liberet per tot iam dies repertum fuisse; quin etiam, que solum ad vite solatium hucusque invente fuerant, defecerunt aque. Itaque dolor dolori additur, et in hac tribulatione profectio tarda quintum usque diem extenditur. Cum interim Sarraceni reges fama preeunte perterriti, in auxilium regis Yconiorum convenerunt , et habito ereptionis sue consilio, loca angustiarum preoccupant, et unanimiter ad pugnam parati, pro patria vivere sive mori mutua cohortatione decertant. Missis ergo ut mos est in obviam suis exploratoribus. Debilitatem exercitus christiani, inediam quoque et lassitudinem tam virorum quam etiam equorum diligenter exploratam qui missi fuerant summa cum festinatione renuntiant. Iam sol ad occasum declinabat, iam quarta dies finierat, et ecce veniunt qui regi Cunrado et principibus aquam potabilem ad radices cuiusdam montis excelsi nuper se reperisse aiunt. Ad quorum relationem rex opido exhilaratus, clam ut si ita sit videat, ad montem qui plus minusve quattuor miliaribus a castris distabat, cum suis properat. Et eo moram faciente, primus post eum dux Welpho, deinde dux Austrie Heinricus, postremo dux Fridericus qui postea regni suscepit gubernacula, ad extremum episcopi comites et omnes viri robustiores pro desiderio aque festinabant. Plus enim siti quam fame labouraverant, quia in heremo tanta se ferarum copia obtulerat, ut habundanter aliquando totus inde reficeretur exercitus. Principibus itaque cum maxima parte nobilium paulatim ut dictum est et in noctu recedentibus a castris, omnis reliqua multitudo ea spe retenta est, ut illis redeuntibus, ipsi quoque irent ad refocillandam animam resumptis viribus: cum interim in- tempeste noctis silentio clamor in castris oritur, ex inproviso sagittariorum iaculis prodita nefanda Sarracenorum turba, adesse monstratur. Cuilibet ergo temptanti vite consulere et pernici fuga inminenti cervicibus gladio se quolibet modo subtrahere, barbara multitudo christianorum se castris repente infudit, mizeros et vix pre laboure spirantes*

Our annalist was familiar with Horace and with classical accounts of warfare. He was also inclined to offer biblical references to evoke certain resonances in his readers.

One of these is the image of Conrad's army being forty days in the desert. The figure is not to be taken literally. The elements of the account that seem authentic both in their vivacity and their correspondence with the *Annals of Magdeburg* are that the army was suffering terribly from lack of supplies, and that the senior nobility were some distance from the main part of the army when it was attacked. The last annalistic account to be considered here is that of the *Annals of Pöldhe*. This annalist was supportive of King Conrad and positively disposed towards the goals of the crusade. As with the *Annals of Würzburg*, the account here seems to have included eyewitness reports by returned crusaders in its depiction of events. The fact that the account is set down with a few ungrammatical sentences suggests the annalist at Pöldhe might have been copying from another work and introduced some errors.[63] Partly because of this difficulty and partly from the fact that there is no published translation in English it has been unjustly neglected by modern English and American historians.

> After this, having accepted the reply of the
> Greek king with regard to the option of which of
> the three designated regions he [Conrad] wished
> to enter, on the advice of his magnates and
> conducted by Greek guides he took the desert
> route leading to Armenia.
>
> Certain of those who accompanied him on this
> route tell that from the first this was the
> intention of the king on this journey: that with
> the foot soldiers being worn out by starvation,
> inexperienced in war and therefore less aware of
> the dangers—some of them having already
> perished from many different sorts of calamity—
> they ought to hasten to Jerusalem, after they
> had received from him expenses to cover their
> need. When this became widely known [the foot
> soldiers] were said to have fallen immediately
> into so great an agitation of spirits that they

---

artus peregrinorum modo sagittis modo stricto mucrone resolvit. Passim ceduntur Christi cultores ab ydolorum cultoribus, nec erat qui resisteret caedentibus; nulla dabatur lassis requies, nulla quies morientibus. Delentur qui aderant usque ad internitionem, nichilque audiri poterat nisi altus dolor et emissus cum clangore gemitus morientium, nichil ex opposito nisi horrida vox: "In iugulos peregrine!" plebis invicem se caninis quibus- dam rictibus exhortantium. Itaque usquequo quinta demum die sol incalesceret, christiani per devia queque sicut oves errabundi feriuntur, capiuntur.

[63] I have checked the earlier of the two surviving manuscripts, Oxford, Bodleian Library, Laud. Misc. 633, against the edition published in the *Monumenta Germaniae Historica Scriptores*.

decided to set up for themselves a certain Bernard as their leader, saying 'because he disdains to keep the people with him, we refuse to have him as king!'

In order to calm these waves the king gave way to the others and attempted that which he expected would not turn out well and in this he suffered in all respects such troubles as no one would believe, unless he had experience [of them].

Therefore, after wandering through the aforementioned desert for two or three days' march, they found the tents of herdsmen and flocks of sheep, which the commoners, eager for plunder, interpreted as an omen of their future prosperity, but the outcome taught them otherwise.

Having seized what came to hand, they went forth from there. For fourteen days they were following wrong paths through awful wilderness and they fell upon places of dread and vast infertility, where of a plague caused by famine and by certain floods many thousands died. Many perished also from the arrows of the Turcopoles and Saracens. There, also, Bernard, Count of Plötzkau, on a certain rock died with a crowd.

Many also were carried off captive by Persians and Saracens.
After many thousands had been destroyed through these and various other misfortunes, since they could not survive any more—not only men but even the beasts of burden being worn out by the barrenness of the land and not even water could be found to restore life into them—they turned aside from their route in order to relieve the evil of want under the very real likelihood of death.

What is more, most of the Christians died, with the barbarians incessantly throwing darts and surrounding them with noise. Many indeed, because their situation was so oppressive, were longing for death.

An eclipse of the sun took place on the sixth hour of seventh kalends November [26 October].

The faithful who were present narrate that for fourteen days and continuously in the nights, with an effort that can hardly be believed, the king held out against the enemy with arms and on foot. The king, furthermore, being struck on the head by an arrow, was for a long time weakened and in no little discomfort. By the secret judgement of God, which nevertheless is always true, none of the catastrophes passed by our men.

And this above all was most wretched to be seen, when one of the pagans as a joke to amuse his own peo- ple created an intolerable insult to the faithful by taking a helmet from a beheaded Christian and placing it on his own head as victor. Therefore a certain follower of the king, choking with rage, before all the rest set upon the boasting barbarian and took off the head with the helmet and therefore caused grief to the pagan's associates and some measure of consolation for the Christians.[64]

---

[64] *Annales Palidenses, MGH SS 16. 82–3: Post hec ad responsum regis Grecie accepta optione, quam trium adire vellet presignatarum regionum, secundum dispositionem magnatuum suorum previis ductoribus Grecorum arripuit iter deserti, tendens ad Armeniam. Tradunt aliqui vie huius comites, primo regis hanc intentionem fuisse, quo pedites inedia fatigati nec bellorum gnari ideoque minus cauti periculorum, cum iam nonnulli multigena clade perirent, acceptis ab eo pro indigentia sumtibus Ierosolimam properarent; quo propalato tanta mox illi commotione 5 animi prolapsi feruntur, ut Bernhardum quendam deliberarent constituere sibi ducem: 'Nos', aientes, 'quia spernit habere plebem, recusemus et eum sequi regem!' [0]Fluctus hos mitigaturus rex, que non bene Ventura sperabat reliquis consenciens adtemtabat, laboures in his omnibus sustinens, quales neminem nisi expertum credere constat. Prenotatum itaque desertum duorum seu trium dierum itinere perlustrantes, reppererunt tabernacula pastorum et greges ovium, quod vulgus prede cupidum, aliter quam finis docuit, interpretabatur sue deinceps prosperitatis auspicium. Direptis que ad manum occurrerant, exinde 14 diebus per horribilem eremum, avia secuti, locum horroris et vaste solitudinis inciderunt, ubi pestilentia famis et qui- busdam inundationibus multa milia occubuerunt; multi a Turcopolis et Sarracenis sagittis interierunt, ubi et Bernardus comes de Ploceke in quadam petra cum magna multitudine interiit; multi etiam a Persis et Saracenis captivi abducti sunt. His et aliis diversis calamitatibus multis milibus extinctis, quoniam amplius subsistere nequiverunt consumti a sterilitate terre non solum homines sed et iumenta, quippe quibus refocillandis nec aqua potuit inveniri, reflexere viam, malum inopie propiore mortis necessitate levaturi. Enimvero circumstre- pentibus barbaris et tela indesinenter iacientibus, christianorum occubuere plurimi; multis equidem, quia tempus in arto fuit, non minus erat optabile mori. Eclipsis solis facta est 7. Kal. Novembr. hora diei 6. Relacio fidelium est eorum qui intererant, 14 dies continuatis noctibus regem armatum et pedes euntem adversus hostes laboure vix credibili durasse; qui etiam sagitta capite percussus, non modico adtenuatus est incommodo per longum tempus. Occulto autem Dei iudicio semper tamen vero, nil plagarum*

The information provided in this account is fascinating and solves a number of problems. There has been some confusion over the events outside Nicea where the German army divided, with a number of modern accounts suggesting that all the foot soldiers followed Otto of Freising on the coastal route westwards, while the knights of the army accompanied King Conrad on the eastern road. But although the German army certainly did divide and a large contingent set off westwards under the leadership of Otto of Freising, such accounts have a hard time explaining why, when Conrad turned back, it was the foot soldiers who were annihilated while the knights escaped. Why were there large numbers of foot soldiers with Conrad if they had departed with Otto of Freising? The answer, according to the account of the Pöldhe annalist, seems to be that while Conrad proposed such a division, a considerable body of crusaders did not accept his proposal. Indeed, they went so far as to mutiny, setting up a certain Bernard as their leader and departing eastwards in the belief, initially justified, that that they could survive on plunder. The idea that the majority of the German army and not just the knights went eastwards is explicitly supported by Odo of Deuil.[65] It is worth pausing here a moment and noting again what the annalist is telling us. A section of the German army, invited to leave and find their way to Antioch via the coastal route, were in such turmoil of spirits that they repudiated Conrad as their king. How radical was this action? What traditions were at work that gave precedence for such a mutiny? The most striking precedent for the deposition of a German king was that in 1077 by the Saxon and south German nobility, who elected Rudolf of Rheinfelden to challenge Henry IV for the crown.[66] But in 1147, the 'electorate' were a crowd of foot-soldiers, not senior nobles, and there was no rival nobleman chosen to represent the mutinous crusaders. Although Wilhelm Bernhardi believed the 'certain' Bernard mentioned here to be Bernard of Spanheim, elderly Duke of Carinthia, this seems to be a rare error, as Count Bernhard of Truchsen, younger son of Count Englebert of Spanheim (who did not hold the title of Duke of Spanheim), marched west, not east, and later died in the company of Otto of Freising.[67] Nor is the 'certain' Bernard the count of Plötzkau, also mentioned by our annalist, but carefully referred to by his full title, in contrast with the otherwise unknown Bernard.[68] These commoners on the Second Crusade, following the example of the First

---

nostros preteriit. Quod potissimum erat videre mizeria, cum unus gentilium obtruncato christicole galeam auferens, sibi quasi victor inposuit, atque suis inde ludibrium, ita fidelibus intolerabile prebuit obprobrium. Unde quidam regis familiaris, accensus ira, pre aliis tripudiantem barbarum inpetens cum galea caput abstulit, et proinde sociis mesticiam et qualemcunque respirationem christianis tribuit.

[65] OD, p. 88.

[66] I.S. Robinson, *Henry IV of Germany, 1056–1106* (Cambridge, 1999), pp. 153–204.

[67] W. Bernhardi, *Konrad III*, p. 628. For Bernard of Spanheim see *Annales Reicherspergenses*, MGH SS 17. 464. H. Dopsch 'Die steirischen Otakare. Zu ihrer Herkunft und ihren dynastischen Verbindungen' in Gerhard Pferschi (ed.), *Das Werden der Steiermark. Die Zeit der Traungauer* (Veröffentlichungen des steiermärkischen Landesarchives, 10, Graz, Vienna and Cologne, 1980), pp. 116–18; OF, pp. 60–61.

[68] For Bernard, count of Plötzkau, in a crusading context see also *Annales Pegavienses*, MGH SS 16. 250.

Crusaders—who threatened to leave the princes with only the bearer of the Holy Lance as their leader[69]—rather than that of Rudolf, were prepared to organize themselves in opposition to the policy of the nobility. Did this reflect the practice of those who came to join the army having already marched in their own contingents, some which had conducted attacks on Jewish communities? Did it reflect a sense that they saw the expedition as ultimately being under the direction of the pope rather than any secular figure of authority? Unfortunately we cannot take the evidence much further.

What we can conclude with some confidence, due to the consistency of these accounts, is that the turbulent masses of the Second Crusade found themselves in a desperate situation due to the bareness of the late October landscape in the Anatolian heights. Their hope that they would be sustained through pillage had led them to defy the king, who had reluctantly followed their lead. An initial success in finding supplies proved shortlived and the Muslim enemies of the crusaders, led by Mas'ud, monitored the movements of the Christian forces, seeking for opportunities to attack. When—on 26 October 1147—a considerable gap opened up between the commoners and the senior nobles of the German army, with the latter riding away to a source of water, Mas'ud's forces struck. The more lowly Christian troops were annihilated by arrow fire and although the king himself and his nobles did not immediately abandon the foot-soldiers and non-combatants they were forced to do so after the king had been wounded by an arrow and the count of Plötzkau killed. While Conrad and his mounted colleagues survived to recuperate at Constantinople, the more lowly members of the army suffered huge losses. William of Tyre's estimate was that Conrad preserved only about 10% of his army, the other 90% being killed or made captive.[70] William was Chancellor of the Kingdom of Jerusalem from 1174 and Archbishop of Tyre from 1175 to his death c.1185. Thus he was familiar with the traditions of the region, and while his Chronicon took its final form after redrafting in 1184, some thirty-seven years after these events, William explicitly stated that he had heard accounts from those who had participated in the events of the Second Crusade.[71] A careful and meticulous scholar, William might nevertheless have been exaggerating Conrad's losses to emphasize the tragic outcome of an expedition that had appeared to hold the potential dramatically to improve the position of the Latin Kingdom of Jerusalem. Whatever the exact proportion of survivors to captured and slain, there is no doubt that the losses were catastrophic. As the Pöldhe annalist put it, 'when afterwards the king returned to Constantinople, he brought back with him only a few of the great army that he had previously possessed'.[72]

[69] C. Kostick, The Social Structure of the First Crusade pp. 142–43.

[70] William of Tyre, Chronicon, ed. R.B.C. Huygens, CC 63 (Turnhout, 1986), p. 742.

[71] Ibid., p. 747.

[72] Annales Palidenses, MGH SS 16. 83: Postea rex Constantinopolin repetens, paucos admodum de grandi exercitu

The destruction of Conrad's army was not only a consequence of inadequate supply. Other contributing factors were the lack of cohesion in the army from even before its various contingents had assembled; the full-blown mutiny outside Nicea; the king being borne away with the crowds despite his sense that they were headed for disaster; and the commoners and the nobles foraging for themselves in a situation that allowed the division between them to be exploited by Mas'ud. In his recent reflections on the failure of the Second Crusade, G.A. Loud deduces on *a priori* grounds that as a small fighting core of princes and knights survived to reach Jerusalem and attempt an attack on Damascus, 'one would wonder whether the armies of the Second Crusade were any more disorderly, worse led, or more burdened with hangers-on that other medieval expeditions.'[73] Despite the great admiration this author has for the work and scholarship of G.A. Loud, on this occasion—based on treating the *Annals of Würzburg* and the *Annals of Póldhe* as important and unjustly neglected sources—it seems necessary to disagree. The conclusion of this article is, in fact, almost entirely the opposite. Conrad III's army in Anatolia was more disorderly, worse led and more burdened with hangers-on than any other European military expedition since Peter the Hermit's army of the First Crusade.

---

quem prius habuerat secum reduxit.
[73] G.A. Loud, 'Some Reflections on the Failure of the Second Crusade', *Crusades*, 4 (2005), pp. 1–14, here p. 3.

The more I wanted to understand how environment, warfare and politics came together in the medieval period, the more I was drawn to seeking information about climate from sources that are not usually taken into account by historians, such as tree rings and ice cores. The establishment of reliable chronologies based on these proxies for climate information has come on in leaps and bounds in the twenty-first century. Armed with data from these sources historians have new tools for contextualising events: even events concerned with theology.

Saints Lives are the most common type of medieval text. Hagiography was a popular genre for both readers and writers. They are typically studied outside of a political context and certainly outside an environmental context. Rather, scholars are highly fixated on the subliminal messages in the imagery of the texts. Conferences on hagiography present papers on such topics as *Male Anxiety in the Life of Saint Cecilia: Examining England from Ælfric to Chaucer* or *Shaping Space and Time in Different Uses of the Old English Translation of Saint Christopher.*

Having sat down properly with the thirty-eight volumes of *MGH* I was ambitiously compiling a chronology of all interesting environmental reports 400 – 1000 CE when I came to a life of St Mansuy by Adso of Montier-en-Der. What struck me about the events described in the text was that they were very vivid and realistically presented. My intuition was that we were not being presented with fictitious challenges resolved by the wonderful powers of the saint, but actual ones concerning drought and plague. How could I test this hypothesis? By seeing if the local tree rings confirmed the drought. The ever generous Francis Ludlow drew on his expertise to check for me and the match was extraordinary, as you'll see.

Not only does this mean we can understand the circumstances in which this particular text was written far more accurately than had been the case and not only did it now reveal a hidden conflict between reformers and concervatives in and around the monastery, but it confirms the value of a methodology that has never before been applied to such texts. A methodology that has only recently become available thanks to advances in dendrochronology. Potentially, this could be an entirely new frontier in medieval studies.

A scourge of sickly disaster, having been driven
through the people by the judgment of God, became

red-hot. For with a likeness to the plague of the groin that formerly swept away the people of Italy, a certain lateral pain with a renewed bud was strewn everywhere. And advancing with fatal success, the plague spread far and wide to the borders of the regions, and thus from an evil beginning there was a serious accumulation of sicknesses: the commoners died, the notable people perished. With no differentiation between the genders or the social orders the streams of dead were rolled along the ground.[1]

A fundamental difficulty that all medieval historians face as they examine their source texts is that of assessing the extent to which the material under study expresses a new idea or carries new information, as opposed to it being merely a repetition of long-establish formulations. A more subtle challenge still is in recognizing the traditions within which an author is writing, but simultaneously appreciating how he or she is adapting ideas that seem to be mere *topoi* in order to apply them in a fresh and original manner. Thus, the apparent contradiction in two medieval authors who share a close intellectual and theological framework urging the destruction of one another can often be resolved by appreciating their respective recasting of the common idea. In one of his typically precise and insightful discussions of eleventh-century church reform, for example, I.S. Robinson shows that both the pro-papal party and the imperial polemicists invoked the idea that in the past the Church had basked in a 'golden age' that was now lost. The rival factions differed fundamentally, however, in their understanding of when that happy period was and in how to define its main features.[2]

One prolific tenth-century author whom it is worth analyzing with regard to this dialectic of innovation clothed in conservative literary tradition is Adso, abbot of Montier-en-Der (near Toul, modern day north-eastern France). In particular, in Adso's *Miracles of St Mansuy* there are some statements concerning drought and plague that would be notable, if we could rely upon them as contemporary reports. The current way of thinking about the history of the bubonic plague, for example, is that it came to Europe in two devastating pandemics: the first, the 'Plague of Justinian', breaking out in the Near East in 541; the second the Black Death, which reached Europe in 1348. It is believed that in between these

---

[1] Adso of Montier-en-Der, *Opera Hagiographica*, ed. M. Goullet, *CCCM* 198 (Turnhout, 2003), hereafter *AD*, 166: *Morbosae calamitatis clades acta Dei iudicio per populos incanduerat. Nam instar inguinariae pestis, quae quondam populos Italiae corripuerat, quidam lateralis dolor ubique rediuiuo germine spargitur, ac laetiferis inualescens successibus, regionum finibus late peruagatur, sicque, quodam malo auspicio, serie cumulata morborum, plebes pereunt, populi concidunt, sin differentia utriusque sexus et ordinis, volvuntur agmina mortuorum.*
[2] I.S. Robinson, 'Reform and the Church, 1073 – 1122', in *The New Cambridge Medieval History IV: c. 102 – c. 1198, Part 1*, ed. D. Luscombe and J. Riley-Smith (Cambridge, 2004), 268–334.

two periods there were no further outbreaks of bubonic plague. It would be very significant indeed if Adso were reliably reporting a new episode in the *Miracles of St Mansuy* as this would indicate that rather than disappearing, *Yersinia pestis* lingered in Europe and under certain circumstances could bring about a local epidemic.

Adso was abbot of Montier-en-Der, in the patrimony of Toul, from at least from 17 January 968, when he is mentioned in an act of Count Herbert of Vermandois.[3] He remained in that position until 992, when he retired to make the pilgrimage to Jerusalem. Dying in the course of his journey across the Aegean, Adso was buried on one of the Cyclades islands.[4] The spirit informing Adso's copious writings was that of reform: earlier in the tenth century, Montier-en-Der had been the scene of conflict between reformers inspired by Gorze and those monks loyal to their accustomed practices and to their accustomed relationships with the local aristocracy. Bishop Gauzelin of Toul (922-962) having pushed matters so far as to lead the then current community to disperse, repopulated the monastery of Montier-en-Der with monks from St Evre (Aprus), which had been reformed in 936.[5]

Not only did Adso sustain this reformed monastery as abbot and write polemics against those resistant to reform, whom he labelled ministers of Satan,[6] but he was also part of a network of like-minded scholarly intellectuals, including Abbo of Fleury (c.945–1004); Richer of Reims, the historian (d.c.998); Adalberon, archbishop of Reims (d.989) and Gerbert of Aurillac - Pope Sylvester II (c.946–1003). An avid collector of books, the library at Montier-en-Der while Adso was abbot was an impressive one.[7]

Probably Adso's most popular work – with over 170 medieval copies surviving in manuscript – was his reply to a request of Queen Gerberga of West Francia (c.913–969), the wife of French king Louis IV d'Outremer (936–954) and sister of Otto I 'the Great' (936–973), that Adso explain his thinking on the coming of the Antichrist. The resulting text, *Letter on the Origin and Time of the Antichrist*, was composed between 949 and 954.[8] Flattering the royal authorities, Adso reassured them that the end times were not yet upon the world, because the Franks had inherited the

---

[3] A. Calmet, *Histoire éccliastique et civile de Lorraine*, 4 (Nancy, 1728), 1. *preuves*, col. 380 f.

[4] *AD*, xvi.

[5] For Bishop Gauzelin of Toul and the early-tenth century reform movement see J.B.W. Nightingale, *Monasteries and Patrons in the Gorze Reform: Lotharingia c.850 – 1000* (Oxford, 2001).

[6] Adso, *De ortu et tempore Antichristi: necnon et tractatus qui ab eo dependunt,* ed. D. Verhelst, *CCCM* 45 (Turnhout: Brepols, 1976), p. 22.

[7] See Daniel Verhelst, 'Adso of Montier-en-Der and the Fear of the Year 1000', in *The Apocalyptic Year 1000*, ed. R. Landes, A. Gow and D. van Meter (Oxford, 2003), 81–92.

[8] Adso, *De ortu*; for discussion, see Simon Maclean, 'Reform, Queenship and the End of the World in Tenth-Century France; Adso's "Letter on the Origin and Time of the Antichrist" Reconsidered', *Revue Belge de Philologie et d'Histoire*, 86 (2008), 645–75, where the attribution of the composition of the letter to Adso is called into question.

rightful mantle of the Roman Empire and a new and happy kingdom would come about.[9]

The text under consideration here, *Miracles of St Mansuy,* was written at the invitation of Gerard, bishop of Toul (963–994).[10] As the anonymous later *De diversis casibus Dervensis coenobii et miraculis s. Bercharii* later put it. 'He [Adso] eloquently composed a life of St Mansuy, who was the first to have been sent to this city by Peter the Apostle himself, at the entreaty and command of St. Gerard, bishop of Toul.'[11] Adso's own prologue to the *vita* is a dedication to Gerard.[12]

The saint who provides the subject matter of Adso's work is not to be confused with the saint of the same name who was bishop of Milan from 676–685. Adso's miracle worker was the first bishop of Toul, sent to Gaul around 365 by Pope Damasus I, and not, as Adso, followed by the author of *De diversis* wanted to believe, at the direct instruction of St. Peter. In a metrical opening to his work, Adso describes Mansuy as coming from Ireland, which might well be a more authentic piece of information.[13] The book then is composed in two parts, the first being an entirely fanciful account of the supposed life of Mansuy. From the divine signs, both celestial and earthly, that accompanied Mansuy's early years, to his journey to Rome and ordination by St. Peter, to his mission to Gaul, Adso supplements what little he can have known about the saint with suitable episodes for establishing the miracle-working qualities of his subject.

The centerpiece of the proselytizing efforts of the saint revolve around the story of a very young pagan prince of Toul, who slips into the Moselle one day and is swept away into the depths of the river. With a fine eye for drama, Adso writes of how the whole town mourns for their young prince, with the king (Leon) and queen nearly insensible from grief. Before the funeral is conducted, Mansuy appears in her sleep to the worthy queen (who had for some time been secretly taking instruction in Christianity) and promises that if she faithfully represents him to the king, he will restore the body of the boy so that it can be properly buried. To the astonishment of everyone, especially the king, the saint brings the body of the prince out of the swirling water and then with a spasm, the boy comes back to life on the banks of the river. Having seen the torments of Hell, the boy desires baptism. Immediately, the rest of the

---

[9] See A.A. Latowsky, *Emperor of the World: Charlemagne and the Construction of Imperial Authority 800-1299* (Ithaca, 2013), pp. 71–2.

[10] For Gerard, see J.B.W. Nightingale, 'Bishop Gerard of Toul (963-94) and Attitudes to Episcopal Office', in *Warriors and Churchmen in the High Middle Ages. Essays presented to Karl Leyser,* ed. T. Reuter (London, 1992), 41–62.

[11] *De diversis casibus Dervensis coenobii et miraculis s. Bercharii, Acta Sanctorum ordinis Sancti Benedicti,* ed. L. d'Achéry & J. Mabillon, 9 (Paris, 1668–1701) 2.844–61, here 849: *Hic etiam precibus ac jussione S. Gerardi Tullensis urbis Episcopi vitam B. Mansueti primi dirigente Petro Apostolo ipsius urbis Pontificis disertissime composuit.*

[12] *AD,* 131.

[13] Ibid., 132.

townspeople rushed to throw down their pagan idols, be baptized and with unanimous acclaim elected Mansuy their bishop.[14]

Part two of *Miracles of St Mansuy* is written in just as conventional a fashion as the first, at least so it appears. The section is framed with a self-effacing chapter on the unworthiness of the author, which prepares the reader for edifying examples of the saint's intercession on behalf of his people in the years after his death. And Adso does deliver on this expectation. But he achieves this by skipping several centuries in a series of brief chapters and coming directly to his own times. This is the sense in which we have a novel content in a traditional form: for the closing chapter of the book includes episodes that read rather more like history and polemic than a Saint's Life. This is not to say that the usual post-mortem deeds of the saint are lacking. The early chapters of the second part demonstrate that the relics of St Mansuy are able to bring sight to the blind, to expel demons from the possessed and to cure leprosy.[15]

When we reach the final section, the tone of the text remains the same, but the content becomes far richer in detail and is clearly organized to give a detailed description of the harrowing events of the recent past. One indication that Adso's purpose in writing has taken on a new direction in these chapters is their length. There is a considerable imbalance in favour of the period after 963 and the appointment of Gerard to the bishopric of Toul. It was this Gerard who commissioned *Miracles of St Mansuy* and Adso was clearly very keen to emphasize how important was the saint to the bishop's goals in office. Gerard, former canon of Cologne, on being appointed to the see visited the church in which the relics were kept and vowed to renovate it. The section dealing with this period amounts to a third of the entire work.

With vivid imagery, Adso in this section recounts a series of trials for the community that he must have also experienced in person and which would have tested his responsibilities as abbot. With rain falling only rarely from the sky, the fields became unusually barren; crops began to fail due to arable lands becoming covered with a dry crust. As the earth cracked open, an unbearable heat surged over the toiling men. Almost consumed by the heat and with the land having been burned up completely, Adso recalled in horror that the crops were entirely lost. The reason for these divine punishments was later discovered: a long while before the drought, certain unfaithful people had rebuked God, the cloudless sky was a sign from heaven above, which stretched out unmercifully over the unyielding earth below.

In those days, moreover, with righteous anger shining brightly out of the heavens, by command of bishop Gerard, it was announced to the suffering people that fasts of three days were what was needed to assuage God's wrath. And because mere mortals could not hope to oppose divine vengeance, the community looked to St Mansuy as their protector. A procession of more than two thousand people took place with

---

[14] Ibid.,137–145.
[15] Ibid., 156–7.

the shrine containing the saint's blessed body and the community carried it to the boundaries of their thirsting fields, hoping that with his intervention the heat would not worsen. Giving voice in the highest, with hymns resounding out to the heavens, praising God, and with weeping voices they implored the protection of blessed Mansuy.

On the return of the procession to the church of St Mansuy an enormous crash suddenly reverberated twice from the heavens, interrupting the singing of the psalms and astonishing the souls of every person present. Then the thunderstruck multitude, which on that day had gathered together more than two thousand people from every direction, went to the Church of St-Evre. As they did so, clouds began to gather in the sky and release bountiful rains.

Not long after this miracle, however, God gazed upon the sins of the people and His judgment took the form of a terrible plague. For 'with a likeness to the plague of the groin that once swept away the people of Italy, a certain lateral pain with a renewed bud was strewn everywhere'. The plague spread far and wide to the borders of the regions, rapidly killing huge numbers of people regardless of gender or social order.

Nor were those who had been seized by that kind of suffering permitted to survive in any fashion beyond three days. Once arrived, the plague rushed into Toul in devastating fashion. Gerard, groaning, gave memorials over coffins seen with his own eyes in which seven or ten bodies had been placed so that they might be covered and buried. The bishop was hemmed in with personal danger, with so many people dying around him. At last he came to the decision that once again the protector St Mansuy had to be taken up from his place of rest, so as to be placed between the living and the dead. And so after three days of fasting an assembly of the people gathered together for a second time with the blessed body of the saint. The procession walked to the church at Ecrouves (in the diocese of Toul), where it was believed that blessed Mary mother of God was often given to providing miracles.

United in the presence of the highest empress of Heaven, mother of all persons and naturally of her flock, the fury of the plague was seen to lessen to a small extent. But this did not assuage the panic of the frightened people. So once more an even greater procession took place with the saint's relics, this time along the River Meurte, near its junction with the Moselle, where stood the convent of Bouxières-aux-dames. With choirs in various rows having sung the psalms to raise everyone's spirits, they undertook what was a major march (perhaps five hours in length), to spend the night at the convent, Gerard among them.

Adso, almost certainly an eyewitness, found it impossible to describe how incredible was the multitude of people, crowded together in bands, with all the social orders mixed: whether from villages, from fields or from various regions, all were suddenly uniting as one. From everywhere nuns together with the innumerable flocks of the Christian faithful hurried all the way to the bank of the river Meurthe. Some of the crowds tucked up their loose clothes and waded through water up to the waist and to the admiration of the multitude were able to ford the river. Eventually, with joyful cries they returned Saint Mansuy to his church, all the while offering him prayers and gifts.

At the door of the church, the sun shone with such a powerful heavenly radiance that the whole of the roof was shining brightly. Plainly, it seemed that the saint wished to be buried in that church. Then, very many people began to weep for joy, while they were ignorant as to why these tears had been forced from them, unless it was because with the saint having been moved by the piety of his people he had aroused heavenly flows in the minds of his children. Nor indeed did the bishop himself, who shared the abundance of this wonderful sweetness with the people, refrain from tears.

It seemed to Adso that from then on the plague abated, thanks to the processions, so that plainly the whole people should know that they stood before the house of Israel in divine radiance of the Lord and that for each one of his sheep Saint Mansuy became an excellent helper against adversity in battle.[16]

This long final section of the *Miracles of St Mansuy* presents a challenge to understand and appreciate. Among the questions that arise from this material is one very central one: to what extent are the events described based on real experiences? If they did happen, can they then be dated? Fortunately, there exist both historical sources and natural proxy sources that allow these questions to be answered.

In Monique Goullet's commentary on the text she makes the valid point that the miracle of the exhibition of a saint's relics ending a catastrophic drought is a commonplace.[17] But this does not mean there was no drought. If Adso were inventing a scenario to demonstrate the ability of St Mansuy to alter the natural environment he could just as easily have chosen the opposite effect, that of the saint preventing a flood. Why the ending of a drought? Perhaps because the diocese really had experienced a terrible drying up of the land at some point in the years immediately before Adso composed his *vita*? Certainly, the descriptions of the cracked earth, the dry crust on the earth and the unbearable heat read like those of an eyewitness. Moreover, the existence of a drought in Lotharingia at this time finds corroboration and a date thanks to the annals being kept at the monastery of Corvey, on the banks of the Weser (modern-day Germany).

Another monastery that had joined the Gorze reform, Corvey was home to Widukind (fl. 942–973), whose three-volume history of the Saxons was composed initially around 968. This work, of great importance to modern historians, was already achieving fame in its day, as it was much exploited by other medieval writerss who followed him. Among the other monks who benefited from the high standard of learning at Corvey at this time were those interested in keeping brief yearly records. This practice might well have been inspired directly by Bede, as

[16] Ibid., 162–8.
[17] Ibid., 182.

the manuscript upon which they made their entries derived from Northumbria and possibly Bede's monastery of Wearmouth-Jarrow. Having inherited a manuscript upon which Northumbrian events had been recorded for the eighth century alongside the Anglo-Saxon calculations of Easter, first of all monks at Fulda and then at Werden continued the practice, until in the 960s the manuscript came to Corvey and annalists – anonymous to us – there took up the tradition.[18] There is only one line for the year 981 in the *Annals of Corvey*, but it is a crucial one: *Hoc anno nimia siccitas facta est per totum annum.*[19] (In this year an excessive drought happened for the whole year).

The date of 981 for the drought described so intensely in Adso's *Miracles of St Mansuy* fits very well with the *terminus post quem* for that work. A report given by Adso that Bishop Gerard appointed a certain Adam to be abbot of the community at St. Mansuy can be confirmed by a charter dated 15 October 982.[20] Even if it were several years had passed after this date that Adso wrote the *vita*, the memory of the drought would still a strong one.

Moreover, the presence or otherwise of a drought in northern Europe in 981 can be tested against evidence that is independent of the all-too-fallible written sources thanks to the fact that consecutive tree-ring chronologies have now been constructed that allow for annual precision in their data going back far beyond the tenth century. In particular, it is possible to examine oak tree growths for north-eastern France, for north-eastern Germany and south-eastern Germany. Their evidence is very striking, especially that of the French sequence.

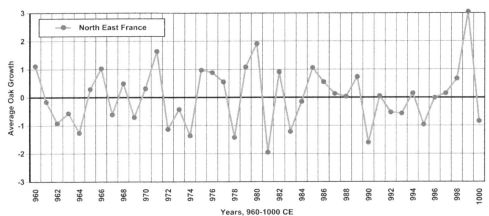

Figure 5. French oak growth patterns from the region around Toul 960 – 1000 AD.[21]

[18] J. Prinz, *Die Corveyer Annalen. Textbearbeitung und Kommentar,* Veröffentlichungen der Historischen Kommission für Westfalen, 10 - Abhandlungen zur Corveyer Geschichtsschreibung, 7 (Münster 1982).
[19] Ibid., p. 39.
[20] *AD*, xxxvi.
[21] My thanks to Dr Francis Ludlow, Marie Sklodowska-Curie Individual Fellow, Trinity College Dublin, for creating this graph, based on data from Ulf Büntgen, *et al.*, '2500

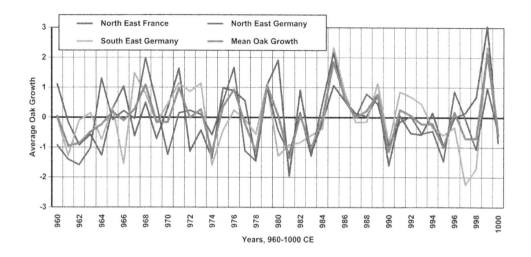

Figure 6. German, French and mean oak growth patterns 960 – 1000 CE.[22]

What the tree-rings testify to is a very difficult year for trees in 981, the worst in the forty years surveyed here. Typically, poor ring growth is a signal for drought, although it is possible for other weather extremes to affect tree growth, such as a local flood, for example, or a protracted winter. By taking into consideration the German chronologies, however, it becomes less likely that the results reflect a local aberration and that what they display is indeed a very strong signal that in 981 northern Europe did indeed suffer from a major drought.

With evidence such as this, historians have an exciting new tool for testing their sources. And put to this test, Adso's *Miracles of St Mansuy* emerges as a text whose description of the terrible impact of a drought is not a *topos*. Combining the information from tree-rings with the report of drought in 981 in the *Annals of Corvey,* the case for the existence of scorching weather that year is very solid. With this knowledge, it becomes possible to gain a new understanding of Adso's methodology in composing his text.

Naturally, Adso's main purpose is that of promoting the cult of St Mansuy by providing the diocese with examples of the power of the relics of the saint to perform miracles. In this regard, the text conforms to very long established traditions; it is formulaic even. But Adso is simultaneously writing on a different level. In his thoughts are the memories of an awful drought, one which, as will be discussed below, was

Years of European Climate Variability and Human Susceptibility', *Science,* 331 (2011), 578–582.
[22] Ibid.

associated with the horrors of famine, horrors that were never too far away from European society in this era. The particular concern that Adso has is not quite that of a historian; this is not the fashioning of a *vita* to preserve a record of events. What seems to be troubling Adso is the impact of the drought (and subsequent plague) on the spiritual confidence of his monks and of the wider community.

If – as Adso accepts without question – the intense suffering of the people of the region arises as a result of the judgment of God, then what was the sin? And what can be done about it? Adso is careful to provide answers to these questions in a work that is not ostensibly about such matters, but which he knows will be read aloud (or sung, in its opening metrical part) before his monks and those of Toul and beyond, especially on 3 September, the feast day of St Mansuy. When the sin that brought the drought was subsequently discovered, it proved to be an act of divine retribution for the *infidelis populus* who a long time before had inveighed against God.[23] The remedy was beyond human management, but fortunately St Mansuy was able to intercede on behalf of the community.

These answers were important for Adso, because the legitimacy of the reform that had been carried out at his monastery with great bitterness was called into question by such a dramatic manifestation of divine disapproval. As a result of his writings, Adso's listeners would be reinforced in their faith and loyalty to the church in two regards. Firstly, it was the unfaithful whose invective against God was the cause of the current disaster. Second, rather than be discouraged in regard to the value of the church in the face of God's wrath, now was the time to rally in great numbers and penitential processions with a saint at the head of them who had the ability to make representation in the heavens. Thus Adso addressed the implications of an all-to-real drought and while providing evidence for the miracle-working powers of the relics of St Mansuy, at the same time reassured the local monastic community of the validity of their practices.

The legacy of the drought, however, was famine and plague. Two other local hagiographies can supplement Adso's information in respect to these subsequent crises: the *Miracles of St Evre* and the *Life of Gerard of Toul*. Once attributed to Adso, but now understood to be a work composed shortly after his death by an anonymous author,[24] the *Miracles of St Evre* has a passage in which a bitter famine is described as attacking nearly the whole people of the diocese. The famine also affected the monks and nuns of the neighbouring towns. Again, bishop Gerard brought together everyone, of whatever social condition and with prayers and hymns, solemnly raised the relics of St. Evre from the grave. With lord Gerard himself presiding, a procession took place that marked the turning point for the hardship of the famine.[25]

---

[23] *AD*, 163.
[24] *AD*, xlvii.
[25] *Ex Miraculis S. Apri*, ed. G. Waitz, *MGH SS* 4 (Hanover, 1841), 520.

Not long after his death, Gerard, the bishop of Toul, who commissioned Adso's work and features in the *Miracles of St. Evre*, became recognised as a saint in his own right and his *vita* was written at the request of one of his successors, Bruno (1002–1054), bishop of Toul. The author chosen to highlight the saintly qualities of Gerard was Widrich, a monk at the monastery of Saint-Evre, a recently reformed monastery whose size and lands had been increased by Gerard. In later years, Widrich would become abbot of St-Evre, St-Mansuy and Moyenmoutier.[26] Bruno, on being elevated to Pope Leo IX (1049-54), issued the first ever Bull of canonization for Gerard and the *Life of Gerard of Toul* was used at the Synod of Rome, 1050, to assist with the making of the case for canonization.[27]

Although belonging to the generation who grew up in the aftermath of the drought, famine and plague, Widrich shows an awareness of these events and incorporates a very vivid account of the outbreak of plague into his text. Having made the point that during the widespread famine of 982 Gerard had given generously to the poor and organized a major procession, Widrich then turned to the subsequent outbreak of plague, the dating of which was probably 983, since it is placed after the famine and before Gerard undertook a pilgrimage to Rome later that year.

Weighed down by their sins, the people of Toul were rebuked by a terrible scourge. By way of punishment, a miserable slaughter filled the streets of the town with human cadavers. With no house free of the dead or dying, all mourned with despair the fleeting nature of life. Then the blessed bishop gathered himself and took responsibility for the people. He was thinking of the various means to treat the disease and of how it would be possible to most quickly rescue the flock with a remedy. Inspired by a divine plan, Gerard announced a three-day fast, and then assembled the people together in a certain square, and with humble and meek worshipful devotion exhumed the glorious bodies of St Mansuy and St Evre, trusting that their protection would lift the imminent peril. With the saints leading the way, in a loud voice the people tearfully prayed around all the streets of the city. But by the hidden judgment of God, the numbers dying of plague swelled on that day, to such an extent that by the time the relics of St Mansuy approached the basilica of the saints, sixteen of the marching multitude joined the grave of the dead.

In order to continue the veneration, however, the bishop of the people did not desist from prayer. With the people having been exhorted to repeat the journey, he visited the crowded monastery of St Evre, and there completed the circuit with the seven penitential psalms, prostrating himself on the ground with the clergy before the bodies of the saints. Rising from there and flooding the earth with his tears, Gerard began the antiphon with the voice of supplication; he maintained it for three hours with people falling down dead in the midst of the multitude. But the

---

[26] I.S. Robinson, *The Papal Reform of the Eleventh Century* (Manchester, 2004), 23–4.
[27] Pope Leo IX, ep.36, *PL* 143, 644–7; E.W. Kemp, *Canonization and Authority in the Western Church* (Oxford, 1948), 62–4.

Almighty for a long time gave a deaf ear to the compassionate tearful prayers of his servant before deciding to end the rage of his plague. Nor did anyone complain about catarrh later in the same year, having become accustomed to being rendered invalid with the plague. But despite this, the virtue of the parade of the magnificent saints was regarded as deservedly legitimate, not because the blessed were believed to be there in any manner but because God with his saints could make the most miraculous works happen.[28]

At the level of miraculous performance, this is a curiously uninspiring account for a work designed to emphasize heavenly approval for the deeds of a saint. When Gerard summoned the people of his diocese together for a ceremony involving the relics of SS. Mansuy and Evre, instead of the plague lessening, it actually intensified and during the long day many people in fact dropped dead. No doubt too many more died in the subsequent days, as it is hard to imagine a worse form of social response to an epidemic than to bring the infected into contact with large numbers of uninfected, especially after all concerned have been weakened by undertaken three days of fasting.

Nor is the conclusion of this episode a rousing endorsement of the powers of the local saints. Nothing good came from their exhibition, but, as Widrich explains, it was still a good idea to parade the relics, not because they were actually present in any manner but because the procession was a demonstration by the community of their belief that God and the saints could make miracles. In other words, it was a demonstration of faith and, echoing Adso, this was a valuable gain in its own right at a time of extreme adversity. Insofar as Gerard was behaving in a saintly manner in this passage, it was not through revealing superhuman powers, but through his model leadership. For Widrich it was naturally a shame that the plague did not abate, but the course of action taken by Gerard was exemplary because the faith of the people was not shaken by the challenge. Gerard's praiseworthy deeds in this episode were that he did not flee the town or passively wait for the plague to abate. He decided to lead ecclesiastical processions and this, while admittedly not effective in medical terms, was valuable for the Church.

Is it possible to tell something of the nature of the plague from the descriptions in Adso and Widrich? From the *Miracles of St Mansuy* in particular, the symptoms very much suggest that *Yersinia pestis* is behind the epidemic. Adso states that it was a plague of the groin – inguinal – like that which once swept away the people of Italy. The term *inguinal* almost certainly derives from the history of Paul of Deacon, who in his entries for 536 and then again for 590 reported that Italy suffered from epidemic outbreaks, the latter being a 'most oppressive plague that they name *inguinaria*. This so devastated the population that from an inestimable multitude hardly any survived.'[29] This plague was responsible

---

[28] Widrich, *Vita S. Gerardi Ep.*, ed. G. Waitz, MGH SS 4 (Hanover, 1841), 449.

[29] Paul the Deacon, *Historia Langobardorum*, ed. L.K. Bethmann & G. Waitz, *MGH S rerum Langobardorum* (Hanover, 1878), III.24, 105: ... *gravissima pestilentia, quam*

for the death of Pope Pelagius II early in 590 and because of this, the section of Paul the Deacon's text describing the plague was much repeated by later writers. It may well have come to Adso via an intermediate source, such as Gregory of Tours, who referred to 'the plague they call *inguinaria*' in his *History of the Franks*[30] and who used the term *inguinaria* again in his work on the miracles of the martyrs, a model text for Adso's own compositions of the same type.[31] There might also possibly be an echo of the early Christian poet Prudentius (d.*c.* 413) present in this description of the plague. Monique Goullet has identified Prudentius as one of Adso's influences.[32] In his *Against Symmachus*, the poet, in explaining that death is not the end, points to nature, where seeds dry up and the dead are committed to a trench 'and though they are buried as in a grave they rise from their tombs and sprout with life anew.'[33]

That Adso was using formulations derived from early Christian Latin works raises once more the question of how much of Adso's description is derivative and how reliable is it for the events he is portraying. Was he simply recycling descriptions inherited from his scholarly reading of past texts? Again, the answer seems to be that Adso certainly did use the work of his predecessors to guide his writings, but that he was addressing very contemporary experience. By explaining that the *inguinal* plague was accompanied by lateral pain and the outbreak of buds all over, he adds details that are not given by Paul the Deacon or Gregory of Tours. Adso's description of the *rediuiuus germen*, 'renewed bud', that sprang up everywhere might well utilize a phrase borrowed from Prudentius.[34] But if so, Adso has reworked the distinctive vocabulary of the poet to suit quite a different purpose; by depicting the life that returns to seeds, rather, he is describing a body covered in swellings.

Other information that is evident from both Adso and Widrich is significant. The plague killed its victims swiftly, within three days, and in very large numbers. The observation that Gerard gave memorials over coffins with seven or even ten bodies crammed into them is very telling, as is the information that there was not one house escaped the outbreak. This epidemic certainly had the kinds of high mortality rates and swift impact associated with the bubonic plague.

---

inguinariam appellant. Quae tanta strage populum devastavit, ut de inaestimabili multitudine vix pauci remanerent.

[30] Gregory of Tours, *Libri Historiarum X*, ed. B. Krusch and W. Levison, *MGH Scriptores rerum Merovingicarum*, 1.1, 2nd edition (Hanover, 1951), X.1, 477: *quam inguinariam vocant.*

[31] Gregory of Tours, *Liber in Gloria Martyrum*, ed. B. Krush, *MGH SS Scriptores rerum Merovingicarum*, 1.2 (Hanover, 1885), 1–111, at 73–4: *Cum autem ad Arvernam regionem lues illa inguinaria adveniret...*

[32] AD, liii–liv.

[33] Prudentius, *Against Symmachus*, ed. and trans. H.J. Thomson, 2 (Cambridge MA, 1949–53), 2.20: *Et more sepuleri obruta de tumulis redivivo germine surgunt.*

[34] AD, 166 ... *ubique rediuiuo germine spargitur.*

The fleas that carry *Yersinia pestis* prefer hosts such as rats and other small animals to humans. But under certain circumstances, when the preferred host is in short supply, the infected fleas will move to a human host. In between outbreaks, fleas with *Yersinia pestis* can reproduce among reservoir populations of burrowing rodents. In such a state – the 'maintenance phase' – *Yersinia pestis* can survive for lengthy periods before attacking human populations once more when the maintenance rodent populations are destroyed for some reason. Perhaps the circumstances of an extreme heatwave and drought in 981 followed by crop failure and grain scarcity in 982 provided the conditions for a disturbance of the rat (or other small animal) population, causing the plague-bearing fleas to seek human hosts, humans whose immune systems were already weakened by the difficulties of those years. Very recent discussion of the Black Death and the information that has been acquired from *Y. pestis* DNA gathered from Black Death plague pits indicates that the great pandemic caused by the pathogen was not due to the appearance of a more virulent strain of the plague but the prevalence of poor health in the population.[35] Adso's account of the *inguinal* plague in the region of Toul in 983 therefore might well be a depiction of the kind of regional outbreaks of plague that, although much less devastating, still occur into modern times, such as that which took place in Los Angeles in 1924.[36]

The text *Miracles of St Mansuy* at one level carries a simple message: St Mansuy was a holy man, to whom God gave the power to work miracles. To convey that message its author, Adso, wrote using tropes and *topoi* with which his listeners would have been very familiar. This is especially true for the first part of the hagiography. Yet at the same time, Adso clearly had contemporary concerns in mind that he wished to address to the local monastic communities. John Nightingale has discussed those concerns that dealt with tensions over property claims.[37] Here, dendrochronological evidence as well as that from historical sources suggests that Adso was also concerned to rationalize a sequence of appalling years that fell upon the region like a nightmare: a severe drought in 981, a famine in 982 and an outbreak of plague in 983. What had the followers of Christ done to deserve such expressions of divine anger? Thanks to the leadership of Bishop Gerard of Toul, the potential for a popular backlash against the reformers, and indeed, against the Christian religion more generally was averted. In particular, Mansuy was a local saint to whom people could rally even when they could not stand before God's wrath.

---

[35] A.G. Carmichael, 'Plague Persistence in Western Europe: A hypothesis', in *Medieval Globe,* 1, Special Double Issue: *Pandemic Disease in the Medieval World* (2014), 157–192.

[36] A.J. Viseltear, 'The Pneumonic Plague Epidemic of 1924 in Los Angeles', *The Yale Journal of Biology and Medicine*, 47 (1974) 47–54.

[37] Nightingale, 'Bishop Gerard of Toul', 44–7.

Reading the text in this fashion, we learn a great deal. Not about St Mansuy, but about the fragility of tenth century northern European society. Adso's world was one of great vulnerability to drought, lacking the resources to avoid a subsequent famine and, worse, a terrible epidemic. That this outbreak might well have been a recurrence of the bubonic plague is a matter of considerable interest to those scientists who today are attempting to understand the historical pattern of epidemics caused by *Yersinia pestis*. What is also evident from the *Miracles of St Mansuy* is a technique through which a reform-minded abbot could address the concerns of his community that had arisen in the wake of these disasters. Of particular relevance to the tradition of intellectual and political church history of which I.S. Robinson is such a master, is how a scholar based around Toul at the end of the tenth century found an effective way to reassure the people of the diocese and encourage them to rally to the Church. In composing this text, Adso adhered to a tradition and structure that would have been readily appreciated and accepted by his listeners. This was very familiar ground, at least in regard to all of the earlier chapters. Yet by the final and easily the most lengthy chapter, Adso shifts the attention of the listener to current events and current arguments. The recent disasters, he assures everyone, were no fault of the church leaders. Indeed, thanks to Bishop Gerard the wrath that had been aroused in God by the faithless was appeased, thanks in particular to Gerard's wisdom in invoking St Mansuy. Above all, the lesson of the saint's miraculous life was for the listener to be unwavering in support for those who had led the local church in recent years.

Chapter 11   The afterlife of Bishop Adhémar of Le Puy

What can Marxists say about religion? Well, perhaps something more than it is the opium of the oppressed. For most of history people have held religious ideas and held them in a fashion that helped them understand the world around them. When the adherents of New Atheism pour scorn on people with reglious views I can't help contrast the present with the past. The idea that religion is irrational and a barrier to clear thinking, or that it is simply a tool for elites to control the oppressed (to be fair to Marx, that wasn't his view, religion also being the heart in a heartless world), just doesn't fit the history and current circumstances of our species.

I'm currently researching Babylonian society and for all their faults, the kings and priests of that world would not reach anywhere near the heights of irrationality that we have currently achieved. Two billionaires with about $200bn each are having a space race, while we have yet to feed, clothe, house and provide clean water to all who need it. We destroy food for the sake of the market. The occasional sacrifice of a 'substitute' king is completely sane in comparison. And at least the kings of the first millenia BCE opened their grain stores at times of famine, instead of allowing speculators to buy up food and raise prices.

Our economic rules, before which we worship as though they were inviolate and Platonic have taken all restraint off abuse of the environment. A frenzy to grab every resource has run away with us and reshaped the planet in a way that is increasingly inimicable to humanity.

My study in the social structure of the First Crusade was not designed simply to find the hidden springs of class conflict but to really try and understand the whole phenomenon, including how in the realm of theology, the people on that expedition understood the universe. An interesting case study arose in this regard with the death of the crusade's main religious voice, the papal legate Adhémar of Le Puy on 28 June 1098. His legacy was fought over in visions that were highly factional, both socially and regionally. And in the reports of his post-mortem return to the crusade we also get a glimpse into the evolution of the Christian theology around what happens to you after death. Adhémar did not go straight to heaven, there to intervene on behalf of the crusaders, but had an ordeal first, a proto-purgatory that suggests the fully worked out notions around that in-between place were still yet to form by the end of the eleventh century CE.

'My brothers should not grieve that my life has
come to an end, because never was I so useful
to them in the past as I will be in the future,
providing they are willing to keep the
commandments of God. As a matter of fact I,
and all my brothers whose life has ended as
mine has, will stay with them, and I will appear
and give them much better advice than
hitherto.'[1]

Bishop Adhémar of Le Puy was the papal legate appointed to journey on
the First Crusade (1096 – 1099) by Pope Urban II.[2] Adhémar led a
sizeable contingent of troops and non-combatants from Provançe, in the
company of the elderly crusader, Count Raymond IV of Toulouse. The
bishop distinguished himself at one of the critical battles of the First
Crusade, that near Dorylaeum 1 July 1097. Adhémar played what was
perhaps an even more critical role in helping prevent the disintegration of
the crusade during its lowest moment. Although the Christian army
captured Antioch on the night of 3 June 1098, within five days they had
themselves become the besieged, with the arrival of an enormous Muslim
army under the command of Kerbogha, atabeg of Mosul. Many prominent
knights abandoned the crusade, letting themselves down over the walls of
the city at knight on ropes. The papal legate was a key figure in
addressing this panic, rallying the princes to make them swear an oath
that they would not abandon the expedition. The victory of the Christian
forces on 28 June 1098 should have secured Adhémar's position as the
most authoritative figure on the crusade, but a plague that subsequently
broke out in the city took his life on 1 August.

Surprisingly, however, this was not the end of Adhémar's
involvement in the leadership of the First Crusade. At least in the sense
that he was popularly believed by the crusaders to have returned to them

---

[1] Raymond of Aguilers, *Historia Francorum qui ceperunt Iherusalem*, ed. John France
(unpublished PhD. thesis: University of Nottingham, 1967). Hereafter RA. I am grateful
to Prof. France for permission to quote from his thesis, which I consider a superior
edition to those of the *Recueil des historiens des croisades Oc.* 3, 235 – 309; *Le 'Liber'
de Raymond d'Aguilers*, ed. J. H. Hill and L. L. Hill (Paris, 1969) and that in Migne,
Patralogia Latina, 155: [Col.0591] - [Col.0668A] to which, nevertheless, references to
the equivalent passages are also given here, as they are more accessible than the
thesis. RA 139; [Col.0620B]: *Et ne doleant, fratres mei, si ego vitam finivi, quoniam
nunquam eis profui tantum quantum prodero, si praecepta Dei servare voluerint. Etenim
cum illis habitabo, et omnes fratres mei qui vitam, ut ego, finierunt; et eis apparebo, et
multo melius quam hactenus consiliabor eos.*
[2] For the role of Bishop Adhémar of Le Puy and his authority on the First Crusade see J.
H. Hill and L. L. Hill, 'Contemporary accounts and the later representation of Adhémar,
Bishop of Le Puy', *Medievalia et Humanistica* 8 (1955), 30 – 8; J. A. Brundage, 'Adhémar
of Puy: the bishop and his critics', *Speculum* 34 (1959), 201 – 12; H. E. Mayer, 'Zur
Beurteilung Adhémars von Le Puy', *Deutsches Archiv für Erforschung des Mittelalters*, 16
(1960), 547 – 52 and I. S. Robinson, *The Papacy 1073 – 1198* (Cambridge, 1990), pp.
350 – 52.

to offer advice and intercede for them with God. The account of Adhémar's experience of the afterlife is told through the work of Raymond of Aguiliers and reveals how the afterlife was perceived by a non-scholastic thinker, but one who was unusually sensitive to the belief that the divine operates in human experience. Raymond's history of the First Crusade was written up in one effort within a year or two of the fall of Jerusalem to the Christian army (15 July 1099).[3] Raymond of Aguilers was a member of the chaplaincy of Count Raymond of Toulouse, raised to the priesthood during the expedition. Crucially, he shared a tent with the key intermediary between this world and the next, a lowly visionary, Peter Bartholomew.

Peter Bartholomew was a servant who had risen to extraordinary prominence during the crusade, by declaring that SS Andrew and Peter had visited him. He claimed that the saints had shown him the location of the Lance that had pierced Christ's side. Although sceptical, not least because, as Collin Morris has shown,[4] Adhémar would have known that the Byzantines claimed to have the same relic at Constantinople, the legate nevertheless utilised the popular enthusiasm for the relic in order to bring about a successful mobilisation of the army against the atabeg of Mosul.

On 3 August 1098, the night after the burial of Adhémar, Peter Bartholomew claimed that the legate had visited him in the chapel of Count Raymond of Toulouse. In the vision, Adhémar explained that he had been in Hell for the period between his death and his burial due his lack of belief in the Holy Lance. While burning in the flames of Hell, the bishop was relieved by the Lord Himself, who presented Adhémar with a robe that protected him from the fire. The robe was that which the legate had given away to a poor person on the occasion of his ordination as bishop of Le Puy.

Adhémar explained that a candle, offered in prayer by the bishop's friends, and three denari that the legate himself had offered to the Holy Lance, were the most effective items in restoring him as he departed Hell. The legate had a message for Bohemond I, prince of Taranto and on of the crusades senior princes: that he was not required to fulfil a vow to take the body of the bishop to Jerusalem. Adhémar then committed his *familia*, his following, to Count Raymond of Toulouse, whose services to them would be rewarded by God. Adhémar explained that none should grieve at his death, because he would stay with them, offering better advice than previously. Those who doubted should open the bishop's tomb where they would see that his face had been entirely burned. The vision of the legate concluded with a warning to all to fear the punishments of Hell and a number of practical commands, including that

[3] RA cxxxix – cxliii.
[4] C. Morris, 'Policy and Visions – The case of the Holy Lance at Antioch' *War and Government in the Middle Ages: essays in honour of J.O. Prestwich*, ed. J. Gillingham and J. C. Holt (Woodbridge, 1984), pp. 33-45.

the Count of Toulouse, together with those of his choosing, appoint a new bishop of Le Puy.[5]

What can we learn of the contemporary concept of the afterlife from this report? Most notably, that there was no neutral space in which the dead bishop resided: no place of purgatory, although there was a purging process.[6] Until he returned to earth to be with and guide the crusade, Adhémar was in Hell. The main reason for this was the fact that he had expressed reservations about the authenticity of the Lance and was therefore punished. Nevertheless, Adhémar's experience in Hell was mediated by both his own past actions and those of the living in a manner that prefigures the development of indulgence. It was the prayers of those who paid for a candle for him and his own contribution for the sake of the Lance that restored Adhémar. It was an act of charity to the poor, the giving away of a robe, that led to Christ himself returning the robe and preventing all harm but for burns to the face that, according to Adhémar's confession, had rightfully been earned through the legate's scepticism regarding the Lance.

Some nine months later, in April 1099, Count Raymond of Toulouse held up the crusade at a deeply unpopular effort to besiege the city of Arqa. By this time the visionary, Peter Bartholomew, was expressing near uncritical support for the goals of Count Raymond and this cost him his life. Arnulf, Chaplain to Robert I Count of Normandy challenged the authenticity of the Lance and the visions of Peter Bartholomew,[7] leading to a dramatic trial by fire and the eventual death of Peter. In his extensive reporting of this episode, three more references to the afterlife of Bishop Adhémar were detailed by the historian Raymond of Aguilers.

Raymond wrote that in the debate about the authenticity of the Lance, the legate visited another Provencal priest, Peter Desiderius.[8] 'I saw the bishop of Le Puy after his death,' said Desiderius, 'and the blessed Nicholas with him, and after saying many things the bishop said this to me: "I am in a choir with the blessed Nicholas, but because I doubted the Lance of the Lord, I, whom in particular ought to have believed, was led to Hell. And there the hair on the right of my head and half my beard was burned. And although I am not suffering punishment,

[5] RA 138 – 140; [Col.0619D]. The See of Le Puy was not filled until 1102, when Pontious de Tournon was appointed.

[6] For the wider context to this issue see Jacques Le Goff, *The Birth of Purgatory* (Chicago: University Press, 1984) and the critique by A. J. Gurevich, 'Popular and Scholarly Medieval Traditions: Notes in the Margins of Jacques Le Goff's Book', *Journal of Medieval History* 9 (1983): 71-90.

[7] For Arnulf, chaplain to Robert I, duke of Normandy before becoming patriarch of Jerusalem in 1099 and again from 1112 to 1115. See R. Foreville, 'Un chef de la première croisade: Arnulf Malecouronne,' *Bulletin Philologique et Historique du Comité des Travaux Historiques et Scientifiques* (1953 –4), pp. 377 – 90. See also B. Hamilton, *The Latin Church in the Crusader States* (London, 1980), pp. 12 – 13.

[8] For references to Peter Desiderius see J. Riley-Smith, *The First Crusaders*, (Cambridge, 1997), p. 216.

nevertheless, I cannot see God clearly until my hairs and beard grow back as they were."[9]

This time Adhémar was portrayed as visiting the crusaders, rather than being invisible amongst them. His true, celestial, home was given as among a chorus with St Nicholas. The association of Nicholas, the fourth century bishop of Myra (South West Turkey), with the crusade is probably connected to the translation of the saint's relics to the south Italian port of Bari in 1087. A new church to house the relics was being built at the time of the crusade and Pope Urban II held a council there in 1098. Interestingly, some of the sculptures of the church at Bari exactly match those of a frieze at the abbey of St Gilles, Gard.[10] Count Raymond of Toulouse was also count of Saint Gilles, suggesting that the appearance of Nicholas in this vision might represent something more than the growing popularity of the fourth century saint. It seems as though there might have been a specific Provençal interest in the presence of Nicholas' relics at Bari.

Likewise, the Normans of southern Italy held St Nicholas in such great veneration that after the victory of the First Crusade over Kerbogha, atabeg of Mosul (28 June 1098), Bohemond I of Taranto, the leader of the Italian Normans, sent a pious donation to the church of St Nicholas at Bari, namely Kerbogha's tent.[11] For very many of the participants of the crusade then, it would have seemed appropriate that Adhémar was now keeping the company of St Nicholas.

The vision of Peter Desiderius repeated the depiction of Adhémar as having suffered burns in Hell for having doubted the lance and added that there is a further punishment in that the legate was not be allowed to see God until his beard and hair had regrown. As with the vision of Peter Bartholomew, there was no spatial concept of purgatory, but there was a sense that the afterlife had rewards or punishments that were not absolute judgements: that ones condition could be altered.

There is an apparent paradox here between the idea of eternal life and having a corporeal nature, but this dichotomy would have been more evident in the light of subsequent scholastic theology. Raymond of Aguilers, a priest of relatively low social status, addressing the popular element among the crusaders, was no dialectician. For him the passage of time in the afterlife directly matched human experience, to judge by the fact that the celestial Adhémar expected his hair and beard to grow in the same manner as if he was still alive.

---

[9] RA 230 – 1; [Col.0639A]: 'Ego vidi post obitum eius episcopum Podiensem et beatum Nicolaum cum eo, et post multa alia, dixit mihi episcopus haec "Ego sum in uno choro cum beato Nicolao, sed quia de lancea Domini dubitavi, qui maxime credere debuissem, deductus sum in infernum, ibique capilli mei ex hac parte capitis dextera, et medietas barbae combusta est, et licet in poena non sim, tamen clare Deum videre non potero, donec capilli et barba sicut ante fuerant, mihi [Col.0639B] succreverint."'

[10] A. Kingsley, 'Bari, Modena and St.- Gilles', The Burlington Magazine for Connoisseurs, (1923), pp. 58 - 67.

[11] Monte Cassino Chronicle, RHC Oc. 3, 206.

The second reference to the afterlife of Adhémar that emerged in the debate about the authenticity of the Holy Lance and the visions of Peter Bartholomew, was a report by Raymond of Aguilers that while sick in Antioch in the summer of 1098, a priest and member of the following of Adhémar, Bertrand of Le Puy,[12] saw the legate. Accompanying the Bishop of Le Puy was Heraclius,[13] his standard bearer, who had been struck in the face by an arrow at the battle against Kerbogha. Adhémar told Bertrand that he was sick because he did not believe in the Lance of the Lord. Although Bertrand protested that he believed in the Lance as much as he did in the passion of the Lord, the legate replied that this was not enough.[14]

Again the main theme of the vision was its insistence on the importance of the Holy Lance. It also reveals, as with the vision of Peter Bartholomew, that it was popularly believed that fallen crusaders gathered together again in the afterlife, with the Bishop here being depicted as being reunited with his standard bearer.

The third reference to Adhémar to be recorded as a result of the controversy over the Holy Lance was a rather poignant moment as Peter Bartholomew lay dying in the tent of the chaplaincy of Count Raymond of Toulouse. Peter challenged Raymond of Aguilers, asking him why, in his secret thoughts, had he joined with those who wanted Peter to undergo the trial by fire. Raymond would not admit the truth of this accusation until Peter said his knowledge was certain, for there was a night when the blessed Virgin Mary and the Bishop of Le Puy revealed to Peter what Raymond was denying.[15] What we learn concerning the afterlife of the legate here is that Adhémar kept company with the Virgin Mary and could see into the thoughts of the living.

Thus far we have Peter Bartholomew, Bernard of Le Puy and Peter Desiderius claiming to have met with Adhémar after the legate's death. A fourth visionary, the Provencal priest, Stephen of Valence,[16] also saw the Bishop, around 18 April 1099, during the siege of ʿArqah in a major vision once more recorded by Raymond of Aguilers.

The Bishop of Le Puy appeared to Stephen of Valence and struck him with a rod to get his attention as he was returning home during the night. Adhémar reprimanded Stephen for twice neglecting instructions regarding the cross that the bishop used to carry in front of the army. The legate desired that Stephen obtain the cross that had been left in Latakia, without which, according to the blessed Mary, the Christians would lack wisdom. When Stephen heard the name Mary, he asked to see her and she was revealed, in her wonderful form and attire. With her were the blessed Agatha and an unnamed virgin with two candles.

---

[12] Otherwise unknown.

[13] For references to Heraclius I of Polignac see J. Riley-Smith, *The First Crusaders* p. 211

[14] RA 239 – 242; [Col.0640C - 0640D].

[15] RA 256; [Col.0643A].

[16] For references to Stephen of Valence see J. Riley – Smith, *First Crusaders*, p. 223.

Stephen then asked Adhémar could he have a candle in order to bring it to Count Raymond of Toulouse, to prove the vision to those sceptics who denied that the legate's beard and hair were burnt in Hell and many other things. Adhémar in turn made this request to Mary, who sent him back to Stephen with a refusal, but with the instruction that a small ring owned by Stephen was useless to him, but it would be valuable to Count Raymond if in the future he solicited the Lady who sent it to him in times of need.

Finally, Stephen asked Adhémar did he have any instruction for his brother, William Hugh of Monteil. The legate answered that William should ask the bishop elect of Le Puy to say three masses for the souls of their parents. Adhémar added that in future, the Holy Lance should not be displayed, except by a priest clad in sacred vestments and the cross should be carried in front. The legate then demonstrated this, holding the cross on a spear, with a man in priestly robes following behind with the Lance in his hands. At this point Adhémar began the antiphon *Rejoice, Mary: you alone in the entire world have destroyed all heresies*, whereupon numberless men in hundreds and thousands joined in and the holy group departed.[17]

The main content of this vision concerned a reorganisation of the political centre of gravity of the crusade. The vision was designed to appeal above all to those Southern French followers of the Bishop of Le Puy who had joined the *familia* of the Count after the death of their lord. The subordination of the Holy Lance to the cross of the dead legate was in fact a powerful symbol that the Bishop's following should no longer defer to their Provençal comrades. The vision took place during a siege that many outside the immediate following of Count Raymond of Toulouse saw as a diversion from the true goal of the expedition.

The policy of Count Raymond at this time was to step up the siege of 'Arqah and await assistance from the Byzantine Emperor, Alexius I Comnenus. Raymond of Aguilers noted that the majority of people rejected this perspective, but the crusade remained at an impasse due to the large entourage of Count Raymond.[18] Prayers, fasting and alms for the people were proclaimed in the hope of resolving the situation, and this sense of crisis formed the background to the vision of Stephen of Valence.

Although the implicit message, therefore, of Stephen's vision was a political one concerning the leadership of the expedition, it does provide further evidence for how contemporaries understood the afterlife of Bishop Adhémar. In reporting the vision, Stephen of Valence confirmed the story that the bishop had been scarred in Hell. He placed the bishop in the company of the Virgin Mary and strengthened their association by having the bishop lead a celestial host in the then contemporary popular Easter antiphon, *Rejoice, Virgin Mary*.

---

[17] RA 325 – 6; [Col. 0654D - 0655B].
[18] RA 266; [Col.0645A].

The final two appearances of Adhémar in the work of Raymond of Aguilers confirm that he remained a popular figure among the crusaders; both took place around the time of the capture of Jerusalem. The first was a reappearance of the legate before Peter Desiderius with an instruction to deal with the sense of discouragement that existed among Christian forces thwarted in their initial attacks on the city. Adhémar told Peter Desiderius to speak to the princes and all the people, telling them to be sanctified from their unclean acts, after which they should go around Jerusalem in bare feet. Should they do this and attack the city with vigour, they would capture the city in nine days.[19] After this vision was discussed in the chancery of Count Raymond of Toulouse, it was decided to ask the Christian army to behave in this way, but not announce the source of the instruction, through fear that it would be disbelieved.

The bare-footed walk of the crusaders around the Jerusalem is a famous incident and it is interesting here that the clergy advocating this course of action felt that there might be some resistance to the idea by the crusaders. This is the second reference to scepticism at the validity of the visions, the first being the concern of Stephen of Valance above, to obtain proof of his vision.

The many stories that subsequently arose, which placed Adhémar to the fore in the decisive attack on the city, show that whatever scepticism existed concerning the visions was not so strong as to preclude a popular belief the legate was with the Christian army at the culmination of the expedition. As Raymond of Aguilers recorded in his final report on the afterlife of the legate: 'On this day lord Adhémar, the bishop of Le Puy, was seen by many in the city. Indeed, many of them bore witness that he was the first to go climbing the walls; he was urging his companions and the people that they should climb.'[20]

The seven visions of Bishop Adhémar of Le Puy on the First Crusade had complex meanings for contemporaries. They intertwined commentary on the particular political situation with deeper-rooted notions of the afterlife.[21] Between them, the visions allow the afterlife of the bishop to be reconstructed with a certain amount of vivacity. Adhémar spent two days in Hell, during which time, the legate's suffering was alleviated by the Lord himself intervening: presenting the bishop with a protective cowl that the bishop had once given away as a charitable act. Importantly for later theological developments within Christian views of the afterlife, the visions also show that, for contemporaries, the prayers of the living had a beneficial affect on the condition of the departed. Once freed from Hell, Adhémar returned to the crusade, at times marching with it invisible, at

---

[19] RA 325 – 6; [Col. 0654D - 0655B].
[20] RA 348; [Col.0660A]: *In hac die dominus Ademarus, Podiensis episcopus a multis in civitate visus est. Etiam multi de eo testantur, quod ipse primus murum ascendens, ad ascendendum socios atque populum invitabat.*
[21] For further analysis of the political content of the visions, see C. Kostick, *The Social Structure of the First Crusade* (Leiden, 2008), Chapter 6.

other times appearing with celestial company, including the other martyrs of the expedition, St Nicholas and the Virgin Mary. He assisted the crusade with the capture of Jerusalem; at which point his interventions in the affairs of living humans came to an end.

Jacques Le Geoff has made a strong case for believing that the clergy did not have a worked out notion of purgatory until the late twelfth century. A. J. Guerevich in reply has pointed out that it was nevertheless the case that it was popularly believed that a person could earn the Heaven after a period of punishment for their sins, assisted by the prayers of the living.[22] What the history of Raymond of Aguilers reveals is that while he had no notion of a place of purgatory, Raymond did have a concept of the afterlife that allowed a person to move from Hell to obtaining the company of God and the saints. Perhaps the strongest impression created by the reports concerning Adhémar is that of continuity between the world of the living and the deceased. For the visionaries and historians such as Raymond of Aguilers, there was perceived to be a direct continuity between the activities of the legate while alive and after his death, even to the belief that his burnt hair and beard were in the process of growing back. Their afterlife had a Heaven (from which at various times St Nicholas, Mary and the Lord descended) and Hell (to which Adhémar was temporarily condemned), but it also co-existed with the timeframe and immediate experiences of the living. For those experiencing and believing the visions of the First Crusade, the afterlife was not something transcendental and abstract, but a state of being in which the dead could walk alongside and assist the living.

---

[22] See above, n. 6.

Stephen J Gould wrote the most marvellous book reviews and he once explained that his approach was not to focus on the book but be inspired by the contents of the book to focus on a topic worth exploring. Sometimes the book itself would hardly feature in his essay. This makes Gould's reviews very entertaining and well worth reading. By contrast I would estimate over ninety-percent of academic reviews in academic journals are not worth reading.

Typically, they take two approaches. One is the review written by a junior figure in the field, trying to bulk up his or her publications CV. The review, especially if it is of a senior figure in the field, is never contentious and rarely goes beyond summarising the contents of the book and declaring it to be a valuable addition to the field. The other kind of review is by the senior figure in the field who is at pains to assert their authority and whose opinion of the book rises in direct proportion to how often they have been cited in it. Sometimes, this kind of review is contentious, but only in the scenario where the reviewer has not been given the attention he or she feels they deserve.

In my reviews, I have tried at least to identify what arguments the book is addressing and to express where I stand on those arguments.

Crusaders and Settlers in the Latin East. By Jonathan Riley-Smith. Burlington, Vt.: Ashgate Publishing, 2008. ISBN 978-0-7546-5967-9. Notes. Index. Pp. 380. $124.50.

The Variorum Collected Studies Series bring together in one volume the seminal essays of eminent historians. It is of real value that the key crusading essays of Jonathan Riley-Smith have been published in this series, for when it comes to scholarly writing about the crusades there is no single figure more prominent in the field. Here are gathered a selection of his articles from 1972 onwards, with a definite preponderance of works written after 2000.

What Jonathan Riley-Smith is best known for is for leading a paradigmatic shift in the conception of the crusades, at least for a generation of Anglo-American historians. Formerly, the dominant view of crusading activity was a negative one, shaped by Enlightenment historians such as Gibbon, who saw the crusaders as disguising rapacious desire with their religious justifications. The idea that crusaders were essentially cynics in search of wealth was given a new impetus in the early twentieth century, when they were seen as colonialists in search of wealth and land.

The pendulum has now swung over to a much more positive view of crusaders in the sense that Jonathan Riley-Smith and his former research students have pointed to the lack of evidence to support the 'materialist' perspective of the crusades. Instead, they have scoured the charter evidence to demonstrate that a genuine piety and desire to serve Christ drove men and women to risk their lives and fortunes on crusading enterprises. The most famous article in this collection is that which defined the paradigm: 'Crusading as an act of love' (1980).

Supporters of Jonathan Riley-Smith, particularly his former research students, believe that the explanatory power provided by a focus on devotional motivation for the crusades is so great that it has decisively replaced the materialist perspective and further, that it is unlikely that their new approach will be overturned.[1] Jonathan Riley-Smith himself does not go so far as claim this, perhaps because as the opening essay here shows, he is all too aware that historiography evolves through shifts in approach from one generation to the next and whilst each shift enriches the subject, it would be rash indeed to think that any one paradigm represents the final word on the correct methodology for approaching any historical subject. And indeed, already there are signs, especially from continental historians, that the most fervent period of writings from the devotional motivation perspective has run its course.[2]

In any case, it is clear from the full range of subjects on which he has published that Jonathan Riley-Smith's contribution to the subject matter of the crusades is far wider in method and scope than the argument for which he is most famous. Several of the essays collected here – the majority even – could be broadly considered to be materialist (in the philosophical sense) in that they are close investigations of social or political structures rather than the intellectual mindset of the crusader. So, for example, four papers, written over a span of thirty years, examine the government and politics of the Latin Kingdom of Jerusalem.

For the military historian, the essay that will probably be of most interest is the chapter 'Casualties and the Number of Knights on the First Crusade,' with its detailed prosopographical appendix. Historians of the First Crusade have speculated rather widely on the numbers of participants, with room for such speculation being created by the inconsistency of the sources. Jonathan Riley-Smith avoids a 'pick and choose' approach to the sources by assembling as thorough a list of known crusaders as possible and extrapolating some figures from them, leading to his conclusion that around 5,000 knights took part in the First Crusade.

The other essay most likely to interest military historians is that entitled 'Were the Templars guilty?'. Published in 2004, this is a rather

---

[1] N. Housely, *Contesting the Crusades* (Oxford, 2006), p. 79.
[2] See for example J. Flori, 'Ideology and Motivations in the First Crusade' in H. Nicholson ed., *The Crusades* (Basingstoke, 2005), pp. 15 – 36.

iconoclastic essay as Jonathan Riley-Smith argues against the modern consensus that evidence against the Templars was fabricated in order to dispossess the order of their wealth. Instead, as he puts it 'I have come to believe that the evidence cannot all be dismissed out of hand or interpreted solely as the construct of an ambitious government.'

All in all this is an important and useful collection and furthermore one which as well as providing ready reference to key articles in crusading scholarship can be read for pleasure thanks to Jonathan Riley-Smith's lucid writing style.

The First Crusade: The Call from the East. By Peter Frankopan. Cambridge, Mass.: Belknap Press of Havard University Press, 2012. ISBN 978-0-674-05994. Maps. Illustrations. List of abbreviations. Notes. Further reading. Nidex. Pp. xxi, 262. $29.95.

The battle of Manzikert 1071 - where the Seljuk sultan Alp Arslan won a major victory over the Romanus IV Diogenes, the Byzantine emperor - has long been considered one of the most decisive battles in history. And rightly so, in that thereafter Anatolia was dominated by the Turks. But very often it is argued that another important consequence of the battle is that the defeat led the Byzantines to seek assistance from Western knights and thus Manzikert was a key event in creating the crusading movement.

The problem with this argument is that the First Crusade was not announced until 1095. The intervening years, between 1071 and 1095 were not ones of constantly worsening crisis for the Byzantine Empire, where their appeal for aid grew louder and louder, until it met with an answer. To see matters thus is to look back through a telescope from 1095 at 1071 and miss all the ups and downs of Byzantine politics in the intervening years.

With so many books having been written on the First Crusade, it is easy to assume that there is nothing new to say on the subject. But with Peter Frankopan's *The First Crusade: The Call from the East* we have a genuinely important new contribution to our understanding of the crusade. The particular strength of the author is in regard to the Greek sources and he very skillfully makes the most of less well-known material, such as the various Greek sources edited by Paul Gautier.

One of Frankopan's main contentions - and a convincing one - is that there were very specific reasons for Alexios's call for western aid in 1094 that had arisen only over the course of a few months and that for some time after his coming to power in 1075 the empire had stabilised and, indeed, prospered. But in 1094, with the death of a key ally in Syria and a mounting financial crisis, Alexios addressed the papacy and the knights of Europe and appealed to them for assistance. This view of events avoids the simplistic 'Manzikert triggered the crusades' argument as well as offering a much more nuanced view of Alexios's goals than is usually provided in narratives of the First Crusade.

There is, however, a problem with the rest of the book, a problem that I suspect might have arisen from the publisher's marketing concerns, which is that the excellent opening chapters are followed by a rather rushed narrative of the crusade that falls far below that of say, John France's classic account, *Victory in the East*. Worse, the sophisticated treatment of the Greek sources that the author offers early in the book is lacking for the Latin and Muslim sources. For example, Frankopan's narrative of the events 1096-1099 places a great deal of reliance upon Ibn al-Athir without ever discussing the author, or even noting that he was writing his chronicle in Mosul over a hundred years after the period. An unsuspecting reader might well be misled by phrases that describe al-Athir as 'writing after 1092' and 'a well-informed commentator' to believe the source was much closer to events than is the case. And this is just one of example from many of the author introducing late material without the kind of source criticism needed for a successful scholarly book.

In short, this book falls between two stools, it has elements that are of a very high level of scholarship, which would make it an important work for undergraduates and researchers, but the original insights are placed in a rather lightweight narrative of the First Crusade. In my view, the many interesting and original insights of the author would have been better presented thematically rather than chronologically and developed with an eye on the community of scholars rather than a popular audience.

Mamlūks and Crusaders – Men of the Sword and Men of the Pen by Robert Irwin (Variorum Collected Studies) xiv, 368 pp. Surrey and Burlington, VT: Ashgate, 2010. £95. ISBN 978-1-4094-0775-1.

The Variorum series brings together in one volume previously published essays by eminent historians and the value of these anthologies is that not only are seminal articles made more accessible, but readers can appreciate the full extent of the historian's oeuvre. In the case of Robert Irwin, this Variorum collection emphasises just how familiar the author is with a huge body of medieval Arabic literature and how capable he is of drawing original and important historical formulations from a study of these texts.

I am primarily a crusade historian and while the book's title is a little misleading - of the twenty-three essays reproduced here, only six are directly concerned with the crusade – there is no doubting the importance of Robert Irwin's contribution to the field. It is well established that the evolution of crusading studies has suffered from a lack of participation by scholars equipped with the language skills and contextual knowledge to make the most of medieval Arabic sources. For the Latin sources we have a considerable – and ever increasing – body of scholarship that has engaged in widespread debates and as a result has generated a deep appreciation of the nuances of the texts under examination. For many of the key Arabic sources, we are lacking modern scholarly editions and translations, let alone a thriving culture of scholarly debate over how the texts should be read. As Irwin himself puts it in his entertaining survey of Western scholarship's engagement with the medieval Arabic sources for the crusades, 'far too few Arabic (and Persian and Turkish) sources have been brought into play. Few sources have been looked at except the obvious chronicles and biographical dictionaries. On the whole, the chronicles have been used merely to provide information to confirm or supplement the western materials. There has been little attempt to, as it were, get inside those sources and recreate the Einfühlung of the Muslim counter-crusade.'

The anthology provides an excellent case study demonstrating what is possible in regard to medieval Arabic source analysis in Irwin's evaluation of Usamah ibn Munquidh's twelfth century autobiographical guide to the ways of the world. Usamah's is a much-quoted text, mainly for its lively passages on the contrasts between Christian and Muslim practices in his day, but until Irwin's study few scholars would have appreciated the literary traditions informing the construction of the text and – more importantly for those seeking historical information in it – the considerable biases and lacunae in regard to Usamah's own involvement in Egyptian affairs.

Robert Irwin is a novelist as well as a historian and this impacts on the anthology in two ways. Firstly, all of the essays are very readable. Not all – or rather, many – of the Variorium series publications can be read from cover to cover for pleasure. But when the historian is unafraid of writing sentences like, 'although Creswell was Wiet's furious enemy and rival, this was not really Wiet's fault, since what Creswell especially hated about Wiet was that the latter was French', or 'in his studies, Berthereau was somewhat hindered by the assistance of a villainous and idle Syrian Arabic speaker called Joseph Chahin', the reader looks forward to the next authorial judgement. Secondly, Irwin is fascinated by the colourful, extraordinary, and adventurous elements of texts as well as the wider Arabic traditions of storytelling. This does not lead to self-indulgence. In Irwin's hands investigations of literary themes can be a route to knowledge of the activities of all manner of professions whose deeds are rarely featured in histories and chronicles concerned with the actions of the ruling elite.

As I write this review, hundreds of thousands of people are demonstrating in Cairo and this creates a strong resonance with some of the essays in this anthology, not least Irwin's study of the Futuwwa. The futuwwa was an institution that evolved in Arabic culture from being a tenth century means of providing young warriors with feasting, hospitality and good fellowship on their travels, to being a body of thugs who, especially in Cairo, were considered disreputable rogues by early modern times, running small-time rackets and controlling districts that needed to be monitored carefully by the elite. For these districts proved to be centres of opposition to the authorities, whether Turks or Bonaparte's troops. As Irwin concludes, 'the defence of poor and humble citizens from the oppression of the alien Turkish soldiery was surely one of the most important roles of futuwwa lodges and similar groups.'

The chronological arrangement of the essays maps Robert Irwin's interests and shows his growing engagement with and authority on Mamlūk history. Here are essays on the historiography of the subject, on individual sources, on the political struggles of particular rulers and periods and one reassessing the commonly held argument – derived from David Ayalon's influential 1956 study – that the failure of the Mamlūks to adopt the use of firearms contributed to the demise of the Mamlūk Sultanate.

An anthology of this sort runs the risk that it draws attention to a scholar's tendency (which we all engage in to some degree) to draw on the same material from one essay to the next, but Robert Irwin's interests and expertise are so wide-ranging that such a practice is hardly noticeable in the collection. And although the same framing device about the unique appropriateness of an aphorism by Sir Lewis Namier is used in two essays in regard to two different texts, this is a terribly minor flaw in an otherwise sparkling collection of learned and stimulating essays.

Britain, Ireland & the Crusades, *c.*1000-1300. By Kathryn Hurlock. Houndmills, Basingstoke, Hampshire, U.U.: Palgrave Macmillan, 2013. ISBN 978-0-230-2986-4. Maps. List of abbreviations. Chronology. Notes. Bibliography. Index. Pp. xxi, 221. £20.99.

This is a book whose goal is to gather all the crusading material relating to medieval England, Wales, Scotland, and Ireland, and organise it according to certain themes: recruitment and funding; participation; political crusades; domestic impact; and military orders. Such a methodology might seem like a modern way to discuss crusading, in contrast, say, to adopting a chronological approach, but in fact this book has a distinctly nineteenth century feel. The reason for this, I think, is that an effective thematic approach to crusading has to be unconstrained by geographical boundary.

Potentially, thanks to the strength of the book, which is the amassing of a considerable body of material concerning the particular regions of its focus, this could be a useful reference book. But in dispersing the material into themeatic chapters, very little is gained yet something is lost. Instead of, say, all the findings concerning Scotland and the Third Crusade being placed in relationship to one another in one section, they are broken up throughout the book.

If the structure of the book gave rise to new insights with regard to each theme, then the author's approach would be justified. At the end of each chapter is a section entitled 'conclusions', but all we get here is a summary of the material that has been presented in each chapter and almost nothing by way of analysis.

If I were given this book at the proposal stage, I would certainly want to see it published, but I would ask the author to take a deep breath; to stand above the dogged accumulation of crusade-related evidence, and pose questions that the specifically English, Welsh, Scottish, and Irish content is best fitted to answer.

For example, historians of medieval Ireland would be very interested in this book, if it used the subject of the crusades as a means to investigate the differences and similarities between the response to crusading in the Gaelic ruled part of the country and the Anglo-Norman realm.

Where the book does offer analysis, such as its discussions of how the idea of crusading could be promoted by those in authority as a means of removing troublesome lords, or of how those in revolt against a monarch could adapt crusading ideas in order to justify their actions, it is very good. But the case studies from which such arguments are derived are complex and I feel they would be more persuasive if the reader were offered distinct chronlogical sections on the civil war in England of 1135-54, or the struggle of Henry II with his sons, for example.

Moreoever, it is hard to have a meaningful discussion of the role of knights, or women, or criminals, say, when these categories are treated as static over the three hundred years of the book's interest. Naturally, there were enormous changes in the social structures of the societies under investigation and the author cannot formulate questions such as: 'does a study of the response to crusading tell us something of the evolution of women's role in medieval society?', when each theme is presented as a block with no internal evolution over time.

The chapter on 'political' crusades is based on the dubious premise that those crusades against the papacy's enemies within Christendom were of a qualitatively different sort to the crusades against non-Christians. This division runs the risk of downplaying the strategic utilisation of crusading by the papacy in its struggle with Christian opponents in every crusade from the First Crusade onwards. All crusades had a 'political' dimension in the sense that the author means here.

Several works cited, or partially cited, in footnotes do not appear in the bibliography. And sometimes footnotes are missing. Those historians, for example, who have searched hard for evidence of participation from Ireland in the First Crusade will be fascinated to read that crusaders from Ireland 'fought in the entourage of the French Lord of Thouars', but statements like this require a reference.

In brief, reading this book was like looking at shards of a broken mirror and wishing that the pieces were reassembled.

Letters from the East: Crusaders, Pilgrims and Settlers in the 12th – 13th Centuries. Translated by Malcolm Barber & Keith Bate.

Burlington, Vt.: Ashgate, 2010. ISBN 978-0-7546-6356-0. Maps. Chronology. List of abbreviations. Sources. Index. Pp. xvi, 188. $89.95.

Despite an increasing interest in the subject of the crusades in the past decade and a growth in the number of researchers addressing the topic, there is still a great need for more translations to make the sources available to both students and interested members of the public. One glaring absence in the canon of works available to those using the English language has been the crusade-related letters of the era. But now we have translations of 82 letters from the Near East, mostly written to prominent Western European figures and mostly translated from Latin originals. The letters cover the period 1097 – 1306.

I suspect that the majority of people using the book will be doing so to look at the letters concerning particular events, say the fall of Jerusalem to the Christians in 1099, or Saladin's victory at Hattin in 1187. But there is something to be said for reading the book from cover to cover, for by doing so, the reader really gains a vivid flavour of the ebbs and flows of the struggle for the Holy Land.

From a military point of view there are some wonderful eyewitness accounts of battles and sieges. For example, the letters of James of Vitry, Bishop of Acre, to Pope Honorius III in 1218 concerning the attack on Damietta by the Fifth Crusade in 1219 have details of improvised siege machinery, such as a rotatable bridge that the crusaders build on top of two ships, on which was put a ladder and fortifications, and the whole then manoeuvred to attack a tower that controlled the entrance to the Nile. The letter of John Sarrasin, Chamberlain of France, in 1249 when Louis IX made his attempt on Damietta has a detailed account of the king's amphibious operation to land his army, with scenes of knights wading through the waves, immersed up to their armpits. And the poignant letter of the badly wounded John of Villiers, Master of the Hospital, after he had been dragged away from the fall of Acre to a Mamluk army on 18 May 1291 reads like a dramatic scene from a novel, with its account of desperate last stands by knights who knew that they were doomed.

As well as having extensive coverage of tactical incidents like these, this book is essential reading for those wanting to understand the strategic questions facing the Christian Kingdom of Jerusalem. The increasingly panicked tone of the letters from the 1160s support a view endorsed by many modern historians, but which dates back to the belief of William of Tyre, Chancellor of the Kingdom, that control of Cairo was the key issue. When, 8 January 1169, the declining Fatamid power finally fell, it did so to a general of the already powerful Nur al-Din, ruler of Mosul and Damascus, and not to a Christian army.

The material in these letters is also extremely rich in regard to other topics. Church historians and theologians will be delighted to have ready access to accounts of the various religious movements and practices of the regions. Social historians will also relish a great many of the letters. I was struck by a comment made in a letter of 1244, that formerly Christian peasants in the region of Acre were joining the Khwarazmian Turks. Given the Muslim sources which lament the fact that a hundred years earlier many peasants preferred Christian rulers, this suggests there might have been another dynamic to the rise and fall of the Christian lordships, one connected to their level of exploitation of the farmers.

This book is ideal for undergraduates and for non-scholars who enjoy reading about the crusades. It falls short of being an essential tool for more advanced research, not because of any failing in the translation - which to judge from the letters I am familiar with is excellent, close enough to being literal to capture the tone of the author, without being wooden – but because the apparatus (footnotes etc) is rather minimal and also because it is not a comprehensive collection.

Le vassal, le fief et l'écrit: Pratiques d'écriture et enjeux documentaires dans le champ de la féodalité (XIe-XVe s.). Jean-François Nieus, ed., Actes de la journée d'étude organisée à Louvain-la-Neuve le 15 avril 2005. (Textes, Études, Congrès, 23.) Louvain-la-Neuve: Université catholique de Louvain, 2007. Paper. Pp. 218; black-and-white figures, tables, and maps. €30. Distributed by Brepols, Turnhout, Belgium.

When Susan Reynolds published *Fiefs and Vassals: The Medieval Evidence Reinterpreted* (New York and Oxford: Oxford University Press, 1994) the study of feudal relations in medieval Europe went into a crisis. Partly because of shortcomings in the Ganshof-esque models and partly because right across the discipline of history there was a swing away from structural analyses towards analyses of mentalities, 'feudalism' became a word to be avoided. Not that anyone had a better term for the relationship between a lord and his (or much more rarely her) knightly followers, but rather, historians began to look over their shoulders and prevaricate when they came to point where they would once have written or spoken about feudal relations without question.

There is, of course, a considerable difference between the modern label for a particular set of medieval practices and the way in which contemporaries refered to their own actions. Marc Bloch and his followers were well aware that 'feudal' and 'feudalism' were originally legal terms, taken over from the courts of the eighteenth century to become, as Bloch put it, 'rather awkward labels for a type of social structure which was itself rather ill-defined.' But Bloch nevertheless employed the terms without choking in the way that some modern historical writing does, on the grounds that even if the term 'feudal' was employed to characterize societies in which the fief was certainly not the most significant feature, we are obliged, like all the sciences, to draw find generalisations drawn from the 'confused vocabulary of daily life.' In other words, his view was that the term was imprecise, but functional.

The difficulty created by the wave of enthusiasm for Reynold's book was that from a demolition of overly simplistic generalisations about feudalism, the momentum of the attack continued to an all-out assault on the notion of vassalage, the role of the fief and the meaning of the ritual of hommage. And in the wake of the wave was only debris. As Dirk Heirbaut writes here at the end of his study on Flemish feudalism 1000 – 1300, 'the great Belgian historian of feudalism, F. – L. Ganshof, and his contemporaries once built up a wonderful contruct of medieval feudalism. In recent years, historians have been destroying this work. There were right in that the old models did not correspond to medieval realities and neglected geographical and chronological contexts, but they have only left ruins, they have built no new constructs of their own.'

Perhaps it would be more accurate to say there have been several attempts to offer alternative constructs, but that none have been particularly successful, because despite all the fraying at the edge of the term 'feudal', no other term and no other model effectively encapsulates the situation in which a knight, in return for a fief, performs an act of submission and promises to serve the fief-giver. The pendulum is now swinging back towards what, in this reviewer's opinion, is a more helpful position.

A conference held in Louvain-la- Neuve in 2005 firmly grasped the nettle and began to investigate feudal relations after something of a hiatus had developed in such studies (with the exception of Germany). A selection of papers from the conference has now been published and what the book achieves is a reinstatement of the validity and importance of investigating feudal relationships. Not that these studies represent a simple regression to the pre-Reynolds state of affairs. The crisis of the structural models of feudalism and the debate around the terms 'fief' and 'vassal' has led this new generation of scholars to be extremely careful about their language and their conclusions. The specialist work evident in these essays demonstrates an awareness of the necessity of nuance in the discourse of feudalism. Simply through the juxtaposition of studies of the Langeudoc in the eleventh and twelfth centuries; the north of France from the end of the twelfth to the middle of the thirteenth century; Rouergue and the Cévennes in the fourteenth century; and Burgundy in the fifteenth, the book acknowledges the diversity of experience across different geographical regions and across different time frames.

All the essays in this collection demonstrate an awareness of the need to treat the source material with great care. Yet at the same time, it is refreshing that these investigations go beyond lamenting the lack of contemporary materials to use what is available to derive effective conclusions. From the earliest documents describing feudal relationships, to the replacement of the traditional forms of diplomatic by lords beginning to issue charters of infeudation here and there in the thirteenth century; from twelfth century inventories to the subsequent gradual appearance of the 'book of fiefs' of the thirteenth century, the study of a variety of categories of document testifies to the evolution of feudal practices.

It will always be possible to argue that inconsistencies in the sources mean modern discussion of feudal relationships is invalid. But what is very welcome about this book is that a group of scholars including Jean-François Nieus, Gérard Giordanengo, Hélène Débax, Dirk Heirbaut, Emmanuel Johans, Karl-Heinz Spiess, Antheun Janse, Jean-Marie Yante and René Noël are nevertheless undettered and have ushered in a new phase of investigation into a fundamental and important phenomon whose historical core resists complete deconstruction: feudalism.

The Irish Church, its Reform and the English Invasion
Donnchadh Ó Corráin, Four Courts Press, €35, ISBN 9781846826672

Discussions about medieval Ireland have often been highly politicised and contested. In the early twentieth century, activists for independence, from Arthur Griffith to James Connolly, became passionate in their engagement with Ireland's medieval past in order to support Eoin Mac Neill in his polemical exchanges with Henry Orpen (the former being seen as the national champion in opposition to the imperial bias of the latter). Donnchadh Ó Corráin's new book very much belongs to this tradition of vigorous and purposeful writing about medieval Ireland. In a relatively compressed framework (122 pages) with coruscating sentences, it attempts to carry an argument, the core of which is this: the impact of the Gregorian reform was a disaster for Ireland and the Irish church.

Personally, I would rather read a short history in which the passions of the author are clear and in which something is being said than a work that is saying very little at great length. This is true even when I don't agree with the author, as is the case here.

The structure of Ó Corráin's argument is as follows. In Ireland, before the coming of the 'English', the church had its flaws, but it was relatively free from the practice of lay appointments to senior positions (not least because of the dynastic nature of many foundations). The early Irish church, too, had an infrastructure that provided the material basis for impressive levels of learning and sophisticated scholarship.

In the Continental church, however, a revolution took place in the second half of the eleventh century, which saw ardent reformers such as Hildebrand (Gregory VII) take control of the papacy and attempt to impose changes on the church, regardless of the cost. As Ó Corráin observes when writing about St Malachy, 'reformers are none other than those who want one's position, power and property because of an absolute conviction that they can and will devote them to proper ends. The uncompassionate sacrifice of individuals and institutions is part of the business.'

In Ó Corráin's view, the reform papacy was ill informed about Ireland and more than willing to achieve its goals here through the intervention of the English crown. *Laudabiliter satis* was a papal privilege given to Henry II of England by Pope Adrian IV in 1155 and it became the justification for the king's arrival in Ireland in 1171 to claim the subjugation of the Irish rulers. The pope at this point, Alexander III, urged the Irish bishops to ally themselves with Henry, which they duly did, at enormous cost. The once independent and culturally vibrant Irish church became a tool of English royal policy and, by diverting revenues towards the episcopacy, undermined the basis of indigenous scholarship.

In making this argument Ó Corráin sidesteps two very important issues by relegating them to footnotes. One is whether *Laudabiliter satis* is a forgery. The strongest case for believing that the document did not exist in the form in which we have it was made by Professor Anne Duggan (see *History Ireland* 13.3, May/June 2005), and I don't believe that writing 'Duggan's reconstruction of *Laudabiliter satis* is a step too far' in a footnote is in any way an adequate means of addressing the issue— especially since, having given a nod to the debate, Ó Corráin then uses the document throughout his book as though there was no question of its authenticity.

'No surviving documents indicate the effect of *Laudabiliter satis* on the Irish church', writes Ó Corráin, but, 'evidently, it had a serious negative effect on its leaders, men keenly and naively loyal to a papacy that seems, in a short time, to have lost confidence in them.' I think the reason why no effect is visible in the sources is that the privilege did not exist, at least in the doctored form that we have from Gerald of Wales, a known forger.

The other issue is that of using the term 'English' to describe an invasion that did, indeed, transform the Irish church, at least in the east and south of the country. The footnote reads: 'The term "English" is here used as an umbrella term for Norman, Anglo-Norman, Cambro-Norman, Fleming, Welsh, Saxon, Breton, English, etc.'. Again, I think that this is too important a discussion to leave to a footnote, because there is a lot at stake in your choice of term for the invaders. Quite apart from the fact that 'English' resonates anachronistically with a much more imperialist phase of British history, there is an underlying issue to do with social structure that has implications for whether the invaders should be considered English or Anglo-Norman.

In Ó Corráin's view, there is no substantial difference in this period between the social structures of Ireland, England, France, Germany, Italy, etc. Frequently, he addresses the justifications given by reformers and invaders for involvement in Ireland by demonstrating that the ills and grievances that were levelled against the Irish could just as reasonably be aimed at other countries. To some extent this is useful, a healthy corrective to negative notions about Irish society derived from the propaganda of the invaders. But to argue, as this book does, that Ireland therefore was essentially similar to the rest of Europe is to use Ó Corráin's deep knowledge of the sources to cherry-pick examples that are in fact misleading.

When we look at the situation in broad terms, in the generality, it has to be recognised that there were significant differences between Ireland and the Norman world. Ireland, for instance, was predominantly a cattle economy, with considerable reliance on slave labour. The Normans devoted much more land to grain production, and in their realms serfs provided the bulk of the workforce.

The difference between slavery and serfdom is significant (not least to members of these orders). In addition, arising from these economic differences are notable cultural consequences. One important example is the castle. It made sense for the Normans to construct castles, not just as forts on river crossings but also as residences for lords and knights and as administrative centres for the control of land and labour. In their conquered territories, e.g. in England after 1066 and southern Italy from c. 1000, castles covered the landscape densely in a way that was not the case in Ireland until after 1169. This is not to say that one system was superior to the other, but it is important to recognise that in the twelfth century Ireland's social structure was not the same as that in England and northern France.

Because he does not address—or believe in—any deep-rooted differences between Ireland and the Norman world, Ó Corráin struggles to account for the transformation of the Irish church when these two systems collided. For me, the reorganisation of the Irish church mirrors the extent to which land use, inheritance and marriage had evolved in the Anglo-Norman world.

What reason can Ó Corráin find for the transformation? Only one, which arises from Ó Corráin's antipathy to the Gregorian reformers. 'Is it possible they [Irish bishops] saw conquest as the only means of bringing about that change and deliberately chose it, at the urgings of the reformed papacy? ... they were prepared to envisage a social revolution that entailed the overthrow of their own ruling cadre and the rise of a foreign land-holding class loyal (at least in theory) to an absent king—all in the interest of an international mother church and an unrealistic programme of perceived moral betterment.'

Although advanced with the reservation 'is it possible?', this is the book's core belief and one that appears throughout the text, especially in Ó Corráin's entertaining judgements of figures like Pope Alexander III or Bernard of Clairvaux. A small layer of clergy (strategically located at the top of the Irish church) had such a desire to end lay control of church offices and estates that they were led to heed the urgings of Europe's leading reformers and back Henry II.

Such a scenario is not impossible. After all, something like it occurred when Henry III journeyed to Rome in 1046. Unable to find a credible pope to make him emperor (there were three at the time), Henry emancipated the Roman church from the grip of the local aristocracy and inadvertently created a dynamic that allowed reformers the freedom to pursue goals that would bring civil war to Germany within a generation.

Even in this story, however, there is an interaction between the ideologically driven reform movement and contemporary social developments, not least in the widespread proliferation of Cluniacal monasteries that provided the reformers with nearly their entire cadre. In the Irish case, the relationship of church reform to the Anglo-Norman invasion is far less significant than Ó Corráin would have it. Note how important a proper assessment of *Laudabiliter* is to the issue. If we discount *Laudabiliter*, we see no further promotion by the papacy of Adrian IV's idea that the English crown should have authority in Ireland. A succession of seven reform synods within Ireland between 1157 and 1167 (one with a papal legate present) suggests instead approval for a process of reform internal to Ireland.

The impetus behind the invasion of Ireland was cruder and simpler than the runaway reform thesis. The invaders belonged to a long line of warlords who had nothing other than a pragmatic interest in religion. Finding themselves at the head of a social and economic structure that allowed for a distinct military advantage over their neighbours, these adventurers had no scruple about muscling in on any region that failed to keep up; 1169 should be seen as part of a continuum with 1059–64 (Apulia and Calabria), 1066 (England), 1098 (Antioch) and 1130 (Sicily).

For me, therefore, the central argument of this book is back to front. If we start with an understanding of the social and economic differences between Ireland and the Norman world, then we have a better understanding of why there would be conflict over divergent practices in the church. I think this provides a clearer basis for interpreting the policy of the Irish bishops than does seeing them as the religious equivalents of Diarmait Mac Murchada.

I've recently read a collection of history essays by James M. McPherson, the splendid historian of the US Civil War. *Drawn with the Sword* not only has a range of terrific essays on figures like Lincoln and Grant, it also has a very interesting final chapter written in 1995, 'What's the Matter with History'. In this chapter, he makes the case that history writing is in crisis because if you write popular history, you are considered lacking in *gravitas*. Professional historians, through their management of conferences and editorship of scholarly journals, exert a pressure that is harmful to the production of great works of narrative history. It is often therefore left to those outside academia to write the really compelling accounts of history.

There's a lot of truth in this argument and it remains forceful more than twenty-five years later. But in addition to the question of peer pressure, I think there's at least one other consideration in play here. It's not easy for an academically trained historian to write a riveting book. Given the historian's awareness of how contentious any particular assesstion is (there might be decades of debate over the subject of just one sentence) it is very hard for the historian to avoid writing with constant caveats and qualifications. It is even harder to imaginatively reconstruct dialogue and thus a powerful dramatic tool is knocked out of the hands of the historian anxious not to stray beyond the knowable.

When I think about my own favourite works of history, I find that in several instances, despite McPherson's observation, they are written by academics, often late in their careers when they can synthesise decades of reading and thinking about their subjects. And they are works which although sometimes presenting the ambiguities of the source material aren't afraid to make judgements. I'm thinking of McPherson's own *Battle Cry of Freedom*, or in my own field, Georges Duby's *William Marshal: the Flower of Chivalry*, Bernard Hamilton's *The Leper King and His Heirs*, and I.S. Robinson's under-appreciated *Henry IV of Germany 1056-1106*.

All the same, it can't be a co-incidence that my favourite historical work of all is that of an engaged participant rather than a professional historian: Leon Trotsky's *The History of the Russian Revolution*. Admittedly, it is exceptional that someone with the writing skills of Trotsky, who was also at the centre of the key events, should find themselves in a personal situation where they can gather sources and have the time to write up their experience as history. And it is very much history, not memoir. For the latter, there is his autobiography, *My Life*, also a terrific read.

Twice in my writings on medieval history, I've grappled with the challenge of trying to write a compelling narrative of events. Once, with an account of the siege of Jeruslam in 1099 and the other of the invasion of Ireland by Strongbow. In both cases, my goal was to entertain and judge as well as account. Certainly, the crusader conquest of Jerusalem deserves a vivid text, the story being full of extraordinary characters and of tipping points that could have gone either way, to spell life or death for thousands of people.

For the Norman invasion of Ireland I was also addressing a wild period of history in which personal hatreds, passions and close-fought battles led to fundamental changes in the lives of everyone in Ireland. But I was also addressing an argument. In the light of the subjection of Ireland to the British empire, it seems obvious to locate the origin of that colonial relationship to 1169 and the Norman invasion of Ireland. Yet the English state was far from being the imperial power it would be even by the time of Elizabeth I, say, when the case for seeing Ireland as a colony of England's is much stronger. Four hundred years before Elizabeth, empires were still medieval ones, where small layers of people at the very top of society struggled for military dominance without the kind of state apparatus and civil authority to cohere all the conquered people into a nation. Henry II of England, for example, king at the time of the invasion of Ireland was ruler of a dominion that contained the western half of France.

England itself was far from settled into a coherent country with uniform language and laws. French-speaking Norman warriors had taken over after their victory at Hastings in 1066 and the language of the elite remained a form of French by the invasion of Ireland.

In my view, a better framework for understanding the Norman invasion of Ireland is to see it as the end of an era, not the start of one. From the time that Vikings settled in northern France a new polity emerged with economic and military advantages that for about two-hundred years gave even small numbers of Normans the capacity to conquer the rulers of other territories in Europe, north Africa and the Near East. The last of these adventures was Strongbow's enterprise in Ireland. What were these advantages? I explain them in the following opening chapters to my book Strongbow: the Norman Invasion of Ireland.

It wouldn't be fair to my publishers, O'Brien Press, to take the story any further, to the actual events of the invasion but if you did want to read on, you can get the book from your library or purchase it via https://obrien.ie/strongbow-the-norman-invasion-of-ireland.

Preface

May 1169. Dispersed groups of armoured men are wielding long axes in a meadow on the southwest border of Leinster. They are sweating in the sunshine and would welcome the opportunity to rest in the shade of a nearby line of trees. It is not timber that these men are hacking but heads from the several hundred corpses that are lying in the tall grass. Blood has been sprayed over the yellow marigolds and buttercups and has collected in dark, scarlet pools. Longhaired, bearded, or bald, the severed heads are picked up and brought to be counted and paid for at a distinct gathering of soldiers, whose banners are as colourful as the spring flowers. There, one man in particular dominates the scene.

Diarmait Mac Murchada, King of Leinster, cannot contain his feelings of satisfaction as the pile of heads before him grows. His teeth are clenched and a bitter, vindictive joy is evidently coursing through him. From time to time the king leaps into the air, clasping his arms above his head in glee. Despite the gore, Diarmait recognises the features of men whom he hated passionately and revels in the fact that they will never defy him again. Their threats have proven empty. Their cruelties towards Diarmait have been answered. In the vicious life and death struggle that has over the years favoured one side and then the other, Diarmait has ultimately emerged victorious. It is finished with now and forever.

Beside the king are three knights clad entirely in chainmail: from the coif over their heads - currently thrown back so they can feel refreshed after their exertions - to their feet. Their names are Robert fitz Stephen, Maurice de Prendergast and Hervey de Montmorency and they are conscious of being foreigners in this land. If these knights think the behaviour of the king is unbecoming, they are wise enough not to display their disapproval. Instead they look on with apparent equanimity as the elderly man jumps around the grisly display, the satisfaction of vengeance fulfilled evidently providing him with boundless energy.

The King of Leinster is a tall man who at fifty-nine years of age still retains some of the muscular physique of his youth. But his bearded face also bears the lines of a man who has brooded in sorrow and anger for many years. And Diarmait's voice, once capable of giving a roar as loud as a charging bull, is husky now, worn out from the din of battle. Of his many sorrows, one of the greatest was the blinding of his eldest son, Énna Mac Murchada. It was the men of Osraige who had made Énna their prisoner and, after holding their captive for two years, it was they who had put out his eyes and made him ineligible to ever inherit the kingship. It is the same warriors of Osraige who carried out this mutilation whose bodies are lying still under the blue sky and whose sightless eyes roll as their heads are tossed onto the bloody heap.

As he turns over the ruined faces to examine them, one in particular excites Diarmait more than all the others. He grabs it by the hair and holds it up for all in the field to see. Everyone pauses to watch. With a husky laugh of triumph, Diarmait suddenly lunges at the head and bites the nose and cheeks of his defeated foe. This action will reassure his superstitious warriors that the ghosts of the slain will not return to haunt them.

The King of Leinster had a lot of enemies; at one time nearly the whole of Ireland was united against him. But the fact that his neighbours from Osraige had joined in the coalition to oust him had been a particularly heavy blow and Diarmait had hardly dared dream that the day would come when he could make the traitors pay. Now they were dead and their corpses were his to abuse. Let the word spread throughout the land: Diarmait Mac Murchada is back. If you had been one of those traitors who had turned against him and drove him to seek the assistance of foreigners, then you would shiver at the news of the King of Leinster savaging the features of his old enemies. It could be your head in his hands before long.

Out of sight of the Irish king, the three Norman lords exchange glances with each other and look back to the far end of the field where a handful of knights and a much larger number of archers are gathered after the battle. Before that morning's conflict began, Robert fitz Stephen had addressed the Norman army. The handsome, clean-shaven knight had emphasised the justice of Diarmait's campaign; the treacherous nature of the men of Osraige, who had committed a crime when they had taken over half of Diarmait's former lands; and the honourable nature of the King of Leinster. If that attempt to exalt their nominal overlord as a model of chivalry now appears rather false, there are nevertheless no shocked stares or insubordinate mutterings from among Robert's followers.

These soldiers from South Wales are hard men with a professional commitment to war and no illusions as to the character of the princes who lead them. And that morning there had been another point made by Robert in his rallying speech that had struck home and made them more loyal to Diarmait's cause than any of the king's own Irish followers. 'Perhaps,' Robert had said, 'the outcome of this present action will be that the five divisions of the island will be reduced to one, and sovereignty over the whole kingdom will devolve upon us in future. If victory is won and Mac Murchada is restored with the aid of our arms, if by our present assaults the kingdom of Ireland is forever preserved for us and for our descendants then what renown we shall win!'

Renown, yes, and a comfortable living as the recipients of the wealth that made its way up from those who worked the land and cattle to those who lived in halls and castles. There was opportunity, here in Ireland, to supplant the local nobles. That was the real appeal of Robert's speech. Let Diarmait behave as a pagan king of biblical times if he wished. It didn't matter. What was important about this campaign was that after Diarmait was gone, it would be their turn to enjoy the fruits of victory.

Chapter 1: *Normanitas*

In the autumn of 911 the foundations of a duchy were laid whose warriors were to become the pre-eminent fighting forces in Europe for over two hundred years. Despite their very modest origins, from Palestine to Ireland Norman knights would conquer kingdoms and make empires tremble. At the small town of Saint Clair on the river Epte – a tributary of the Seine – Charles, king of the Franks, whose unaffected manners earned him the nickname 'the Simple', came to agreement with a Viking troop that they should desist from their depredations upon the French and instead, settle the land. For more than a generation the descendants of the great emperor Charlemagne had been humbled by raids of swift-moving Viking armies. The Norsemen were difficult to contain and even when cornered and forced into battle they proved to be ferocious warriors, clad as they were in sturdy chainmail hauberks and wielding iron weapons of the highest craftsmanship.

The leader of the Vikings who met with Charles was a warrior called Hrólfr (Latinised by those who subsequently came to write about him as 'Rollo'). Hrólfr was a massive man, so bulky in fact that no horse could carry him far and thus he earned the nickname, 'the walker'. The band of Vikings that Hrólfr led were more than a short-lived raiding party, their comradeship was a way of life and they had stood together for more than twenty years: sailing, raiding, fighting on either side of the English Channel and living off the tribute that the nobles of France and England offered up to appease their violence. The initial impulse that led Hrólfr to raise his banner – whose design was the left wing of a red bird - and for hundreds of warriors to rally to it was a desire to live freely.

Back in Norway, a king had for the first time fought his way to such power that the whole country was obliged to serve him. Harald Finehair, it was said, had been spurned as a teenager by the high-spirited Gyda, who had replied to his advances that she would only become his wife if he could rule Norway with as little opposition as the kings of Denmark and Sweden faced in their realms. On hearing this, Harald vowed that he would win Gyda and that he would not cut or comb his hair until he did so. When at last his goal was fulfilled, it was the revelation that after cleaning and unknotting Harald's hair was actually a striking, bright blonde that earned the king his nickname.

Subduing one small Norse kingdom after another, Harald rallied a sizeable section of the defeated Viking elite to him by crushing the free farming class as he marched. The king imposed such taxes upon the bonder that those the king appointed *jarl* could live better under Harald than they had managed independently of him. But Vikings prided themselves as much on their freedom as on their consumption of food and drink so the stronger that Harald Finehair became, the more entire communities of warriors took ship, to settle the Faeroes and Iceland and to trouble northern Europe.

One summer Hrólfr returned from Russia and raided territory that had fallen under King Harald's sway. In consequence, Hrólfr was banished and no amount of pleading from his high-born mother could reverse the decision. As a result she made a prediction:

> *Evil it is by such a wolf,*
> *Noble prince, to be bitten;*
> *He will not spare the flock*
> *If he is driven to the woods.*

The wolf crossed the North Sea to the Hebrides, gathered more ships, and on 17 November 876 planted his giant frame firmly on the heavy soil of northern France. For the Christian church a nightmare had arrived; not only did the Viking army plunder directly from the churches and monasteries but the royal authorities drew on church wealth to buy off attacks on towns. The church had accumulated a great deal of wealth in the form of precious ornaments and delicate works of art, but this was now all taken from them. If there was one positive effect to derive from the pagan Vikings' lack of appreciation of such cultural artefacts it was that the Norsemen released into circulation once more the church's gold and silver; melting it down to make ingots for trade. The commodity that the Vikings were most interested in was iron. The Vikings cared more for iron than any other metal, because iron made their ships sturdy, their armour strong, and their swords the finest weapons in Europe. Those settlements in the former Carolingian province of Neustria that were now under Viking control began to prosper, with a lively trade and flourishing of craftsmanship.

Accepting that the Norsemen were here to stay, Charles the Simple decided to try to end the pattern of raids and tribute-giving for once and for all. A treaty made at Saint Clair gave all the land from the river Epte to the sea to the Norsemen and as a result this land became known as Normandy. In return for this grant, Hrólfr was to be baptised a Christian, take Charles's daughter Gisela as his wife, and accept the French king as his overlord. A twelfth century verse history of this moment, however, reports a striking incident that is said to have taken place when Hrólfr came to make his submission, an incident that testified to the continued determination of the Viking host to assert their freedom.

Surrounded by his nobles and the senior figures of the French church, Charles met Hrólfr to ratify their agreement. But for Charles the meeting got off on the wrong foot, literally. The French king attempted to impose his authority from the beginning by having his heralds explain that before discussions could begin, the Vikings should show due deference to the monarch by kissing his foot. After some murmuring on the Viking side, one of their warriors strode forward and bent down. Then clasping Charles firmly by the ankle stood up again and raised the royal foot, causing the king to dangle in a most undignified manner. The Viking warrior then fulfilled his obligation of kissing the king's foot, before letting go of Charles who collapsed back towards the cries of consternation and outrage coming from the royal entourage. But scandalised as they were, the French nobility could not retaliate, not while they needed the good will of the leaders of the Viking army.

Despite their very different attitude towards authority, the Vikings and the French came to an agreement. The Vikings did not exactly turn their swords into ploughshares, they still needed to be able to mobilise an army to face their neighbours or the possibility of attack by rival Viking fleets, but they did take up farming in a land that was far more fertile than the rocky mountains of Norway. Whereas yields of grain crops were rarely more than three to one in Scandinavia at the time, the fields of Normandy returned up to fourteen times the grain sown. And the Vikings knew all about the use of a heavy iron-tipped plough to break through the thick clods of northern soil and get the most from the land.

Elsewhere in France, a great deal of aristocratic disdain existed towards those who performed manual labour. But the early records from Normandy show a keen interest by owners in their tools; they made extensive lists of their iron tipped mattocks, spades, hoes and other equipment. Hrólfr himself announced decrees to ensure that farmers need not fear the loss of their ploughs or tools from theft.

According to one medieval historian, a farmer's wife thought to take advantage of this ruling and when her husband left ploughshare, coulter, and tools behind in the field as he went to rest, she moved them all to a secret location and the farmer, naturally, thought that they had been stolen. Facing ruin, the farmer went to Hrólfr, who gave him the considerable sum of five *solidi*. But the duke did not leave the matter there and had the incident investigated further; suspicion fell upon the wife and she was forced to take the ordeal of hot iron to prove her innocence. When she failed that, she was whipped until she confessed her crime. The duke then asked the farmer, 'did you know your wife was the thief?' and the farmer answered, 'yes, I did.' At this Hrólfr said, 'you wicked man, your mouth condemns you,' and he ordered both to be hanged. The severity of punishment for theft in Normandy in Hrólfr's time was such that a story grew up claiming that when he left golden bracelets hanging from an oak tree after removing them for a meal, the gold remained safe and untouched for three years.

One of the most significant revolutions in the Norman way of life compared to that of their neighbours was the effective abolition of slavery. Slavery did exist in Normandy up until the mid-eleventh century, but in the form of a few slaves serving in the homes of the rich, rather than large numbers of slaves working in gangs on the fields, or, as in the Irish case, working with herds of cattle. Not that the Norman elite had a benign attitude to their workforce, it was just that they found the system of serfdom a more efficient one than that of slavery. When a gang of slaves goes out to work the land, they don't care whether tools get broken or not, or whether the field can be expanded through new drainage systems, or whether it is worth doing the backbreaking work of cutting bushes and shifting rocks to bring more land into use by the plough. A slave resents every task. A serf or a crop-paying farmer on the other hand, one whose land was granted to their children and grandchildren (albeit on making a payment to the lord), is immeasurably more motivated to improve the yields of their seed and livestock. Not quite slaves, the serf did at least have a stake in the crop, taking a share for themselves.

The life of a serf was better than that of a slave, but barely. To be a serf was to surrender yourself to the lord who owned the land and from the point that you ceremonially attended him with a rope around your neck you no longer had any freedom to leave the land or even marry without the lord's consent. And the lords were brutal in maintaining their grip on the lower classes. When the Norman peasantry tried to resist new exploitative burdens, such as taxes on the use of traditional paths and river ways, their overlords could be very severe. In 996, Rodolf, count of Ivry, and his nephew Duke Richard II of Normandy, caught peasant delegates in the act of assembling to discuss methods of rebellion against such new impositions, the lords had the hands and feet of the peasants cut off. The point of this particular form of harsh punishment was that these impudent serfs would live on, a burden to their communities and a warning to anyone who dared to resist the knightly class.

From Vikings to Normans

With generous revenues and a military force capable of seeing off those who might rob them, the former Vikings slowly, over the next four or five generations, inter-married and prospered and in the process they reinvented themselves. By the middle of the eleventh century the consistent development of their farms and their efficiency at squeezing the lower classes had provided the Norman knight with the wealth for developing the finest arms and armour west of Constantinople and for breeding the stoutest warhorses on the continent. The Normans took a direct interest in the development of their farms and especially in the purchase and breeding of horses. The destrier, so-called because it was led by the right hand (*dextra*) of a squire, was a powerful beast, capable of carrying an armoured warrior into battle. Costing some thirty times more than a palfrey – a light horse suitable for couriers – muscular destriers in the fields and stables of the knights were one of the most visible forms of the growing wealth of Normandy. The Vikings had long known of the use of the stirrup and treated stirrups as precious items, to judge by the fact that their riding equipment, made from bronze or iron, often accompanied their owner in burial. But it was on the grassy fields Normandy rather than the mountainsides of Norway that the art of fighting from horseback was perfected. Within a few generations, from Spain to Byzantium, the Normans were praised as masters of horsemanship, riding horses that had been trained to be surefooted in the tumult of battle and to turn at the touch of a hand.

Culturally, the Norman elite had changed over the years. They still remembered their Viking origins and Norse was used as a language among them for several generations. Viking zoomorphic art, the swirling-tailed animals that decorated metal goods and cloth, remained popular in Norman crafts. But by the eleventh century it was clear there had been great changes since Hrólfr's day.

Socially, the former warriors had copied developments among their continental neighbours, and where they could achieve it, the richer amongst them had become a distinct nobility, concentrating on improving their knightly skills by riding to the hunt almost every day that they were not actually riding to war. Not all the descendants of Hrólfr's Viking army had become lords of the labour of others, many were still free farmers of varying degrees of wealth but on the whole, the aristocracy of Normandy by the end of the first millennium could trace their origins back to Viking ancestors.

In their religion, there was an enormous contrast between the pagan values of the original invaders and their descendants. As part of his agreement with King Charles the Simple, Hrólfr had been baptised. As a result the practice of beheading captured Christians in honour of the old gods came to an immediate halt. Indeed, at the end of his life Hrólfr distributed a hundred pounds of gold through the churches in honour of the Christian God. Was he genuinely converted? It would appear so judging by these donations. Hrólfr's conversion in order to sign the key treaty was clearly a political decision, but the distribution of great wealth back to the church – albeit in the face of death - he once plundered shows a great deal of respect for the religion.

Understandably, though, it took the church some time to regain its confidence and function once more in Normandy. For much of the ninth and tenth centuries, bishops, such as those of Avranches, Bayeux, Lisieux, and Sées, were not appointed or if they were, lived in exile. But when the Christian religion was consolidated among the Norman nobility, the new lords began to compete with each other in their efforts to endow monasteries and churches. Evidence for just how skilled the masons and carpenters of Normandy were at this time remains in the landscape even today, especially in the form of the restored church buildings of the eleventh century. Huge stone buildings, employing the latest techniques in construction, sprang up over the duchy as each magnate established his own religious foundation.

These clerical and monastic communities provided an important service for the new Norman nobility in addition to that of spiritual welfare. A religious endowment provided a setting for the retirement and final resting place of a knight and his descendants. The clergy were also essential in estate management, being literate where the knight, typically, was not. In marked contrast to the Irish lay nobility, which included poets with extraordinary technical prowess, the Norman knight generally did not trouble to learn to read.

One knight who might have come to an early appreciation of the practical value of written records was William the Bastard, later 'Conqueror'. As a young lad of seven, William, along with several other boys, was summoned to a meeting at which his father, Duke Robert the Magnificent had just reached agreement with Humphrey de Vieilles over the foundation of a monastery at Saint-Pierre at Préaux. Duke Robert smacked his son hard in the face. Humphrey did the same to young Richard of Lillebonne, who was carrying the Duke's greaves. When Richard asked Humphrey why this strong blow had been struck, Humphrey answered, 'because you are younger than me and perhaps you will live a long time and you will be a witness of this business whenever there is need.' For good measure the adults then gave a solid crack to

Hugh, son of Count Waleran of Meulan. Hitting youths was not a very efficient method of record keeping but perhaps William was to learn from this hard lesson: in later life he was to commission the greatest documentary survey of people and property of the medieval era: the Domesday Book.

Over time the dukes of Normandy found in the clergy useful and effective allies in the suppression of the near-constant warfare that threatened the stability of the political structures of the region. At large assemblies of knights, clergy and free farmers in the time of William the Conqueror, decrees were passed announcing general 'truce' and 'peace' legislation: the former outlawing warfare on all days but Tuesdays and Wednesdays, the later banning attacks on the unarmed and their property. The penalty for ignoring these decrees was excommunication and a heavy fine, payable to the church.

Castles

One striking symbol of the restless efforts by lords to promote themselves at the expense of their rivals was the rapid proliferation of castle-building. The Norman knights led the world in the development of the castle, largely because they had the resources to invest in the considerable labour and craftsmanship required. But Normandy, too, had social conditions that impelled the art of castle construction forward. Although tactically the castle is a defensive building, strategically, the castle is used offensively. By locating a castle in disputed land and on river crossing points, a lord fashions a base from which his knights can range far and wide into enemy territory and from which they can demand revenues from the local peasantry. In a word, a castle means domination. At least forty castles were erected in Normandy before 1066 and there would have been many more, but for William the Conqueror's intervention, halting castle construction except at his discretion. William decreed that:

No one in Normandy might dig a fosse in the open country of more than one shovel's throw in depth nor set more than one line of palisade, and that without battlements or alures [wooden walkways]. And no one might make a fortification on rock or island and no one might raise a castle in Normandy and no one in Normandy might withhold the possession of his castle from the lord of Normandy if he wishes to take it into his hand.

In Ireland in the eleventh and early twelfth centuries there did not exist the same drive to build castles. Clearly, those lords who founded such impressive constructions as the monasteries of Mellifont or Baltinglass had the resources and the access to skilled artisans necessary to build castles. But why would they, when the source of wealth in Ireland was mobile? Build a castle near enemy territory and the enemy would simply move their herds of cattle away from it. Nor were there administrative structures in Ireland which were centralised in the same way as, for example, the English financial centre at Winchester or governmental centre at London. When the Normans conquered England, they immediately built castles in both cities to ensure control of them. But the retinues and functionaries of Irish kings, like the kings themselves, were itinerant. They had favoured residences, of course, but like their wealth, they were constantly mobile.

In a mistaken belief that Irish society before the coming of the Normans was sufficiently like that of northern Europe to warrant an expectation that the Irish aristocracy used castles as their primary residences, some historians and archaeologists have looked for evidence of for pre-Norman castles. They have searched in vain and they will continue to do so. The only possible exceptions being the various Uí Chonchobair fortresses described with the loan words *caistél* or *caislén* located beside rivers, where control of such key crossing points might have repaid the investment of the king. But even if – as they certainly could have – the Uí Chonchobair rulers had hired experts in castle construction and built something similar to a Norman ringwork or motte, it would still have served a rather different function to the castle as it was developed in Normandy. There is no suggestion by the Irish sources of these forts being residences for lords or centres of administration. For a Norman knight, by contrast, establishing jurisdiction over a 'fief' allotted to him by his lord, meant creating a fortified residence to control the revenues of those ploughing the land and to threaten the revenues of those within riding distance. And if the fief were on conquered territory in England, Wales, Italy, Palestine, or Ireland, there was no question but that the residence would be a castle. The generation living at the time of the conquest of England would see over a hundred castles appear on the landscape and by the time the Normans came to Ireland a century later, there were over 1,000 castles in England.

The early Norman castle was a wood and earth affair. It came in two basic forms, either that of a ringwork, where the defensive system depended entirely on the ditch and palisade that surrounded the stables and residential buildings, or a motte and bailey, where the main defence was a high mound (the motte) on top of which perched a wooden tower for additional height advantage to the defenders. In the latter form of castle, the residences and other buildings were usually at the foot of the hill surrounded by a ditch and palisade (the bailey). By 1066, the Normans had become adept at throwing up a motte castle in a hurry. When they invaded England, for example, they built a castle at Hastings within fifteen days. Once their foothold on a territory was consolidated, the Normans then built more substantial structures out of stone.

The same pattern was even more evident in the partial conquest of Ireland a hundred years later, where about five hundred earth and timber castles were constructed within the space of a decade or two and covered the eastern half of the country. Having secured their presence in Ireland in this way, the Anglo-Normans then built more permanent and much more impressive stone castles, such as that at Trim, which was constructed on top of the early timber ringwork castle.

Conquests

If there was a golden rule of European high politics in the period from 1000 to 1200 AD, it was not to let the Normans become involved in your realm. For not only were they the finest warriors in Europe, they were also intensely ambitious, restless, and devoted to the goal of achieving fame. Wherever a Norman force encountered weakness among an existing ruling élite whether friend or foe, they ended up supplanting the old aristocracy and taking their land.

Despite intense rivalry between them, the Normans also knew when to band together to take advantage of an opportunity. They had no fear of the sea, having inherited from their Viking forbears the techniques of building seaworthy craft capable of transporting their cavalry, as well as a knowledge of weather, tide and coastal landscape. As a result, the Normans made some extraordinary conquests, including the amphibious invasions of England, Sicily and Ireland.

William the Conqueror

The most famous Norman leader both in his day and in modern times was William, who in later life was known as 'the Conqueror', but who from childhood was termed 'the Bastard'. For William was born from a liaison between Duke Robert the Magnificent of Normandy and Herleva, the daughter of a lowly leather worker. Drawing on a traditional motief of heroic literature, one medieval historian retrospectively embelished the episode with significance by writing that the couple slept together and Herleva awoke with a start, saying that she had dreamed of a tree that grew from her body towards the sky, until the whole of Normandy was in its shadow. Whether or not Herleva did tell her lover of her dreams, impressing him with their prophetic implications, the duke took responsibility for Herleva and later married her. This did not prevent William's enemies from mocking him in regard to his grandfather's profession. When, around the year 1050, he was besieging the town and castle of Alençon, a group of knights and foot soldiers cried down from a stockade at William's troops, banging on the protective leather hides:

The skin, the skin of the tanner
That belongs to William's trade!

Such taunting was rather reckless, since as soon as the town's outer defences were overcome, William picked out those involved and had their hands and feet cut off. The feet were then catapulted into the castle to demoralise the defenders.

Partly because of his lowly origins on his mother's side, but more due to the desire of all Norman lords to throw off any authority above them, William faced enormous challenges in becoming an effective ruler of the duchy. Duke Robert left on a pilgrimage to Jerusalem in 1035, when William was just eight years old. William's father never came back, dying on the return journey at Nicaea. And although the Norman lords had all sworn loyalty to the boy in front of the archbishop of Rouen at Fécamp, they immediately set about fighting one another and building castles to protect their independence. At one point, in 1042, when William was fourteen or fifteen, a conspiracy to murder the young Duke nearly caught him unawares. One evening after hunting in Valognes he was woken by a jester called Goles beating on the walls of his room.

'Open up,' Goles cried, 'open up! You will all be killed, get up, get up! Where are you lying William? Why are you sleeping? If you are attacked here, you will soon be killed. Your enemies are arming themselves. If they can find you here, you will never get out of the Cotentin and not live till the morning.'

With just breeches and shirt and a cloak around his shoulders, William grabbed a horse and set off. In great fear and distress the teenager could not risk going to any major town until he knew who remained loyal to him. With the pursuit close behind, William came to the castle at Reys, where he was relieved to find that Hubert of Reys was willing to aid him. Sending William on with his three sons as escort, Hubert met the rebel party and while pretending to share their goals, escorted them down the wrong path, allowing William the time he needed to reach safety.

The turning point for William's extraordinarily successful rise to power was a battle, that of Val-ès-Dunes, near Caen, in 1047. There, on a wide, sloping battlefield William, aided by King Henry I of France, met his enemies. Before the battle began a significant incident took place. Ralph Taisson had once been a part of the rebel army and had sworn to strike William if he got the chance. Now, however, along with hundred and forty knights, he wanted to reconcile himself to the Duke. Riding up to William, Ralph took off his gauntlet and slapped the young man with it, saying –

'I am acquitting myself of what I swore. I swore I would strike you as soon as I found you. I have struck you in order to acquit myself of my oath, because I do not wish to perjure myself.'

'My thanks to you for this blow,' replied William. And the two fought together thereafter.

The press of this battle was particularly fierce, with knights in tight formation clashing against one another. Lances sought openings in armour; maces and swords clattered against shields. No one wanted to earn the ignominy of fleeing and so on both sides they persevered despite the blood and horror. William and Henry were in the thick of the press and at one point the French king was unseated by a blow from a lance. Only the strength of the hauberk that he was wearing saved Henry from death and the proud peasants of Cotentin remembered the fall of the king hundreds of years later, with the couplet: 'from the Cotentin came the lance, which struck down the King of France.' Despite being trampled in the mud, Henry was raised back up to his saddle and rallied his knights, riding around to make sure they could see him and thus quell the rumour that he was dead.

It was rare for the most senior lords of a realm to be killed in eleventh and twelfth century European battles. Normally, their opponents would prefer to capture them alive. But whether because of the near-death of the King of France or the bitterness engendered by the rebels' previous attempt to assassinate William, the duke and his allies showed no mercy once they got the upper hand. As men fleeing the battle were killed while trying to cross rivers, their bodies floated off downstream in such numbers that all the local watermills became choked for miles around.

After Val-ès-Dunes, William was never seriously challenged again and his authority was such that he could undertake the adventure for which he became famous, the conquest of England.

1066

England was a country with vastly greater wealth and resources than Normandy; it had also gone much further in the eleventh century in the formation of a central administration than had its neighbours. Under the impact of a succession of Danish raids demanding tribute, the English kings had developed a strong tax collecting system. A secular judicial system too, that operated via local courts and the testimony of worthy men, was more sophisticated than that prevailing elsewhere in Europe, with the possible exception of Ireland. But in the mid-eleventh century England was suffering from political instability that undermined these strengths and invited the attention of foreign predators, not just in Normandy but also in Norway.

From 1042, Edward the Confessor had ruled in England, having spent most of his life in exile in Normandy. His connection with Normandy was something that Edward considered to be of great value, for he looked to the Normans to give him the strength to defy the powerful English earls who otherwise dominated the throne. Edward appointed three Norman bishops to sees in England and also made Ralph the Timid Earl of Hereford. The new king's particular target in this approach was his most powerful vassal, Godwin, Earl of Wessex. Godwin's influence in England was such that despite Edward's reluctance, the king was obliged to take Godwin's daughter, Edith, as his queen. But in 1051, feeling that his position was now strong enough, Edward struck out at Godwin, outlawing the earl's sons and threatening Godwin himself. Edward had miscalculated, the two other great earls of the English kingdom, Leofric earl of Mercia and Siward of Northumbria, were uneasy about the king's favouring of Norman appointees and allowed Godwin to make a comeback. Godwin was restored to all his positions in 1052 and the queen to the royal bedchamber.

The absence of a royal heir meant the question of who should succeed Edward became a central one in English politics and one that drew in the Duke of Normandy. For William was related to the king's mother and that gave him a distant claim on the royal throne. There were others with a much better claim, such as the young Edgar Atheling, the only other male relative of Edward's father King Æthelred. But at least William had some connection to the royal dynasty, while the main power in England, Harold, Godwin's son, had no inherited claim at all to the title. Unfortunately for Harold an ill-fated voyage saw him forced to land in Normandy in 1064, where immediately William sent men to bring the English earl to the ducal court. William interrogated Harold as to the situation in England and before letting him go, famously obliged Harold to take an oath recognising William's claim to the crown.

On the 4 or 5 January 1066, Edward the Confessor died. On the day he was buried, Harold Godwinson was made king. Edgar Atheling was passed over, being only fourteen and having no forces under his command. For England needed a capable military commander. Not only was William of Normandy planning to mount an invasion to back his claim to the throne, but the greatest adventurer of the century, Harald Hardrada, King of Norway, had taken up with Harold's estranged brother Tostig and was also assembling a fleet. Harald Hardrada was a ferocious warrior who had fought his way around the Mediterranean as a leader of the élite Byzantine Varangian Guard before coming home through Russia to claim the crown of Norway.

Early in September 1066, two fleets were poised to attack England. It is testimony to the tremendous resources available to Duke William that he could afford to wait nearly two months before sailing. Not only did he want favourable weather, but he did not want to be the first to face the English army. For this strategic advantage and in the hope that the new English king could not afford to keep his fleet mobilised, William was willing to pay the living costs of the thousands of knights and footsoldiers who had assembled at the estuary of the river Dives.

Harald Hardrada therefore sailed first, gathering more troops from the Shetlands and then sailing down the east coast of England and inland at the Humber to camp at Stamford Bridge, just outside of York. With surprising speed, Harold Godwinson raced north and on 25 September 1066 caught the Norse king unprepared, with many of the Vikings having left their armour with the fleet, several miles off. While the Vikings formed their shield wall and sent a contingent back to get their armour, the English attacked. The fighting was fierce and it took the English army some time to wear down their opponents. Only when Harald Hardrada took an arrow to the throat and fell, did it seem as though Harold Godwinson had won. But then the Norse reinforcements arrived to prolong the struggle. Due to the heat of the day and their lack of water, these men who had run from the ships were exhausted and they too fell to the English axes.

Stamford Bridge was a great victory for Harold Godwinson and one that would have given him the platform to become a powerful and successful ruler of England. But the chance to savour his achievement was short-lived. Three days after the battle, the Normans set sail.

William's invasion was a triumph of Norman logistical ability. Some seven thousand knights, along with their horses; thousands of archers; tens of thousands of arrows; all their armour and weapons; and hundreds of craftsmen and all their tools were safely brought across the Channel to Pevensey in Sussex. Then the army was moved to Hastings and it was there, on 14 October 1066, a battle took place consequences of which would completely overshadow the battle of Stamford Bridge.

Having marched swiftly from London, Harold hoped to catch William unawares, as he had the Vikings at Stamford Bridge three weeks earlier. The Normans, however, had put on their armour every day since arriving in England and were not to be caught by surprise. At around nine in the morning the two armies eyed one another from opposing hillsides. From William's perspective, the arrival of the English king was welcome news. Clearly, a confrontation had to happen and the sooner the better. The longer it was delayed, the more chance Harold could gather in troops from right across England.

In terms of the quality of the two armies, the Normans had two great advantages. They had powerful warhorses and knights trained to ride in formation and they also had a great superiority in the numbers of archers and the technology of their bows. It was probably this latter aspect of the Norman army that won the day for them at Hastings. For the English army, with its core of iron-clad housecarls, was well able to defend itself against cavalry charges. Sending their own horses to the rear, the English formed up on a hill a 'shield wall' that bristled with axes and spears, proving impenetrable to repeated charges by the Norman cavalry. What the threat of the Norman knights did create, however, was a great immobility in the English ranks. Fear of allowing the cavalry a breakthrough meant that the shield wall had to be held tight, even while the Norman archers were creeping close to the English lines. Slowly but surely over a long day, the clouds of arrows made a slaughter of the poorly armoured and also found their mark in numbers of housecarls. Despite strong iron helms, the English warriors were vulnerable at their eyes, mouths, and the neck above the top of their chain hauberks.

Not that the Normans were always in control of the battle. When the Norman knights' efforts to break down the shield wall came to nothing, their formations were disrupted and after being repulsed, they began to turn tail, especially when the rumour began to spread that William had been killed. When sections of English warriors broke from the shield wall to scatter the Normans, it seemed that they were on the verge of victory. But as the less experienced 'thegns' in Harold's army were drawn far from the hill and away from the more heavily armoured and experienced housecarls, the joy of the English troops at their apparent success turned to horror as the Norman cavalry rallied as one, turned and cut down their former pursuers. This pattern of Norman cavalry appearing to flee, but regrouping to turn on their attackers repeated itself several times over the day, and bled the English army dry.

At one point during the day-long battle, Gryth, Harold's brother, had come face to face with the Duke of Normandy and having successfully thrown a spear at William's great stallion, had forced the Norman ruler to dismount. But the other riders with William overran Gryth's position before the Duke was in any great danger, killing the English prince. William then demanded the horse of a nearby knight of Le Mans, who reluctantly yielded the mount. Not that it fared any better than William's favoured steed. For a second time William's horse fell beneath him, this time due to 'the son of Hellox', a lightly armoured Englishman, who followed up his attack by going hand to hand with the Norman duke. With the second disappearance of William into the fray, rumours began to spread that he had been killed and the Normans, along with their Breton and French allies, were losing heart in face of the bloody resolution of the English shield wall. But William had overcome his assailant and riding to his aid came Eustace of Boulogne, who willingly dismounted and helped the duke back in to the saddle. William then rode around his troops, helm tipped back so that all could see he still lived.

By evening the outcome was still in the balance, although in terms of attrition, English losses throughout the day had been higher than their Norman attackers. King Harold and his bodyguard were in a tight knot at the top of the hill, still suffering from the constant rain of arrows, when William demanded yet another effort from his knights and led the decisive charge. At last, the English shield wall disintegrated and the mounted knights could utilise the advantage of height and power to the full. Riding through the last stand of the housecarls, the Normans toppled the English dragon banner and trampled over piles of bodies, among which lay that of Harold Godwinson. After months of preparation and one day of ferociously violent fighting, William had won himself a crown. As a result of victory in this battle the path was opened to a thoroughgoing conquest of England and the replacement of the aristocracy of the country with new, Norman, rulers.

Robert Guiscard

While William was proving the superiority of Norman horsemanship and fighting technique in the north of Europe the same lesson was evident in the south. In some ways the achievements of Robert of Hauteville, nicknamed 'Guiscard' – the cunning - and his brothers in Italy and Sicily were more impressive than those of William, for William had begun life in a high position, whereas Robert had almost nothing, just his sword and a genius for the art of war.

Around the turn of the millennium, a number of Norman knights had been returning from pilgrimage to Jerusalem and were in southern Italy, when their services were called upon as mercenaries. The region was torn by warfare. Arab armies landed and attacked from Sicily; the Byzantine Empire held a number of cities on the east coast; the King of Germany – the western emperor - often took an interest in the region; as did the papacy; while the Italian lords of Lombardy were bitter rivals among themselves for the land. Some of the Norman warriors remained to make the most of the opportunity for well-paid employment as fighters, but others returned home to spread the word: here was a land of opportunity. The call to go to southern Italy was particularly well received by a minor aristocratic family in the diocese of Coutances: that of Tancred, Lord of Hauteville. With five sons from his first marriage and seven from his second, Tancred had brought up a band of brothers with few prospects in Normandy. One of them stayed to manage the inheritance, the rest departed to try their luck in war.

When he arrived in Italy in 1047 or 1048, with five knights and thirty foot soldiers, Robert Guiscard came to join a force of Normans led by his older half-brother Drogo. Fraternal loyalty did not mean easy gains for Robert and he was put to the test by being sent, with his small number of troops, against Byzantine controlled towns and villages. As with the English and the Irish at the time, the southern Italians were not accustomed to the use of castles. They built forts at the major towns, but did not control the surrounding land through the construction of castles. Robert, however, was a master of the strategic use of the castle and he built a small but effective motte-and-bailey at Scribla (today 'Il Torrione' in the commune of Spezzano Albanese) and soon afterwards another at San Marco Argentano. With these castles as his base, Robert was able to raid far along the valley of the river Follone, and divert rents away from the Byzantines, while at the same time he could retreat and defend himself when his opponents mustered strong forces to try to deal with him.

As Robert strove to master the upper valley of the river Follone, the call came to rally all Normans and French warriors in southern Italy, for Pope Leo IX himself was leading an army from Rome to get rid of them before they become too strong. It was unprecedented for a pope to act as general for an army, but Leo IX was not afraid of innovation. Having striven to emancipate the papacy and the senior Roman clergy from the control of the local aristocratic families, in 1053 Leo IX felt the time had come to rid Italy of the disruptive Normans. With contingents sent by the Byzantines and some Swabian cavalry sent by the western emperor, along with troops from the Italian lords whose power was disintegrating from the manoeuvres of the Normans, the pope led his army to Civitate. There, on 17 June 1053, the pope was humiliated.

The far more accomplished Norman cavalry cut the papal allies to pieces, with only the Swabians showing any discipline. While all other troops scattered, the Germans held steady with the pope until the last, but this bravery earned them only death and a later papal pronunciation that they had earned a place in heaven. Of the Norman leaders, it was Robert Guiscard who attracted the most praise for his conduct in the battle, showing both a strong grasp of cavalry tactics and individual bravery when called upon to do so.

Having captured Leo IX, the Normans were careful to treat the Pope with the greatest respect. There was no need to look for vengeance, instead this was an opportunity. Back in Normandy the descendants of pagan Vikings had learned that the church was an invaluable ally in the governances of the duchy. Now the former mercenaries had a chance to create the same kind of relationship with the Italian church. Cleverly, the Normans pledged themselves to be servants of the Pope and offered to make annual payments to the church. As a result, Leo IX had considerable incentive to accept they were a legitimate part of the political landscape and allow monasteries such as the vibrant community at Monte Cassino to provide the Normans with church services and competent administrators.

Success followed success and as Robert's elder brothers died or retired, he became the leader of a now significant Norman presence in Southern Italy. When his younger brother Roger arrived in the early 1060s with fresh forces from Normandy, the two brothers came to an agreement to share all that they conquered. Their military actions began by securing Calabria but their ambition was extraordinary. Their next goal was to take the island of Sicily from its Arab and Berber rulers and after that, well the Byzantines had been beaten in Italy, could they be beaten in Greece too?

In 1059, a new pope, Nicholas, revolutionised the papal attitude towards the Normans by winning over the cardinals to a pro-Norman policy. His thinking was that the traditional military support of the papacy, the German king, was unlikely to be able to assist the church, given that Henry IV was only nine years old and the kingdom riven by factions attempting to hold the regency. Without imperial assistance, it was almost inevitable that that papacy would fall under the sway of the local Italian aristocracy, as it had for centuries. So in 1059 a synod was held in Melfi, the strongpoint of Norman Apulia. There the Normans swore to assist the papacy with their troops and regular financial tribute, the pope in turn recognised Richard of Aversa, son of the first Norman to have risen to prominence in the region, Rainulf, count of Aversa from 1029, as the legitimate prince of Capua, while Robert was invested 'Duke of Apulia and Calabria, as well as Sicily yet to be conquered'.

A duke, with equal status to that of William back in Normandy, recognised as such by the pope and Robert Guiscard was still only forty-four. There was plenty of vigour in his frame and ambition in his heart. So in the year following the new agreement with the papacy, Robert and Roger set about building ships and testing the defences of Sicily. Although nominally vassals of the Zirid sultan of Mehdia in north Africa, the Muslim rulers of the island were effectively autonomous. They were, however, bitterly divided: the west of the island was ruled by an emir called Abd-Allah ibn Manqut; the south and centre by Ibn al-Hawwas; and the east by Ibn Maklati. None of the three rivals was able to dominate the whole island and soon their rivalry produced an opening for the Normans.

Ibn Maklati was deposed by an upstart emir, Ibn Timnah, and killed in his capital city of Catania. To consolidate his new position, Ibn Timnah married the widow of Ibn Maklati but, understandably, his new wife did not appreciate the changed circumstances and assassination of her husband. Matters came to a head in a drunken night of attempted murder, after which Ibn Maklati's widow fled to the protection of her brother, the ruler of the south of the island, Ibn al-Hawwas, whom she encouraged to war upon Ibn Timnah. A series of events that had already carried a curious foreshadowing of those which took place in Ireland a hundred years later, then became an even more explicit prediction of the future, when the success of Ibn al-Hawwas forced Ibn Timnah to flee westwards across the sea to Calabria. There he offered the Normans lordship of Sicily if they would help him back into power.

Before Roger and Robert fully committed their forces to such a risky venture, they sent reconnaissance parties over to the island. From the skirmishes that ensued, one fact became clear: small numbers of Norman soldiers could defeat considerably larger Muslim forces. The Muslim knight could easily outperform their Norman opponent with the bow, but when it came to hand-to-hand fighting, their heavier armour, their horses trained for close combat, and their ability to charge with the lance saw the Normans triumph. In May 1061, the Norman invasion began in earnest. While Robert manoeuvred with the larger part of their fleet off the coast of Calabria, to draw away the Muslim war galleys, Roger crossed to Sicily at night with three hundred knights. These proved enough to capture Messina, with its vital harbour, and as a result the Muslim admirals became demoralised. It was no longer realistic to hope to intercept the Normans, who now simply had to wait for the Muslim fleet to leave the Straits of Messina, which they had to do to take on water or to seek shelter from rough weather. Then the the Normans could sail across the short distance to the secure harbour.

Once Robert had arrived with the full army, the two brothers consolidated the defences of Messina and set out with about a thousand knights and the same number of foot soldiers, guided by Ibn Timnah and his followers. Their target was the strongest of the Muslim emirs, Ibn al-Hawwas, whom they encountered in the summer of 1061 on the banks of the River Dittaino, east of Castrogiovanni. There, despite being considerably outnumbered, the Normans battled hard and eventually scattered the Muslim army. This was a remarkable success and their advance had been rapid up to this point, but the full conquest of the island took another thirty years. The main reason for this being that Roger, and more especially Robert, were needed back in Italy, where the struggle to oust the Byzantines from the country was ongoing. With Messina as a bridgehead the Normans could return to Sicily and keep the pressure on the other emirs, until such time as a decisive campaign became feasible.

The eventual domination of Sicily by the Normans was mostly the work of Roger; Robert Guiscard came to the island only twice more, for he had raised his eyes even higher and was looking towards the east and the possibility of becoming an emperor. First, though, there were still some Italian princes whom Robert could strongarm out of their lordships. As the Norman armies ground down the local nobility and took over their land, they once more fell out of favour with the papacy. In particular, the fiery and determined Gregory VII was furious with Robert for dispossessing a key papal supporter, Gisulf, of his city of Salerno, which had capitulated to Robert in 1077. Excommunicate for several years, Robert nevertheless returned to papal favour for the simple reason that his was the strongest army in the region. After Gregory VII had embroiled himself in a mighty conflict in Germany, one that led to a bitter civil war and a real risk that Henry IV would march on Rome to rid himself of the most outspoken voice of rebellion, Gregory needed to reconcile the Normans. Robert was once more Duke of Apulia and Calabria by grace of God.

From Robert's point of view, peace with the papacy was equally important, for a very alluring prospect had arisen. While the Normans had been driving the Byzantine forces out of Italy, most notably capturing the eastern coastal city of Bari in 1071, Seljuk Turks had caused the disintegration of imperial power in Anatolia. The efforts of Emperor Romanus IV to halt Turkish advances led to a battle in the same year, at Manzikert in Armenia. The result of the battle was a catastrophe for the Byzantines and the emperor himself was captured. The crisis for the empire now deepened, with imperial finances in a state of collapse as all their wealthiest dependencies no longer felt compelled to pay tribute to Constantinople. The bezant, the imperial gold coin that was the standard for the Mediterranean, collapsed in value as it was debased.

Already one adventurous Norman had sought to take advantage of the disintegration of Byzantine power. Having once fought alongside the Hautevilles in southern Italy, Roussel of Bailleul had moved east to serve on behalf of the Byzantines in Asia Minor as a mercenary leader of a band of warriors at whose core was a body of Norman knights. Turning on his former employers, Roussel plundered the eastern states of the empire and defeated the Byzantine generals sent against him, creating a principality for himself based on Ankara. Roussel was undone, however, by the Turks, who in return for recognition of their conquests, agreed to a peace treaty with the Byzantine emperor at the heart of which was an agreement to destroy the Norman usurper. Despite a period in prison in Constantinople, Roussel was released in 1077 because the Byzantine emperor, Michael VII Dukas, desperately needed Norman military support to deal with a rebellion. But Roussel once more turned against his employers, joining the rebellion and once more was defeated by a

Byzantine treaty with the Turks. This time there was to be no comeback; Roussel was executed after being brought back to Constantinople.

What Roussel's wild career had proven to Robert Guiscard was that the Byzantines were no longer the mighty power they once had been. Moreover, the Byzantine elite made the mistake of asking for military aid and offering a marriage alliance. It was never a good idea to whet the appetite of a Norman lord. Michael VII offered his younger brother as husband for one of Robert's seven daughters in return for the services of the Norman general and his knights. In order to test the Byzantines, Robert delayed an answer, looking to see what else they might offer him. In March 1074, the Byzantine offer was indeed improved. The marriage alliance would be between Michael VII's own son, then a baby, Constantine, and one of Robert's daughters. In addition, Robert Guiscard, the once lowly knight of Hauteville, was offered the highest position available to someone not born to the purple, that of the court rank of nobilissimus. Robert agreed and his daughter, re-christened Helena by the Greeks, arrived in Constantinople in 1076.

In March 1078, Michael VII's career ended, as did that of so many Byzantine emperors in this period, through a military coup directed against him. Unlike many of his predecessors and successors, Michael avoided execution or blinding and retired to be a monk of St John Studios in Constantinople. The new emperor, Nikephoros III Botaniates had a more hostile approach to the Normans of southern Italy and broke off all dealings with Robert. They were done with him, but Robert was not done with the Byzantines.

Backing an impostor claiming to be Michael VII, Robert began to mobilise his army and prepare to invade Greece, with the object of putting his puppet on the throne and rescuing his daughter. Sending his eldest son, Bohemond, across the Adriatic in March 1081 to establish a beachhead on the island of Corfu, Robert followed two months later with a force of around 1,300 knights and many more foot soldiers. The conquest of the island was completed by 21 May 1081. The Norman fleet then conducted the army to Albania but here, in a rare occurrence for a Norman amphibious operation, they misjudged the weather and were caught by a summer storm. Despite losing part of his army, Robert landed sufficient troops in Albania that he could march on Durazzo, a port town that had the potential to unlock the empire as Messina had Sicily.

By this time, Robert's opponent had changed, due to yet another coup. Alexios I Comnenus was now on the imperial throne and in Alexios, Robert met a skilled adversary. Moreover, many of Robert's military cadres, the veterans of his campaigns in Italy, thought this too risky an enterprise and had not crossed the Adriatic with him, sending younger relations in their stead.

Of the hundreds of problems facing the empire, Alexios treated the Norman invasion as the most urgent. Raising funds by the risky act of melting down gold and silver owned by the church, the new emperor brought an army to the relief of Durazzo. He also negotiated a treaty with

Venice, whose fleet proved crucial in cutting off the Normans from their home territories. The situation looked to be a dangerous one for Robert, but his first encounter with Alexios proved favourable to the Normans. By utilising their cavalry skills to the full, the Normans lured the Varangian guard, the mercenary shock troops of the Greek army, into a premature charge. Many of the Varangians were Anglo-Saxons who had fled William's conquests in England, only to find the same enemy in Greece. Isolated, they were cut down and the Greek army thrown back, allowing Robert to enter Durazzo after an eight month siege.

News from Italy meant that Robert could not press the attack on Greece in person. He was needed to put down rebellions in Apulia and guard against the German king, Henry IV, who had crossed the Alps. Leaving Bohemond in charge of the campaign, Robert found he was kept fully stretched for the next three years and could not reinforce Bohemond as he wished. His son, however, proved very competent in keeping control of Durazzo and twice obliged Alexios to withdraw from attempts to take the city.

One of the issues facing Robert in 1083 was that his ally and nominal overlord, Pope Gregory VII, was in desperate straits, with the German army engaged in a persistent effort to take Rome: even managing to breach the walls of the city in 1084. Aided by his brother Roger, who sent Muslim as well as Norman troops from Sicily, Robert marched on Rome. Henry IV, probably wisely, was not attracted to the idea of a pitched battle with the famous Norman warriors and withdrew, allowing Robert to rescue Gregory. The Norman troops in Rome, however, enraged the citizens by their looting and serious unrest broke out, resulting in a major fire that raged through the city. Hated for having brought about this disaster, Gregory VII could never return to Rome and died in May 1085 in exile under Robert's protection at Salerno.

At last able to return once more to his most ambitious project, Robert crossed the Adriatic and resumed battle with Alexios. Here the intervention of Venetian fleets cost him dear, cutting his supplies in the winter of 1084 and contributing to a terrible outbreak of disease that claimed the lives of some five hundred knights. Bohemond was struck down and returned to Salerno, where he recovered. But Robert himself fell victim to sickness in the summer of 1085 and died of fever on the island of Cephalonia.

Although Robert Guiscard fell just short of becoming the effective ruler of the Byzantine empire, his career was an incredible one all the same. That a poor knight could set out on his travels from Normandy as a teenager and become a ruler of huge swathes of territory in Italy, that the papacy would honour him as a duke, and that he could challenge for the rule of the Byzantine empire is testimony to the extraordinary economic and military advantages the Normans had over their neighbours.

Bohemond

It was intended that the first born child of Robert Guiscard was to be called Mark at his baptism, but the stocky size of the infant boy was so impressive that he was given the nickname Bohemond, 'the giant', and the child grew into a man of a stature that deserved such a name. San Marco Argentano, the second castle constructed by Robert Guiscard, was the birthplace of Bohemond and as eldest son, he might have expected to inherit all of his father's lands. But although Bohemond was entrusted with the leadership of Robert's troops and fleets, he had a rival for the role of leader of the Italian Normans. For Robert married a second time, to the daughter of the ruler of Salerno (before Robert went on to capture the city) and by Sichelgaita, he had a son, Roger Borsa, who stood to gain all of the inheritance.

In 1096, Bohemond was in alliance with his uncle, Roger I of Sicily, against his rival half-brother, besieging the city of Amalfi. Suddenly, the possibility of an extraordinary new adventure opened to Bohemond. Warriors began travelling through Italy on their way to Constantinople to join up with a mighty crusade – the first of its kind – to liberate Jerusalem and place the Holy City in Christian hands. Seizing on the excitement generated by the crusade, Bohemond, along with his young nephew Tancred, offered to lead those Italian Normans who wished to take part. Demonstratively, he cut up his most valuable cloak to make crosses. Hundreds of knights who had been vassals of his uncle rallied to his banner. Lamenting the loss of his army, Roger was forced to abandon the siege of Amalfi and return to Sicily.

The First Crusade was a chaotic enterprise, with perhaps as many as 100,000 participants, many of whom were non combatants: farmers, their wives, children, the elderly, monks and nuns. Because of its disparate nature, there was no overall command structure, although the papal legate, Adhemar of Le Puy, was held in great respect. But of all the warriors on the crusade, it was Bohemond and his Norman followers who came to dominate military decisions. Whenever the crusade faced a military threat, it was Bohemond who was chosen to direct the army.

The son of Robert Guiscard earned this respect above all for his ability to match the tactics of the Turkish opponents of the crusading army. At the core of the Turkish fighting forces were light cavalry whose riding ability equalled that of the Normans, albeit in a different style. For a Turkish warrior was trained to fire a powerful horn and sinew composite bow over his shoulder while riding away from the enemy. Again and again, these riders had destroyed enemy armies by luring them into false charges by feigned retreat, only to turn and encircle their enemies when the momentum of the charge was lost. Qilij Arslān I, sultan of Rūm met the crusading army near Dorylaeum in central Anatolia on 1 July 1097 and in a storm of dust, his 10,000 riders attempted to draw the Christian army out of position.

In Bohemond, however, the crusaders had a leader thoroughly aware of the tactic of the feigned retreat. Norman cavalry had practised it often enough and Bohemond himself had used it to destroy the Byzantine

Varangian guard in 1081. Mounted rows of Norman knights formed the centre of the Christian defences, weathering the storms of arrows, assisted by women bringing water up from the rear for thirsty men and horses. The moment Bohemond was waiting for was the arrival of the crusade rearguard, several hours away, and although impetuous troops – including those of Tancred – were drawn into rash charges, the discipline of the Christian army held. Late in the afternoon the Turks were shocked to find that their opponents, immobile for so long, were now moving into action, reinforced by the fresh arrivals. Worse, they were outflanked. Adhemar of Le Puy had come around the far side of a mountain to intercept the Turkish riders as they withdrew from battle. From a feigned retreat, Qilij Arslān's army was suddenly in genuine rout and many of his troops fell to the Christian lances. The path towards Jerusalem was open.

It was during the siege of Antioch, however, that Bohemond showed that not only was he a master of the cavalry charge, but also he had craftiness worthy of his father. Antioch was a rich city, a slave trading entrepôt on the river Orentes, secure behind walls that rose up the sides of a mountain. Although past its most glorious days, Antioch was still a major trading centre and a near autonomous Seljuk garrison was based there under the command of Yaghī Siyān. The Christian forces had arrived at Antioch on 21 October 1097 and they were not to capture the city until 3 June 1098.

During this long siege, a number of battles were fought against relieving Muslim armies, perhaps the most crucial being that of 9 February 1098 against the forces of Ridwan ruler of Aleppo. The night before, an emergency council of the princes of the crusade had taken place. All agreed that the crisis called for one person to command the entire crusading forces and that person should be Bohemond. The Norman lord did not hesitate and despite the risk, ordered all the available knights to mount up that night and ride out in darkness in order to set up an ambush. The total Christian force was less than a thousand riders.

As dawn came, so did a light rain, ideal weather for Bohemond's plan; for rain reduced the effectiveness of the Muslim bow. While Ridwan's army approached, confident the Christians were still some twelve miles away, the crusader cavalry rode over the crest of a large hill and utterly surprised the Muslim army with a thunderous charge. To create the impression that the crusaders were there in great numbers, all the banners had been brought from the camp. This ruse and the ferocity of the charge was a complete success. The vanguard of Ridwan's army recoiled back upon the main force, adding confusion to fear. Not that victory was assured for the Christians. Outnumbered some twelve to one, the momentum of the first charge was not enough to win the battle and the fighting grew fierce. Sensing the critical moment had come, Bohemond now committed his Norman reserves, leading them into the thick of battle. The sight of the red banner flying high, moving deep among the Muslim force rallied the whole Christian army and the Muslim enemy riders scattered. Bohemond had secured an extraordinary victory, with very few losses to the remaining knights of the crusade.

Antioch fell on 3 June 1097 in a manner that echoed Robert Guiscard's capture of Durrazo after a long siege. A traitor from within the city, named Firouz, had approached Bohemond with an offer to allow the Norman lord into the city in return for rewards and protection. Bohemond played his hand very cleverly, hiding the knowledge of this offer from the rest of the Christian army. An enormous Turkish army under Kerbogha, atabeg of Mosul, was on the march and only when the Christian scouts had confirmed its proximity did Bohemond ask for a meeting of all the princes of the crusade. Before revealing his plan, Bohemond asked all the others swear an oath that whoever could deliver the city should become ruler of it. Nearly all of the princes agreed: after all, the situation was so desperate that if Bohemond could get them into Antioch, he would be saving the crusade and would deserve to become lord of the city.

Once the Christians had secured the city and seen off Kerbogha's army, they recuperated for several months, before moving off towards Jerusalem. Bohemond, however, and most of his Norman followers, remained in Antioch, the capital of a new principality. There he ruled, part Norman prince, part oriental emir. The fame of Bohemond's deeds spread throughout Europe, to the great pride of the Normans and, indeed, all of France. In 1105, Bohemond went to France in search of a bride and enjoyed a triumphal reception throughout the land, culminating in his marriage to Constance, daughter of King Philip I. Success in battle had made Bohemond a prince and now even the descendants of Charlemagne honoured him by giving him a princess as a bride.

For several generations, the Normans were the most powerful warriors in Europe and beyond. Their great destriers, heavy protective chainmail surcoats, skilled horsemanship, their improvements to the bow, and above all, their use of castles, allowed them to wrestle their way to power everywhere the opportunity presented itself. Not only did they have these technical advantages in warfare, but they also had a pugnacious spirit to match. Norman knights valued bravery, ambition, feats of arms, guile and above all, success. They were not chivalrous, in the later sense of the term, they were pragmatic. Whether by ruse, intimidation, marriage, or ferocity in battle, what mattered was the result. Each of them held a belief that they could end their lives in far better position than that to which they had been born. And in the cases of William the Bastard, Robert Guiscard and Bohemond they had clear examples of just how dramatic an advance was possible.

The last of Norman adventurers in this tradition was a lord called Strongbow and his opportunity to sieze a realm came as a result of a political crisis in Ireland.

Conclusion

I called this book *Marxism and Medieval History* to try to bring it to the attention of readers who are both sympathetic to the writings of Marx and interested in medieval history. If you're such a reader, then I hope you enjoyed some of the essays at least. It's more of a dip into different topics than a book to read from cover to cover. I have written books in the latter spirit and as indicated in the last chapter, you might be interested in my *Strongbow: the Norman Invasion of Ireland* and *The Siege of Jerusalem: Crusade and Conquest in 1099*.

Despite the title, I'm not sure whether the contents are Marxist history. They are essays by someone who greatly admires Marx, has read and studied Marx, and who does what he can to help bring about a transformation of the world from capitalist to socialist. No doubt this background has an impact on how I study and write about history. Yet when I see that a Chinese University has advertised for a professor of Marxist History, I have to wonder what kind of history that person does. Presumably at the job interview you praise China as being a model Marxist country and write history accordingly: the kind of history where great men (usually) are great because they confirm to the world historic tasks of their day, as assigned by the forces and relations of production.

To my view, that's not history at all, it's a kind of game where you become expert in a certain vocabulary and canon of works which you reference not to communicate insight and understanding of people in the past but that you are loyal to the cause. This game playing with Marx's concepts is not confined to the cause of the Chinese state, of course. There are plenty of other states and also 'Marxist' political parties that have a similar programmatic approach to writing history.

When I put these essays together in this book, it occurred to me that there are techniques available to a historian now that were not available to Marx and Engels. So inevitably, even the most orthodox of Marxist historians is going to research history in a different fashion to how it was practiced in the mid-nineteenth century. In order to try to understand the sociology of William of Tyre, for instance, I availed of massive databases that had become available on CD-ROM more or less in the year I needed them. Of course, these are online now, allowing an even more rapid and thorough search for key phrases.

Similarly, a whole new dimension of context has opened up for historians with the availability of an accurate model of past climate and of severe weather events like droughts and floods. I don't think this has yet been appreciated enough by most historians, although we are close to achieving something of a tipping point where all works will take into consideration the environment of the past: not only because of the creation of more accurate ice-core and tree-ring chronologies but because we are all more sensitive to extreme weather events now we are witnessing them with greater and greater frequency.

Some of the essays here have embraced these new possibilities. Others have explored certain historic situations with great sympathy for the poor, the visionary, the woman. What I don't think I ever did in trying to answer such questions as occurred to me was to deploy a ready-made toolkit of Marxist concepts. As I argue in the critique of David Laibman's *Deep History*, generalisations about history have to arise from the particular moment and not be imposed upon it. There is a world in every grain of sand.

Whether Marx and Engels would recognise these essays as broadly in the spirit of their own writings I'm not sure. I'd like to think so.

Printed in Great Britain
by Amazon